Street Life under a Roof

INTERPRETATIONS OF CULTURE
IN THE NEW MILLENNIUM

Norman E. Whitten Jr., General Editor

A list of books in the series appears at the end of the book.

Street Life under a Roof

Youth Homelessness in South Africa

EMILY MARGARETTEN

University of Illinois Press

URBANA, CHICAGO, AND SPRINGFIELD

Library of Congress Control Number: 2015946976
ISBN 978-0-252-03960-7 (hardcover)
ISBN 978-0-252-08111-8 (paperback)
ISBN 978-0-252-09769-0 (e-book)

To Michael and Marian

Contents

Illustrations

Acknowledgments

This book is the outcome of years of help and hospitality from the young women and men of Point Place. My gratitude is immense. *Ngiyabonga, abangani bami.*

To those not from Point Place but who were an important part of my fieldwork experiences in Durban, too—Keith Breckenridge, Catherine Burns, Jeff Guy, Meghan Healy-Clancy, Jason Hickel, Helmut Holst, Mark Hunter, Lesley Lewis, Andy MacDonald, Gerhard Maré, Sarah Mathis, Julie Parle, Renée Reynolds, Ilana van Wyk, and Thembisa Waetjen—a big thank you for your friendship, conversations, and housing! At the University of KwaZulu-Natal, my instructors in isiZulu, Mary Gordon, Msawakhe Hlengwa, Zoliswa Mali, Nelson Ntshangase, and Mpume Zondi, made language learning a pleasure and a possibility. And this includes Sandra Sanneh as well! To the organizers and participants of the History and African Studies Seminar, I am grateful for your comments and suggestions, which shaped the early drafts of this book. And to the Social Anthropology Department, thank you for the institutional affiliation. Similarly, as a postdoctoral fellow at the University of the Witwatersrand, I benefited immeasurably from the institutional support of the university and from the intellectual insights of my colleagues. To the Social Anthropology Department, David Coplan, Kelly Gillespie, Gavin Steingo, Carol Taylor, Robert Thornton, and Shahid Vawda, I learned much from your dedication to your students. Now that I am a full-time teacher, I recognize the immensity of your hard work!

This research also was made possible by the generous support of several granting agencies, which included a Fulbright-Hays Doctoral Dissertation

Research Abroad Grant, a National Science Foundation Cultural Anthropology Doctoral Dissertation Research Improvement Grant, a fellowship from the Wenner-Gren Foundation for Anthropological Research, and an Andrew Mellon Postdoctoral Fellowship. In addition, I wish to acknowledge the institutional support of Yale University, which provided fellowships not only for my studies in graduate school but also for preliminary fieldwork investigations and language training in South Africa, which included a Foreign Language Area Studies Fellowship.

To the members of Yale's Department of Anthropology (who now are so far afield!), my acknowledgments are many. Foremost to Eric Worby, whose intellectual guidance and mentoring have been invaluable to me. To Kamari Clarke and Mike McGovern, I am deeply grateful for your support. To Isak Niehaus, who, in his visiting year, inspired me with his enthusiasm for South Africa and has been generous with his friendship ever since. To my friends, mentors, and writing and traveling companions: Allison Alexy, Devika Bordia, Seth Curley, Judd Devermont, Joseph Hill, Jennifer Jackson, Libby Jones, Juan Orrantia, Richard Payne, Mieka Ritsema, and Gavin Whitelaw, thank you for the laughter and listening ears. And, to Kay Mansfield, it was an honor to be a Marvelette!

More recently, at Ripon College, I have benefited from the warm welcome of the Anthropology Department. Thank you, Paul Axelrod, Emily Stovel, and Bill Whitehead. To the Ceresco Research Workshop in the Humanities and Human Sciences, it was a pleasure to present the final drafts of this book. And, of course, to my students, who have helped me remember what makes reading ethnography so much fun. Here I also wish to acknowledge my gratitude to the two, as it turns out, not-so-anonymous reviewers of this book, Adam Ashforth and Mark Hunter. I am indebted to you for your comments, suggestions, and insights, and, as the following pages reveal, for your scholarship. Here, too, a special thanks to Norm Whitten and Danny Nassett, editors at the University of Illinois Press. I never imagined that walking past a book booth at a conference would lead to such productivity! And to Jane Lyle, thank you for your keen eye and insightful edits to this manuscript.

Over the years, portions of this book have benefited from the comments and suggestions of anonymous reviewers. Sections of the introduction and chapter two appeared as an article, "Standing (K)in: Street Youth and Street Relatedness in South Africa," in the journal *City & Society* 23, Supplement 1 (September 2011): 45–65. Chapter one appeared as an article, "Street Life under a Roof," in the journal *Anthropology and Humanism* 34, no. 2 (December 2009): 163–178. Chapter five appeared as an article, "uGogo: Residing with the Spectral in South Africa," in *Transition Magazine*, no. 104 (2011): 2–7, and is reprinted with permission from Indiana University Press. Sections of chapter six appeared as an essay, "Parting Homes in KwaZulu-Natal," in *Ekhaya: The Politics of Home in KwaZulu-Natal*, edited by Meghan Healy-Clancy and Jason Hickel (Pietermaritzburg: University of KwaZulu-Natal Press, 2014), 190–314, and is reprinted with permission from the University of KwaZulu-Natal Press.

Finally, I would like to acknowledge the love and support of Michael Mahoney, whose enthusiasm for South Africa has meant the world to me. And, to my family, who have helped me through it all. Thank you for everything.

Introduction

Vignette One: Vigilante Justice and Street Rehabilitation

"Did you hear what happened to me over the weekend?" A group of young men and women are relaxing in a shaded park on a Sunday afternoon. It is the end of summer in Durban, a South African city known for its subtropical climate and expansive beaches along the Indian Ocean. I am sitting near the group and overhear the story. The young woman explains to her companions that a teenage boy stole her purse while she was sunbathing on the beach. The purse contained the wallets, cell phones, and car keys of her friends, too. A few seconds after the theft, the woman realized what had happened and jumped up from her towel. She saw the teenager with her purse and shouted for help. A mob set upon the boy, who fell to the ground, trying to protect himself from the blows to his body and head.

"Ay, it was vigilante justice," a young man remarks.

"They were angry," the woman answers. "They hurt him badly." She goes on to say that they brought the teenager to the police station. She decided not to press charges, though, for he already had suffered enough from the beating. The police also said that there was not much else they could do, for the boy had returned the purse to her with all the contents in it. As a final warning, they planned to drive him far out "to the bush," where it would take him several days to walk back to the city, possibly longer because of his injuries.

"They do that for those big conferences," another girl muses. She is referring to a practice in which police officers round up street kids from the beachfront and dump them in remote places when there is an influx of visiting foreigners and dignitaries to the city. The group is quiet, contemplating her statement as well as the mob beating of the teenage boy.

Figure 1. The South African provinces. Durban is located in the province of KwaZulu-Natal along the Indian Ocean.

The young man who spoke of vigilante justice remarks, "There's no chance for rehabilitation, is there?" The others nod in agreement.

Vignette Two: Urban Renewal and Unsightly Buildings

It is crowded in the Durban International Convention Center, its conference hall filled with reporters and delegates wearing well-pressed suits and, in many cases, police uniforms. They mill around the room, amicably greet-

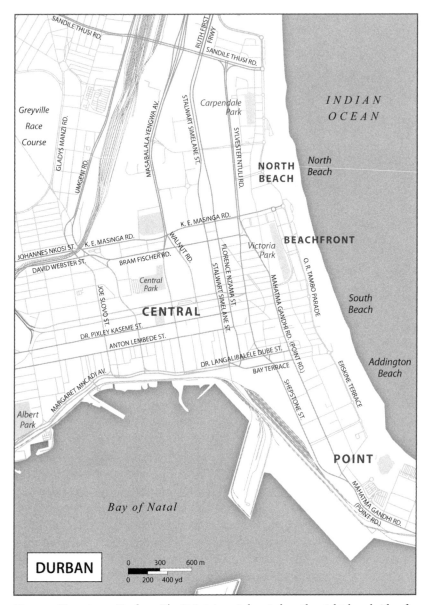

Figure 2. Downtown Durban. The Point Area is located on the right-hand side of the map. It covers the land that extends past Addington Beach but also is used as a shorthand designation for the part of the city that goes inland from Addington Beach and continues on Point Road parallel to South Beach.

Figure 3. The Durban beachfront.

ing one another before taking their seats in rows of evenly spaced chairs. The delegates—representatives from the Departments of Health and Social Welfare and the Chambers of Tourism and Business—are there to attend an inaugural "Safety and Security Summit." I have come with an older street youth named Shorty. Many of his friends intended to join us, but on seeing the large number of law enforcement officers, they lost their nerve and left the building. Shorty is not worried, for he does not have an outstanding warrant for his arrest. He is there to learn what the city plans for him and his friends.

In her presentation to the audience, a municipal official informs us about what these plans entail.[1] She focuses on a flagship project of the Safety and Security Summit—a project that aims to "rehabilitate" the city center by addressing one "bad" building at a time. The initiative will start with a condemned apartment complex in a downtrodden part of the city known as the Point Area. As she explains it, the building is an "eyesore," a place of social degradation and bad hygiene that accommodates thieves, drug lords, sex workers, and street youth; it hosts a cache of stolen firearms, too. Shorty and I look at each other, amused. The woman's description is highly sensationalized, and her last statement is entirely untrue.

After the formal speeches, the audience is encouraged to ask questions. People state their affiliations and make various suggestions. Shorty waits until hands are no longer being raised. He stands up and then announces to the room, "I'm from that building you want to close down, that building called Point Place."

The audience laughs, but this does not deter Shorty.

"I've grown up on the streets. I've been living in Point Place for years now." The din lessens.

"I've nowhere else to go. Point Place is my home." Shorty pauses, carefully choosing his words. "Yes, I've committed crimes, you see, to survive. My friends, too, they've committed crimes. We want to change. But how can we do this if we're thrown onto the streets?"

Finished with his speech, Shorty sits down. "Amen!" a few people call out, applauding enthusiastically. Soon afterward, with no apparent resolution, the summit ends. Newspaper reporters jostle me to edge closer to Shorty. They want to photograph and interview him. I wait for him to finish. As we leave the room, we pass by a buffet table spread out with meat kebabs, savory samosas, and fresh fruit. Good food is difficult to come by in Point Place, and I ask Shorty if he would like something to eat. "No," he replies with a smile that is both ironic and sincere, "it's a waste of taxpayers' money."

*   *   *

I introduce *Street Life under a Roof* through these ethnographic vignettes to illustrate the institutional inequalities and interpersonal abuses that characterize the lived experiences of youth homelessness in South Africa. The first vignette presents a perspective that is fairly common to South Africa's privileged classes. It describes a group of young men and women who, although sympathetic to the plight of a beaten teenager, believe that "rehabilitation" offers a solution to his criminal acts. Implicit in this view is the assumption that the teenager lacks the capacity to conform to societal norms and therefore requires some type of intervention. The second vignette also presents a perspective on "rehabilitation." In this case it is a municipal official's description of "bad" and unsightly buildings, a description that she extends to the occupants as well. Plans of "rehabilitation" essentially equate to evictions and arrests, by means of which poor black youth—deemed unfit for urban citizenship—are expelled from the city center.

In detailing these forced removals, *Street Life under a Roof* offers a counterview to popular perceptions of youth homelessness. It argues that "rehabilitation" is not needed because these youth share the same aspirations, ideals, and hopes of their wider South African society. They too want to live in a loving and secure home; they want a good education and gainful employment; they want to provide for their dependents—elders and children alike. In sum, they want to carry purses, which impart symbolic and material significance, as they hold wallets, cell phones, and rings of keys to cars, homes, and places of work.

The attainment of these aspirations is unlikely, however, as South Africa has one of the highest measures of income inequality in the world.[2] This inequality, which has a historical basis in the political, social, and economic disenfranchisements of apartheid rule,[3] is reflected most acutely in the national unemployment rate, which hovers around 36.3 percent.[4] This is a striking figure considering that South Africa has a well-developed industry in mining, manufacturing, and agriculture and boasts the largest export-based economy in Africa. It has a strong finance sector, too. Nonetheless, unemployment remains high as the country fails to develop policies to absorb large amounts of unskilled labor—primarily black labor—into its market-driven economy. "Unemployment," as economist Nicoli Nattrass (2007:179) writes, "is now the major driver of poverty and inequality" in South Africa. These inequalities present themselves in categories not only of race, class, and gender, but also of age.[5]

Youth between the ages of fourteen and thirty-five constitute the largest proportion of the unemployed in South Africa. To account for the severity of the situation, the South African government has taken to referring to a specific group of youth, those between the ages of fourteen and twenty-four, with the acronym NEET—Not in Employment, Education, or Training. Approximately 31.4 percent, or 3.3 million youth, fall into the category of NEET, which the government also identifies as "idle youth" (Statistics South Africa 2012a:3).

Idle: "not working, active, or being used: not having any real purpose or value" (Merriam-Webster.com). With respect to formal institutions—like the market economy, education, and training—the definition of "idle" accurately depicts the life circumstances of the young men and women in this book. The majority of them are not employed, in school, or engaged in vocational activities. When asked about their day, many will respond with a shrug and say, "I'm just sitting." Ethnographic evidence from other parts of Africa suggests a similar state of idleness for its youth populations, as they are unable to access desirable jobs or further their aspirations with formal education and training (Mains 2007; Weiss 2009). Moreover, with increasing exposure to global capitalism, media, and commodity goods, these youth find themselves in the position of wanting more with fewer means of legitimate acquisition (Cole 2004; Hansen 2008).

At a macro level, much of this commonality across Africa relates to neo-liberal economic reforms that were advocated by the World Bank and the International Monetary Fund in the 1980s and 1990s. The implementation of structural adjustment programs devalued local currencies, restricted government spending, and privatized state assets, which in turn pushed up the prices of commodity goods, cut social welfare services, and created higher levels of unemployment. Historian Mamadou Diouf (2003:4) links these economic reforms to a bankruptcy in political projects, too, which once promoted African youth as vanguards of national liberation struggles and as icons of postcolonial development and reform. No longer is this the case. As Diouf (2003:5) elaborates:

> This loss of status is reflected in the physical and intellectual collapse of the institutions of supervision and education, the absence of health coverage, and the massive and aggressive presence of young people on the streets, at public garbage dumps, and in urban and rural undergrounds. The reclassification of young people is manifested in hostility toward them. This takes increasingly violent forms which, combined with disdain and indifference on the part of the elites, renders their present difficult and their future unpredictable.

Yet, while African youth find themselves excluded from formal institutions, especially those that promote their wellbeing, this is not to say they have shrunk from the public sphere. If anything, as Diouf (2003:5) writes, their presence is magnified, often violently so, as they turn to urban areas, and more particularly the streets, to defy and appropriate their marginalization by the state and society at large. Hence, recent anthropological studies about youth in postcolonial Africa tend to gravitate toward metaphors of maneuverability to describe their social identities and practices. Youth are "makers and breakers" (De Boeck and Honwana 2005:2), "navigators" (Vigh 2006:31), "generators" (Christiansen et al. 2006:21), and "social shifters" (Durham 2004:592). In each case they are represented as agents of considerable mobility and social change.[6]

With these considerations, this book presents the distinct cultural universe of youth who refuse to accept the bleak prospects of their socioeconomic subjugation. They do so, moreover, through their very movements on the streets, transforming public spaces into domestic spaces. The title of the book, *Street Life under a Roof*, conveys these experiences and patterns of living. It delineates the daily routines, exchanges, and interpersonal relationships that make urban survival not only possible but also meaningful. In this regard, the government's attribution of "idle" to its youth is misleading, for the young men and women in this study do not succumb to inactivity but rather do the

Figure 4. Rooftop graffiti by street youth.

opposite. They set up structures of domesticity at the very edges of public acceptability—in alleyways and gutters, underneath protruding overhangs, in parking lots and condemned buildings. Their shelters—constructed from cardboard boxes, plastic tarps, and oftentimes just blankets—are impervious to idleness, for they undergo constant modification and degradation, and when the state is involved, outright demolition. To draw on the apt metaphor of one law enforcement official, these sites are like mushroom patches: they seem to spring up overnight (helped by rain) and disappear just as quickly. Analytically, one can even extend the metaphor of the mushroom patch to view these shelters as a type of "youthscape"—a geopolitical configuration of cultural spaces connecting youth to one another and to larger globalizing institutions, ideologies, and technologies (Maira and Soep 2005).

Puff and Pass

The stark graffiti shown in figure 4, written on the rooftop of one such shelter, conveys the impermanence of these cultural spaces. "Puff and Pass" refers to drug use, to the smoking of a joint or Mandrax pipe.[7] It also describes the moral economy of the streets, of having very little and sharing with a person, most likely a friend, sitting nearby. The accompanying script "When days are dark, friends are few" offers a cautionary adage. It highlights the volatility of street life as well as the capricious nature of social relationships. To the far left, "[Blank] is a scrub" similarly conveys the disappointments of social relationships, in this case a sexual relationship. Taken from the American hip-hop group TLC and their hit song "No Scrubs," the graffiti presents a commentary on deadbeat boyfriends, on those who cannot fulfill emotional and material commitments. It is notable, too, that the boyfriend's name is removed, literally scrubbed off, erasing an individual identity to leave the scrub as an everyman. These sentiments—"Puff and Pass," "When days are dark, friends are few," and "[Blank] is a scrub"—animate the ensuing chapters of this book. They speak to the centrality of social relationships in the lives of street youth as well as to the structural violence—the poverty, addictions, illnesses, and abuses—that shape the uncertainties of their urban survival. And here perhaps "Puff and Pass" sums it up best, for it emphasizes the transience of street life under a roof, of inhaling, exhaling, and moving on either in life or in death.

*   *   *

Vodacom! Tokyo Cars! Chicken-Licken! Billboards and advertisements abound in the Point Area, but no painted sign, mailbox, or number announces the address of Point Place. In the early mornings, fog rolls in from the Indian Ocean, shrouding the building in mist. With the hazy sun the fog lifts, replaced by car exhaust and the bustle of passing pedestrians. Rarely do they look up to catch a glimpse of the young occupants peering outside. Only the gaping windows, without panes or curtains, reveal that something is amiss.

Point Place is a five-story apartment complex that is located in between Durban's beachfront and central business district. Its proximity to the recreational and commercial sectors of the city makes the building an attractive residence, at least to the untrained eye. For as it stands today, Point Place has no working electricity, running water, or sanitation services. Since the mid-1990s, following the overturn of apartheid rule, a constant stream of tenants has occupied the twelve apartment units within Point Place. The ground floor of the building, once a family restaurant, now operates as a nightclub. The upper residential floors have been cut up, diced up, and leased out so many times that not a single room conforms to its intended blueprint layout. Further confounding this legibility, most of the original owners have moved abroad. As a consequence, the body corporate of Point Place has ceased to exist, making it difficult for the Durban municipality to enforce its housing bylaws. To collect on outstanding debts, in 2001 the municipality cut off all services to and from the building.

At the time of this municipal cutoff, Durban's older street youth faced a shutout of their own kind. The Street Children's Forum—a service provider for children's shelters—lowered the intake age for accepting youth directly off the streets. Overnight, those who were sixteen years of age and older found themselves without affordable accommodation. Unable or unwilling to return home, most of these youth returned to the streets. A few, however, knew about Point Place. They had learned of its whereabouts from a shelter worker who was residing in the building at the time. Sympathetic to their plight, he allowed a group of older boys to enter one of the vacated units. From there they made steady inroads, their numbers growing to incorporate companions on the streets. By 2003, Durban's older street youth—males and females between the ages of fourteen and twenty-nine—had claimed eight out of the twelve apartments within Point Place as their de facto rent-free domain.

In many respects, the youthful occupation of Point Place reflects the shifting demographic of South Africa's inner cities. It reveals the uneasy transitions of a post-apartheid state, the lifting of repressive influx-control laws (which until the mid-1980s restricted Africans' residence in urbanized areas) and the subsequent flight of white residents and capital from the city centers. The structure of Point Place reveals this rapid disinvestment, as does its disconnection from basic municipal services. Yet, while the building's physical disrepair points to the socioeconomic disparities of urban life, its internal composition suggests a different story. For the large number of youth residing here—up to a hundred at any given time—signals an undertaking of enterprise and activity as opposed to abandonment or idleness. It points to a continuation of social connections despite the welfare gaps, disappointments, and setbacks of institutional structures. Ultimately, then, I contend that the Point Place youth—contrary to the assertions of the general public—do not set out to oppose the regulatory practices of the state. Rather, they reside together to mediate the inequalities of urban life. In the process they transform their social dislocations into rich cultural forms of domestic companionship, care, and cohabitation.

* * *

The research for this book spans a decade, from 2000 to 2010, providing a longitudinal view of the lives of street youth in post-apartheid South Africa. While I conducted preliminary investigations of street shelters in the summers of 2000, 2001, and 2002, the majority of my research derives from my two-year field stay in Durban, which occurred between September 2003 and August 2005. In 2008 I returned to South Africa as a postdoctoral fellow at the University of the Witwatersrand. During this time I traveled back and forth from Johannesburg and Durban, spending ten months, until 2010, conducting follow-up research with street youth and their families.

My findings largely draw from the anthropological field methods of participant observation, semistructured and unstructured interviews, informal conversations, and a demographic survey that I administered inside Point Place. I also make extensive use of local newspapers as well as scholarly sources to triangulate my data and frame my analysis. Over the course of my field research, I interviewed approximately one hundred street youth, with a large number of them participating in follow-up and group interviews. I conducted these interviews primarily in isiZulu, the language that is spoken most commonly in the province of KwaZulu-Natal. My knowledge of isiZulu derives from two years of formal language training in graduate school at Yale University as well as an intensive summer language course in South Africa that included rural and township home stays as well.

In addition to interviewing street youth, I spent a significant amount of time traveling to their homes and speaking with their family members. These visits proved invaluable to my research, for they helped me corroborate life stories while providing a better understanding of the love and commitment—and suffering and abuse—that underpin the relationships of youth living in the city. Telling, too, is that during these home visits, their kinsfolk would press photo albums into my hands, showing me pictures of family members—alive, missing, and deceased—while narrating their accomplishments and tribulations. The walls of their living rooms also displayed portraits of kin, honoring and recognizing their presence in the home.

The prominence and, indeed, celebration of these photographs sits uneasily with my obligation not to include identifiable pictures of individuals in my publications, a requirement of the institutional review board that oversaw my fieldwork, which also stipulated that I change the names of my research participants. Therefore, this book displays photographs of places and events devoid of identifiable individuals. My intention is not to marginalize or stigmatize the Point Place youth or their families. I make an exception only with my research assistant, Ofentse, who was invaluable in helping me carry out this project and requested that I include her photograph in my work.

Although I am unable to include identifiable pictures of the Point Place youth, I do my best to convey the substance and style of their communicative praxis: their articulations and deliberations, their reflections and intercessions. My narrative approach draws on what anthropologists Arthur and Joan Kleinman (1996:172) describe as "experience-near" research, as it "interprets patterns of meaning within situations" while also putting forth a "liberating distance" that stems from an "appreciation of shared human conditions." Similar to the Kleinmans' focus on the interpersonal and experiential, Michael Jackson (1996) calls for anthropologists to engage in a project of "radical empiricism," which he describes as "a methodology and discursive style that emphasizes the subject's experience and involvement with others in the construction of knowledge" (Narayan 1993:680). With these insights, I privilege the ethnographic context of lived experiences as I frame my observations and conversations—frequently presented as stylized field notes—through the intonations of the Point Place youth: the rhythms, cadences, and modulations of language and bodily practice that inflect their life stories with feeling and emotion, with sentiments of more than mere survival.

*   *   *

For organizational clarity, I have divided the book into three ethnographic parts. In part 1, "Street Life under a Roof," I discuss my methodological and analytical entrée into the world of street shelters, which began in the year 2000. At the time, I was participating in a social service program at the University of KwaZulu-Natal in Durban. Professors at the university asked me to investigate a children's shelter in the city center, which they were considering as a site for internship programs. The shelter had an unsavory reputation, so before they involved students, they wanted to make sure that children were not kept there by force.[8] Over the course of my investigations, I learned the opposite to be the case: far from a site of detention, it was one of routine eviction, with male adolescents and younger females consistently rejected from the premises. In 2002 these same youth—deemed too old, unruly, or sexually promiscuous to gain access to the welfare services of the state—introduced me to shelters of their own making.

Chapter 1, "Shelter Hopping," traces the institutional displacements and disenfranchisements of Durban's street youth population. It follows their movements from shelter to shelter as they attempt to establish a semblance of stability in a precarious situation of state-sanctioned evictions and arrests. Here I introduce close associates, including my research assistant, Ofentse, who make regular appearances in ensuing chapters. I also outline the centrality of Point Place as a viable yet problematic housing option for older street youth and females. Chapter 1 thus sets up the overarching narrative of *Street Life under a Roof*, in which youth look to each other to mitigate the hardships of their urban poverty.

Chapter 2, "Standing (K)in," draws on an analytical framework of "relatedness" to present the everyday attachments—the kinships, friendships, and sexual partnerships—of the Point Place youth. To convey the fluidity of these relationships, I refer to the idiom of *ukuma*, which in isiZulu means "to stand." Sometimes the youth in this study "stand for one another" (*ukumelana*), while at other times they "stand in the way" (*ukumuma*) of each other. Their various enactments of *ukuma* speak to the hierarchies of urban survival as well as to the commensalities. Hence, while this chapter details the conflicts that occur within Point Place—as seen through a court case drama—it also reveals the practices of solidarity that maintain the Point Place youth on a day-to-day basis. With *ukuma* at the forefront of its investigations, it shows how youth negotiate their standing in society precisely through their relationships with one another—as kin, friends, and lovers.

Part 2, "Domesticities, Intimacies, and Reciprocities," conveys the material and emotional exchanges of love and survival on the streets. I present chapters three and four as companion pieces, meant to complement each other through the respective viewpoints of the Point Place females and males. These chapters continue to focus on the relationships of the Point Place youth while also bringing in broader concerns framed by the socioeconomic and political inequalities of the global AIDS pandemic. At the time of this research, international drug companies restricted the South African government from importing generic and thus affordable drugs to treat HIV/AIDS. Subsequently, the majority of the South African population did not have access to antiretroviral treatment, which also could have helped reduce the transmission of HIV/AIDS. In this context of massive life disparities, chapters three and four discuss the sexual intimacies of the Point Place youth. I argue that the debilitating effects of HIV/AIDS are not a manifestation of youth degeneracy or irresponsibility, but rather should be seen as an outcome of inequality, dependency, and love.

Chapter 3, "Love, Betrayal, and Sexual Intimacy," takes up the challenge of understanding why the Point Place females, who are aware of how HIV/AIDS is transmitted, agree to unprotected intercourse. Certainly material circumstances impinge on their capacity to negotiate condom use, yet this does not fully account for why they distinguish different sexual encounters with different degrees of risk. In short, the Point Place females use condoms with boyfriends who reside outside the building but not with boyfriends who reside within the building. Their construction of "outside" and "inside" boyfriends links up to notions of trust and, more specifically, to acts of *nakana*,[9] which in isiZulu means "to care about or take notice of one another." The Point Place females repeatedly cite the ongoing support of *nakana*—with its emphasis on domestic companionship and reciprocity—as the motivating reason for why they agree to condom-less sex with their Point Place boyfriends. This in turn opens them up to the risks of sexually transmitted infections (STIs), which they view as acceptable when compared to the perils of being unloved or forsaken on the streets.

Chapter 4, "Love, Respect, and Masculinity," discusses *nakana* from the perspective of the Point Place males. Like the females, they, too, link *nakana* to love and acts of reciprocity, which they also connect to a shared living space. While chapter 4 discusses *nakana* in relation to categories of sexual exchange, chapter 5 considers it in relation to models of masculinity. Specifically, it addresses the production of patriarchy inside Point Place, where the males set up a paradoxical living arrangement. Because they do not trust the Point Place females—whom they deem sexually promiscuous—they select girlfriends from outside the building. They bring these girlfriends inside as rooming companions, creating a situation in which an "outside" girlfriend becomes an "inside" girlfriend and therefore a figure to be distrusted. To protect themselves, the Point Place males resort to disciplinarian tactics meant to control the behavior of their sexual partners. Condoms, from their perspective, indicate failure because their girlfriends—deemed trustworthy before entering Point Place—should be HIV free. In this context, unprotected sex is an affirmation of *nakana* as well as a successful dominant masculinity.

Whereas parts 1 and 2 largely focus on the intragenerational fellowships of the city, part 3, "The Power of Home," presents the intergenerational rifts that characterize the home situations of the Point Place youth. In many respects, these rifts reflect the demographic losses of HIV/AIDS in South Africa, as the province of KwaZulu-Natal has the highest HIV prevalence and incidence rates in the country, leaving it with the largest number of AIDS orphans, too. Bereft of material and emotional support, many of these youth—like the Point Place youth—have taken to the streets. Yet, while the impact of HIV/AIDS is profound in KwaZulu-Natal, it tells only part of the story about the estrangements of kinship in the home. Chapters six and seven detail the fragility of these ties, linking the moral dominion of the home to the perceived immoralities of the streets.

Chapter 5, "Residing with the Spectral," reveals the psychological turmoil of street life under a roof. Rather than speak of their losses outright—the losses of kin, friends, and lovers to the violence of poverty and HIV/AIDS—the Point Place youth speak of uGogo, a ghostly grandmother who torments youth to their death by enticing them to jump out of windows. From their narratives of despair and destruction, I explore the various significations of uGogo's presence. Why does she appear to some youth and not others? Is she a witch? An ancestor? A drug-induced hallucination? To answer these questions, I privilege a symbolic analysis of uGogo, linking her floating associations to a broader discussion of spirituality, witchcraft, and death in post-apartheid South Africa.

In chapter 6, "Homecomings," I travel to the townships and rural areas of KwaZulu-Natal to understand the home situations of the Point Place youth. Here I meet their kinsfolk, who explain the reasons for their children's departures. While acknowledging the material constraints of their homes, they also refer to infractions from the past. They speak of unsuitable marital alliances, inactive lineages, and unfulfilled filial obligations. In short, they refer to the estrangements of kin, which include not only the living but also the deceased—or the *amadlozi* (ancestors). Chapter 7 thus presents the power of the home through the intervening authority of the *amadlozi*. From these ties of kinship, it investigates the possibilities of reconciliation, of youth returning to their homes to appease the conflicts of the past and to extend the lifelines of their lineages.

The conclusion to the book summarizes the major themes of *Street Life under a Roof*, emphasizing the connections between everyday relatedness and companionship—or *nakana*—on the streets. It also presents the endings to the stories of the Point Place youth. Notably, a substantial number of them are still seeking shelter in the city center. Chapter 8 thus reviews the housing options for the urban poor, noting the lived disparities between political rhetoric and practice that make the basic right of dignified life, including the right to shelter, an unlikely reality for South Africa's older street youth population.

PART 1

Street Life under a Roof

1   Shelter Hopping

"What are those *creatures* doing here?!"

The taxi driver instinctively hits the brakes. We lurch to a stop. I sink down in my seat, not wanting the boys outside to associate me with this unfolding scene. I need not worry. They teeter away from us, barely registering Rose's outrage.

Slam! Rose gets out of the car. She kicks aside a plastic milk bottle, its contents filled with a yellowing substance, the last remnants of congealed glue.

I step behind Rose, slowly placing one foot in front of the other. We enter a narrow passageway. Towering gray walls obstruct the winter sunlight. A breeze whips through the corridor, causing swirls of grime to reach my eyes, momentarily blinding me and then settling on my skin and in my hair. I feel grit along the enamel of my teeth. Above I hear the rushing noise of cars speeding along the freeway. I tilt my head upward. Spiraling rolls of barbed wire twinkle brightly, harshly. Through their steely points, I can make out billboards: *Coca-Cola! Drive Safely! Arrive Alive!* I look down. A pungent smell emanates from the tarred surface: baked urine. We turn the last corner. The overhead din of traffic is now surpassed by the shrieking clamor of laughing, fighting, crying children.

Rose introduces me to the surrounding kids and care workers. She herself is a manager of the care workers. Within minutes of our arrival, all able bodies scatter. It takes me only a few seconds to realize why, for at every possible juncture Rose has a new demand: "Wake up, wash, clean up, pick up, sweep up . . . do something!" In this onslaught of manic activity, I am forgotten, which allows me to observe my new surroundings.

* * *

Thuthukani (fig. 5) is a children's street shelter located in the metropolis of Durban. Its two-story structure is organized around an open-air courtyard. By standing in the center of the courtyard and turning 360 degrees, I can see every door to every bedroom on both levels. This panopticon effect is a holdover from South Africa's apartheid past. The building originally was constructed as a hostel that was designed to accommodate a flexible labor pool of migrant workers. Today the disciplinary gaze is only partial, for all the doors upstairs are closed, obstructing an insider view. The rooms on the first floor, however, are exposed and accessible to most individuals.

The dining hall—like all of the common rooms—is located on the ground level, its rectangular space filled by rows of aluminum tables and benches. Sound echoes loudly off the surfaces, amplifying even the lowest hum to a reverberating roar. A split door bolted from the inside blocks off the kitchen area. Only a few chosen children may enter here if entrusted with the food preparation and cleanup procedures. The kitchen is sparsely outfitted: a stove, prep counter, sink, and padlocked refrigerator-freezer. The pantry (fig. 6) is not much better. Sacks of sugar and rice sag against the wall, meager spills crunching underfoot. The shelves themselves are empty, covered more by

Figure 5. Thuthukani, a shelter for street children in Durban.

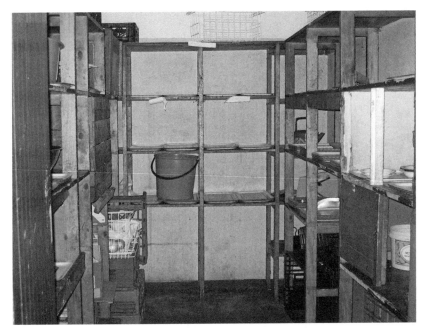

Figure 6. The food pantry at Thuthukani.

rat droppings, cockroaches, and broken crockery than by anything even remotely edible. Food is largely donated, brought in daily by local charities and religious organizations. Bundles of secondhand clothing arrive from these very same people and are lifted from the trunks of their shiny cars. All of this can be seen through the dining room windows.

Children rush forward, grabbing, pulling, and seizing. Shirts, pants, and mismatched shoes burst forth from cardboard boxes. The laundry room located at the far end of the shelter overflows with castoff apparel. The washing machine jumps up and down, vibrating with constant activity. Outside, damp garments and linens hang from every available clothesline, protruding gutter, and desiccated bush. Next to the laundry room is the classroom, also filled to maximum capacity. Desks and chairs occupy the center, with bookshelves and a chalkboard pushed against the sides. Colorful drawings, poems, and educational posters brighten the water-stained walls. When utilized, the room is filled by a distinct demography, children thirteen years and younger. Most of the older kids remain outside, either milling around the shelter or having left the premises altogether. These five sites—the courtyard, dining room, kitchen, laundry room, and classroom—are all excessively visible, regulated by the watchful eyes of adults. The bedrooms remain a separate affair.

Figure 7. A typical bedroom at Thuthukani.

Behind these closed doors, a counterpublic exists (Warner 2002), a space where youth maneuver around the direct surveillance of adults. On first glance the bedrooms appear secure and orderly (fig. 7). They are minimally furnished: a few mattresses with threadbare blankets; the occasional pillow and stuffed animal; perhaps a wooden bureau, office cabinet, or trunk; a collection of assorted toiletries, broken mirrors, cups, candles, and matches. The windows are small. They are situated near the ceiling, which makes it difficult—if not impossible—to look down to the bustling streets below. Burglar bars are fixed on the outside, a permanent solution to the missing panes. Dust, soot, and grime add layer on layer of dinginess to the walls, floors, bedding, and furniture. Magazine cutouts artfully taped to the walls alleviate the dullness of the bedrooms only marginally. Esoteric graffiti— names and places—add a little more personality, leaving signatures that last far longer than the tenure of any single occupant. All this can be seen immediately, exposed by the open swing of a bedroom door. It is only with time—several years' time—that I realize the importance of these rooms as a private domain of interpersonal engagement distinct from the dominant public eye.

*   *   *

I hear a gurgling noise and feel a slight tremble under my feet. Two older girls motion for me to step aside. I look down and see water seeping from an exposed drainage hole. It pushes its way through the crumbling cement. The girls point to a bathroom a few feet away. I recall the recent flush of a toilet, mere background noise to the overall din of playing children. The girls take my hand and lead me toward the reception area. I step over some sleeping boys, new arrivals brought in by the police. Their clothes are ragged and torn; their hair is uncombed, and their faces, feet, and hands are unwashed and covered with scabs and sores. My presence, along with the surrounding noise and sunlight, does not disturb them. I reach the reception area. I see Rose standing next to another woman, Tina. She holds a clipboard.

"Are you able to administer this survey to the children?" Tina asks. It was created in the Netherlands, a questionnaire that monitored the behavioral patterns and aggression levels of schoolchildren. Over the course of several weeks, I am to meet with the Thuthukani children to provide an assessment of their personalities. Tina assigns me an isiZulu interpreter, Miss Patience, one of the care workers from the shelter. I scan the questions: Does the child address you in a monotone? Is the child rude, angry, or agitated? Does the child avoid looking you in the eye? It is my first day, and I already know this will never work.

*   *   *

It is my last day at Thuthukani. Just before I reach the gates, I recognize a group of girls standing outside. One of them is carrying a duffel bag on her back. She is angry. A few others are crying.

"What happened?" I ask.

The night before, several of the girls left the shelter to go clubbing with their boyfriends. When they returned the next morning, the female care workers berated them, saying they no longer were allowed inside Thuthukani. The boys, meanwhile, slipped in unnoticed, neither their presence nor their absence a matter of disapproval.

I tell the girls to wait outside while I find the care workers. I believe that their eviction from the shelter is a misunderstanding. I find the care workers in the kitchen preparing their teatime ritual of fried eggs and buttered bread.

The atmosphere is remarkably calm, even jovial. I ask them what happened the previous night, and I hear a similar story. I am perplexed: "Why aren't the boys sanctioned the same way?"

The room is silent. Angrily, Patience interjects, "The girls bring shame onto the shelter." Their sexuality is an embarrassment, easily detected by the swelling of their bellies.

"But aren't the girls more vulnerable to pregnancy if they're left on the streets?" I inquire.

A debate ensues among the care workers. The male care workers decide that the girls can return to Thuthukani if they give an apology. The female care workers are ambivalent. Resentful of my interference, they refuse to look at me. I walk outside to call the girls and discover that they are gone.

Wiseman, one of the nightshift workers, believes that the girls walked to the "Golden Mile," a popular beachfront attraction for the Thuthukani kids. We head that way, and I am grateful for his company. The girls, however, are not at the beachfront, the arcades, the shopping centers, or any of the other usual spots.

"The girls may be staying with Nelly," Wiseman speculates. Nelly is the laundry lady from Thuthukani. She often takes children home with her. I had heard of this arrangement before but had not been able to confirm it with any of the care workers. The kids at Thuthukani believe that Nelly is setting up her own *shebeen* (an unlicensed drinking establishment), using the girls to sell beer and attract surrounding township customers. The rumor seems more plausible now, for the girls are nowhere to be found.

I ask Wiseman if I can accompany him to Nelly's home. Although surprised by my request, he agrees. At the time, I am unaware of how my decision will affect my later interactions with Durban's street youth. For in the years to come, these same girls will allow me to gain entry into a new type of living arrangement: Point Place.

*   *   *

Two years later, I am back inside Thuthukani. This particular day I am sitting on top of a deflated tire watching a game of pick-up soccer in the parking lot. The boys are barefoot and the game is fast, for they are playing on asphalt. A young man enters the premises, clearly familiar with the Thuthukani staff and children. I recognize him immediately. His face bears the scar of an injury that I recall quite well, etched in my memory and field journal:

> *The din of shouting boys and girls echoing along the metal tables*
> *leaves me with a headache. I step outside the dining room into the*

courtyard. I make my way to the front reception area hoping it will be calmer. A group of older boys pass by me laughing boisterously, causing me to speculate that I may be part of some inside joke. One of them steps in my path of direction, blocking my way. He casts a shadow against the warm sunlight. I look up into his face and see that part of his nose is missing. Underneath the flapping skin I detect the shiny smoothness of white cartilage. I try not to react. My face must have betrayed something, for the young man promptly asks if I believe in God. I think this may be a test of some sort. Rather than answer, I turn to my dependable cache: paper and pens. He joins me on the front steps, drawing a portrait that is supposed to be me. He signs the picture with his English name, Thomas. He asks me to copy a biblical passage. I oblige, adding some flowers to the verse. Thomas appreciates this. A sparrow lands nearby. It hops gingerly toward the kitchen, pausing at the entrance. Thomas pounces upon the bird. He slams the kitchen door shut. Startled, I am left sitting outside alone.

Two years later, Thomas's nose is whole again. His demeanor, however, remains the same: unpredictable. "My friend, it's me!" He tap dances around the tire.

I stand up. "Yes, I remember!" I am happy to see him. Thomas tells me that he is staying in an apartment building near the beachfront. Wiseman lives there, too, along with other boys and girls chased out of Thuthukani. I inundate Thomas with question after question

He claps his hands in encouragement. "I'll show you!" he offers.

I hesitate.

"Don't worry." He senses my apprehension. "It's in a busy part of town. You can decide when you see it."

I agree, and we set off.

*   *   *

Another year later, I am back inside Thuthukani. I have established myself as an anthropologist and a volunteer. My mind remains preoccupied with Point Place—the building that Thomas showed me a year ago. I am not sure whether it still exists. I know I must wait for a guide. I cannot visit on my own. Until then I engage in my usual routine, my established methodology: I draw pictures with the kids. We create life-history books, filling in blank pages with personal stories. We go on outings. I become an expert on the sidewalk interests of ten-year-old boys: Kung Fu posters, soft-serve ice cream, street vendors, and medicine markets filled with mysterious herbs, potions, and animals, alive and deceased. My eyes take in all these amusements, but my ears remain trained on two words: "Point Place." Finally an occasion arises.

I am organizing donated books, stacking them by size and difficulty level for an older, stoutly built woman whom the children refer to as "Teacher" since she offers basic reading and math lessons. A few of the younger boys are sitting at the desks patiently waiting for their turn at the electric razor. It is haircutting time. I hear a yelp and chairs being scraped against the floor, followed by a chorus of shouting kids. I turn around. One boy tries to run, but Teacher catches him in an iron-fisted clutch. "Turpentine!" she yells.

Confused, I ask what happened. The boys gleefully chant, "*Izintwala, izintwala!*" I do not need my pocket dictionary to figure this one out. I can tell immediately from the boy's shamed expression and the small white bugs falling off the nape of his neck . . . lice. The turpentine is brought in, and Teacher orders the boys to scrub down the tables, floors, and chairs. They use their own T-shirts.

Teacher returns to her cup of instant coffee, muttering in annoyance, "Point Place." I approach the front desk elated by this revelation. Up until now, I have not been able to glean much information from any of the care workers. Whenever I mention the building, my line of inquiry is quickly dismissed: "Why should you be concerned about Point Place? Isn't there enough going on at Thuthukani?"

I try to be casual. "So this boy comes from Point Place?" Teacher nods in answer, still distracted by the defilement of her classroom. "But he's so young," I continue. "Isn't Point Place only for older kids?" Teacher looks up from her mug. I press forward, thinking of Wiseman: "Are there any care workers inside Point Place?"

"There aren't any care workers."

"But who looks after the kids?"

Teacher appraises me for a second and then replies, "They look after themselves." She pauses, "I guess you could call it a true democracy."

I am surprised by her choice of words. If it is mentioned at all, Point Place is usually associated with anarchy, not democracy. The boys, meanwhile, have finished dousing the lice and begin adding their opinions. I pick up fragments of description: dark, smelly, dirty, no toilets. I cannot tell if these are firsthand accounts or shared imaginings learned from others, spoken in the genre of little-boy gossip reminiscent of bedtime stories. Teacher sees that my interest has been piqued. "Talk to Nompilo," she tells me. "She stays inside Point Place."

In the kitchen I find Nompilo, a young woman in her early twenties, leaning on a table, eyes half-closed, obviously bored. Nompilo is the cook at

Thuthukani. She wears a maid's uniform, a purple pinafore with a matching headscarf. A younger girl stands next to her. They are picking mold off rotten strawberries, eating them slowly, savoring them one by one. I address the girls in isiZulu, aware that my formal greeting and bright smile do not fit in this setting. There is a chasm between us, based on race and class differences, which I cannot bridge. They offer me a strawberry, but I decline. My stomach's refusal reinforces the social distance.

"Nompilo," I take a chance, "do you know Point Place?"

"Yes."

I wait for her to continue, but she is silent. "Teacher says you stay there?"

"No." She laughs, embarrassed. "I stay with my family. Point Place is dirty. And the kids," she shakes her head, "they're not good."

"Oh." I don't know what else to add. "Do you think you'll go back?"

Nompilo looks at me suspiciously and then brightens. "Hey, can you organize a job for me?"

I issue my standard response: "I'm a student from overseas. I don't have any contacts in South Africa."

Both girls observe me in brooding silence. The younger one asks for my flip-flops, and I turn away in resignation.

* * *

I am sharing a seat with a young woman named Angel. Apart from the driver, we are the only two remaining passengers on the bus. Angel softly whispers, "*Ngiyasaba ngempela*" (I'm really scared). She is looking out the window, staring at a cluster of shacks situated across the hillside. A group of girls are milling around outside, not daring to venture more than a few yards from the idling bus. I start to worry. When is Wiseman coming back? I again ask Angel why we have stopped here. She explains that we have come to pick up another girl. They are attending the same computer class. This is the reason why I am on the bus as well. These girls all come from Point Place.

It is through Wiseman that I am able to access Point Place. Although he no longer works at Thuthukani, Wiseman remains a close ally of Durban's street youth. He not only resides with them inside Point Place—sharing an apartment with one of the owners—but he also assists the Street Children's Forum (SCF) in short-term pilot projects like the computer training class. Everyone recognizes that Wiseman has "a certain way" with the older kids. Many question his motives. I, too, question Wiseman's motives. Yet this is not a one-sided indictment, for my research agenda and goals also are suspect, often brought into painful relief by Wiseman's probing accusations. Our relationship is contentious and fraught with anxiety. But there is friendship, too, for the two of us have assisted one another, often in the most difficult times. It began with a common interest: visiting Nelly's home. Neither of us has forgotten this, and so when we see each other again by chance at a meeting for street youth, Wiseman invites me back inside Point Place. He tells me about a computer-training course sponsored by the SCF. He asks if I would like to accompany the girls, mainly to motivate them and to make sure they attend the classes together. I am pleased with this arrangement, for it provides me with an opportunity to interact with the Point Place youth. It also allows me unlimited access to the building.

Wiseman returns with the missing girl. She has been staying with her boyfriend, sharing a room in one of the shacks. The girl looks to be dressed better than her peers. Her shoes match her outfit. She barely glances at me before lowering herself onto a seat. The other girls admire her clothes, fake diamond-stud earrings, and pink clasp purse. Just as the bus is ready to leave, the driver cuts the engine. I look through the windows and observe several young men confronting Wiseman. One of them flashes a gun. It is tucked inside the waistband of his pants, partially concealed. The young man pushes his way through the doors, sees me, and stops. I hear the words "Sorry, Miss," and nod in acknowledgment. He continues to the back of the bus. Something is said to the newly arrived girl. She stares straight ahead, her neck taut, her face not registering any emotion. The young man, satisfied with this response, walks off the bus. I now understand why Wiseman has asked me to accompany him to the township. My presence provides a legitimacy to the computer classes that otherwise would be lacking.

I spend my days inside Point Place yet remain an outsider, a foreign observer. To pass the time, I record the details of my surroundings. I count the number of fruit flies circulating overhead. I follow the girls from room to room. I accompany them to the computer classes and to the beachfront. I help them bag candy, cookies, and *umcako* (a chalky white mineral thought to aid digestion and to prevent pregnancy), which they sell to their friends and to pedestrians outside. I ask them basic questions about their lives, backgrounds, and future aspirations. They tolerate me in a bemused way, remarking on my American accent, light eyes, and pale white skin. They tell me that I speak isiZulu like a farm girl. I think this may be an insult. I begin seeing notices. They are plastered to the front gates and entrance walls. They are crumpled in the corners of the foyer, torn and wet, ink running. I read them. They are all the same: eviction notices citing the contravening of numerous health codes, building regulations, and bylaws. I watch the girls set fire to the notices, twisting the paper into fine points to ignite the paraffin stoves. My eyes sting in protest. The girls usher me to the open windows. They change their mind. I am not a farm girl. I am a missus.

* * *

It was in the morning. We were trying to clean the room and then one of my friends came and told us, "Hmm, come and see outside. There are police and soldiers. I think they're coming to close the flat." Then they came. Two men were carrying guns, shouting, "Out! Out! Out!" We asked them to please wait for us to take our clothes. They said, "No, go out! Go out! Go, go, go, go!" We left our clothes inside Point Place. They took our photos. They put us in the police vans and trucks. They took us to the police station. We stayed there 'til the afternoon. And then in the afternoon we went back to the streets. (Thenjiwe, seventeen-year-old female)

They just chased us out, woke us up. Hey, they threw out our clothes. They threw out our bags. Hey, they threw out our food. Hey, they hit us. They used tear gas. I couldn't do nothing. (Chester, twenty-three-year-old male)

When they came, they said we must go out from where we stay because of the things that are happening inside. We're stealing. We're taking other people's chains [jewelry]. They said that we're stealing. They said they're going to lock us up. We must go out. (Zakes, nineteen-year-old male)

Figure 8. A bedroom in Point Place after a police eviction. This room—originally a kitchen for an apartment unit—functioned as a bedroom for street youth. The police pulled everything out of the cabinets and scattered the items across the floor. They were looking for drugs and weapons but found only shoes.

We were waiting for food, talking. Then the police came, Boers and soldiers.[1] They said we must take our things. They had guns. We took our things. We took our things and we left with them. We put other things in the rubbish bins. Other things were thrown out the window into the rubbish truck. We only took small things. And they put us in the police van. They locked us inside there. (Dudu, sixteen-year-old female)

It is early afternoon when I arrive at Point Place. Even before I reach the building, I can see that something has happened; something has gone terribly wrong. The sidewalks are cordoned off. Police cars are flashing red and blue lights. Furniture and clothing are strewn across the pavement. I ask a pedestrian what happened. She tells me that the police invaded Point Place earlier in the morning and forcibly evicted everyone from the building. I feel the weight of my camera in my pocket and pull it out to start snapping photographs. I walk to the front entrance, to the battered gates. The police do not stop me. Perhaps they think I am a journalist? I step inside. The camera offers an objectifying lens, a protective distancing. I move quickly through the apartments, unnerved by the silence. Rooms have been gutted; bedding has been ripped apart, and bureaus are overturned, their contents dumped on the ground. I wind my way up to the rooftop and have a bird's-eye view of the streets below. Several blocks down, I see a slow-moving procession. It is the youth from Point Place making their way back from the police station. I turn and am greeted by a young man. I take his picture.

Jabulani stands tall, hands loosely held at his sides. His eyes are clear, his gaze direct. Razor marks—etched onto his forehead and cheeks—decoratively frame his face. The scarification suggests a traditional upbringing meant to protect Jabulani from illness and harm. His clothes, while slightly threadbare, are well pressed. He wears a loose-fitting dress shirt and brown pleated pants. A belt is cinched tightly at his waist; his white patent shoes are buffed to a high shine. I suspect that Jabulani may be a preacher, one of the apostles who routinely descend upon the building trying to convert kids to their charismatic faith of Christianity. But Jabulani surprises me. He is not an apostle. He works for the city municipality, hired to sweep the streets. An access card is pinned to his shirt. He refers to it with a noticeable sense of pride and accomplishment. Jabulani lives inside Point Place. He works the morning shift and so missed the police invasion. Now he is searching for his identification book, lost in the chaos of the eviction. His despair is momentarily lifted by the thought of the end of the month, the day after tomorrow.

This means payday and the possibility of finding a room to rent. Jabulani plans to take several of the Point Place youth with him. He grins, a lasting impression of hope and optimism.

Outside, the streets are transformed yet again, overflowing with recently evicted residents. They are determined to find their meager possessions. A retired Catholic missionary named Hilda, an excessively talkative but well-meaning elderly white woman, intercepts me. Hilda has tried to assist the Point Place youth in the past, especially the girls, with small entrepreneurial projects. She would like them to sew their own clothes, set up fried-chip stands, or help out in a hair salon. Hilda's efforts usually turn into dismal failures. Even so, unlike the other missionaries who frequent the Point Area, Hilda has not given up completely. She introduces me to one of her more receptive charges, Ofentse. I recognize Ofentse from the streets. She is carrying a baby on her back. Hilda expresses concern over the sleeping child. She asks Ofentse whether she has moved her belongings into the Nest, a nightly paying shelter. Ofentse replies, "No," sees Hilda's disapproval, and quickly modifies her answer to "Not yet." Hilda is unsatisfied with this response. She scolds Ofentse, telling her to think of the baby. Ofentse blinks, pats Hilda on the arm, and declares that she will remain outside a little longer to fight for her rights.

Ofentse stands apart from all the girls I have met so far in both physical appearance and temperament. She is tall, thin, and angular—a striking figure when set next to her shorter, rounder, and softer-featured companions. People often mistake Ofentse's slenderness for illness or even something else. Many think Ofentse possesses a certain type of ancestral power: that of an isangoma. *Others are afraid of her. I have heard people whisper that she is a witch. Ofentse scoffs at these associations, saying that she is too young, too poor, and too afraid of water and blood to suffer the trials of an* isangoma. *Besides, she has a baby to care for. And indeed her little boy, Musa, is well looked after, properly fed and nourished, receiving not only his mother's portions of food but also those of a dozen other kids who supply him with drinks, sweets, and meat. Ofentse's attire sets her apart as well. Unlike the other girls, Ofentse does not seem to care much about what she wears. Her shirts, shorts, and skirts are faded, stained, and secondhand, the colors muted from countless repetitive washings. Her jewelry consists of beads and trinkets picked up from vendors and friends. Ofentse styles her hair differently, too. It is not combed, plaited, or braided but rather is twisted into dreadlocks. Strangers call her Rasta, a name usually reserved for males. Again Ofentse defies expectations, for she does not smoke drugs (apart from the occasional cigarette), drink alcohol, or sniff glue. Certainly Ofentse looks different, yet it is her internal composure—as seen in the way she articulates herself—that so clearly differentiates her from the other Point Place youth.*

Ofentse has no intention of spending the night at the Nest. She sleeps on the streets, with Musa tucked by her side. I know this because I end up sitting next to them, perched on a cardboard box waiting for the sun to rise. The sidewalks are impassable that evening, filled with sleeping bodies, more than a hundred. Pots, pans, plastic tubs, and water jugs are stacked into piles, carefully guarded. I, too, am guarded. A little boy and a younger girl, Mbali, sit near my feet, urging me to close my eyes. If anyone gets too close, they throw stones. On my other side rests Beauty, a girl I know from Thuthukani—one of the girls who went to Nelly's home. She also looks after me. When a stumbling drunk comes close, Beauty shouts for Wiseman. He pulls out a rusty *panga* and chases the man away. I am wide awake. The Nigerians across the street are awake, too, watching for buyers. I see the same car speed up, slow down, and speed up again. It circles the block several times, stopping briefly in front of a nightclub. A tinted window is rolled down. Four men run up to the driver, elbowing for an exchange. The police van parked at the end of the street remains stationary, its headlights directed at us.

4:30 A.M.: The sky begins to brighten. The street sweepers arrive first, carrying their palm-frond brooms; next come the Indian shopkeepers. Metal gates are heaved upward, groaning with the effort. The little boy by my feet leaves and then returns. He shyly offers me a cup of tea. I try to share it with the girl next to me, Mbali, but he knocks the cup from her grasping hand. It is Friday morning. Stores are open, ready for business. I stand up to buy an early edition of the local newspaper, the *Witness* (2003:3):

[Point Place] has floors closed. The landmark [Point Place] building in Durban's Point Road was raided yesterday and three floors ordered closed. Police spokesman Superintendent Vasie Naidu said members of the SA National Defence Force, Metro Police, Fire Department and the Departments of Labour and Health were involved in the operation. The building houses the well-known Chinese restaurant on the ground floor and has accommodation on the upper floors. Naidu said the building has acquired the reputation of providing a safe haven for petty thieves and those involved in smash-and-grab robberies. Police also found a large number of street children living in unsafe, unhealthy conditions. "The residential portion of the building was totally dilapidated. There was no lighting, the place was filthy and there were no fire extinguishers. In addition, there were several water leaks and the sewerage was not working," she said. Naidu said the children were removed to places of safety and the three floors closed.

I look out onto the sidewalk and wonder which children have been removed to places of safety. Mbali reads aloud from the isiZulu newspaper, *Isolezwe* (2003). She translates the words slowly, sounding them out in a halting voice. The front-page headline proclaims, "Crime Tackled: Children Who Were Selling Their Bodies." Her eyes widen at the implications of the article. The other girls click their tongues in protest. Mbali stops reading. They are not prostitutes.

*   *   *

It is late morning when I return to the Point. This time I am prepared for a night on the streets. I have a warm jacket and a toothbrush. I turn the corner to reach the building, and my breath catches. The sidewalks are empty. Different scenarios play out in my mind, all of them involving the police, all of them bad. I feel a presence by my side. It is Angel. She starts twirling in a circle. I assume that she is high. She motions for me to follow. We turn a few more corners, and I see a massive spread of young bodies. They have set up a new sleeping area, protected from both the passing traffic and the approaching rain. It is a dead-end street sandwiched between two warehouses. The extended roofs provide a sheltered covering. Angel directs me to a row of blankets that have been arranged in sections. Ofentse, Beauty, and Mbali are sitting together. Cooking pots and duffel bags partition their space off from the others. They have been waiting for me. Mbali invites me to join them. I smile in grateful acceptance, my social set now demarcated by the edges of their matted blankets.

The following three nights and four days are more of the same. I spend a substantial portion of my time sitting on the blankets, recording observations and talking to my companions. Food donations arrive from Christian and Muslim organizations. The African National Congress Women's League also makes an appearance. Ofentse tells me to observe closely. These women are looking for maids, impressionable young girls who will cook, clean, do laundry, and watch their babies for minimal compensation. Mbali and Angel already have received several offers. The girls laugh at the propositions, telling the women that they are too busy with schoolwork. City officials start to arrive, becoming more concerned about the health implications as each day passes. Pressures from an outraged public are taking a toll as well. On the fifth day, they announce a negotiated settlement: The older youth will be taken to a bowling alley, the younger ones to Thuthukani. From there, kids under sixteen years of age will be sent to other shelters. I look at Ofentse, who is twenty-three and has a baby; Beauty, who is seventeen; Angel, who is seventeen; and Mbali, who is fifteen. They all opt for the bowling alley. It is beginning to rain, and they do not want to spend another night on the streets.

As it so happens, the keys to the bowling alley cannot be found. So we are driven to Thuthukani. This time I enter the premises from a different vantage point. I am not looking out the windows of Rose's hired car but rather am pressed against the mesh grills of a paddy wagon. The back doors open, and I tumble out with everyone else. The care workers are standing nearby anticipating our arrival. Never an enthusiastic bunch, they look especially morose this wet evening. The Point Place youth are visibly more upbeat. They know that it will be difficult to evict them anytime soon, for the municipality is intent on keeping the streets "clean," at least for the present moment.

*   *   *

The Point Place youth are correct. It takes the SCF another three months to find an alternative solution. In the end, they shut down Thuthukani. The SCF attributes the closure to health violations. Still, as one young man (and repeat resident) notes, "There always have been rats and cockroaches inside Thuthukani." To close the shelter down is the only way to remove the Point Place youth—permanently. A news article from a street youth organization called I-Care offers a more forthcoming account:[2]

> Before the criminals moved in, Thuthukani was a temporary haven for Durban's young street children, a sort of one stop shelter where they could be assessed by social workers. However, that refuge was shattered the moment the police closed down a seedy joint [...] in the Point [Area] in October. Authorities allowed 20 displaced adults [...] to stay for three days at Thuthukani in (Alice Street)—and they never left. Instead, more of them moved in and, before long, kids, men and women were living under the same roof. This mix gave rise to a dangerous environment which saw the newcomers virtually seize control of the center. During the day couples whiled away their time having sex in open view, drugs were consumed and dealers brazenly plied their trade. Organized networks of thieves used it as a hide-out from which they hit businesses, homes, and tourists in a wave of smash-and-grabs. The orgy of crime finally came to an end this week when police moved in and ousted the unwanted inhabitants, in the process bagging themselves four suspects in connection with burglary, theft,

and housebreaking. While the operation was considered a success, it highlighted a perennial problem in inner cities—keeping curb dwellers off the streets and in rehabilitation programmes.

The above narration represents the perspective of those in positions of authority, although, admittedly, not those in complete control. It is the dominant discourse, one that is displayed in newspapers, heard on the radio, and circulated on the Internet; one that is reified in board meetings, courtrooms, police stations, rehabilitation centers, health clinics, and hospital wards. It is the public's telling of reality, yet it is not the only one. For the youth of Point Place also offer their own commentary—a constellation of oppositional views and practices that both uphold and challenge the hegemonic expectations of their surroundings.

* * *

It is our first overnight stay inside Thuthukani. Already a care worker has entered the bedroom to explain the rules: (1) no smoking, (2) no sniffing glue, (3) no boyfriends, (4) no speaking to pedestrians outside the windows, (5) no leaving the room to use the toilets, and (6) no disrespecting the staff, with the added clause that care workers reserve the right to hit anyone who disobeys them. Two plastic basins are set down, one for brushing our teeth, the other for relieving ourselves during the night. The care worker leaves, locking the door behind him. The girls immediately light up, causing me to wonder what would happen in the event of a fire. Ofentse, her baby, and Mbali share a sponge mattress on the floor. I curl up at the end of Beauty's bed. Angel is in the corner sniffing from a glue bottle. The other girls pile onto the five remaining beds and into the floor space. They are loud and apparently drunk, fighting over the blankets, pillows, and mattresses. Again I do not sleep. Ofentse does not sleep, either. She has a throbbing toothache. A piece of Kleenex is jammed into her ear. She claims it helps the pain. At 5:00 A.M. a care worker unlocks the door. I rush outside to use the toilet. Ofentse gets up to wash her laundry and has everything drying on the lines by 6:00 A.M.

It is another day, midafternoon, the heat pressing down on us. Beauty lies on her bed slowly breathing in and out, trying not to cough. She has tuberculosis. So does Angel. For now, neither girl is willing to go to the clinic for a test. I am sitting on the floor with Ofentse watching Musa teeter in between the beds, scavenging for items to put into his mouth. The door opens and Hilda walks in. I greet her, but none of the girls do. Hilda gingerly sits down, balancing herself on the edge of a bed frame. She complains about the heat, her tiredness, and the long walk she undertook to visit us. I make appropriate remarks, but the girls still do not engage. Their faces have taken on blank expressions. Hilda continues to make small talk without much success.

"Is this what you've been doing all day, sitting?" she asks.

"Yes," I nod, not sure how to explain that there is activity in being still.

The silence bothers Hilda. She offers a banana to Musa. "But don't mangle it!" she laughingly tells Ofentse.

"Musa prefers his bananas mashed," Ofentse replies.

Hilda looks disbelieving for a second but decides to let it pass. She again mentions her exhaustion.

I cannot resist: "Why don't you lie down on one of the mattresses?"

Hilda looks at me in unspoken horror. A few minutes later she stands up, clearly annoyed by our apathy. On her way out, she puts a hand on Ofentse's head. "Hmm, have you showered recently?"

Ofentse is taken aback by the question. She translates the remark into isiZulu for Beauty, who breaks her cover of being asleep by shouting, "*Bhuka indlela asidontsela ngayo phantsi!*" (See how she brings us down!)

Hilda, although surprised by Beauty's animation, does not understand isiZulu and so does not pick up on the comment. When she finally leaves, Ofentse angrily informs me, "She doesn't have a child, not even one."

*   *   *

I am sitting at a table inside a small luncheonette just around the corner from Thuthukani. Three heaping plates of food are being dished up behind the counter. It takes a while, because the serving ladies are distracted by the television. It is showing one of their favorite soap operas, *Days of Our Lives*. They bring over a one-liter glass bottle of chilled Coke and set it down on the table. Condensation collects along the bottom and pools atop the plastic tablecloth. A recorder and microphone lie exposed, precariously close to the collecting water. The recorder is turned off. None of us are sure how to proceed. It is six weeks into my field stay, and this will be my first formal interview. I explain my objectives to Ofentse and Beauty: "I'm an anthropology student from the United States, and I'm here to conduct research . . ."

Ofentse's face lights up. "Can we talk about the police eviction?"

I switch the recorder on. Ofentse has a natural oratory skill that enables her to narrate well in almost all situations. Because of this, it takes me a few minutes to realize that she is performing. Her answers, while truthful, are spoken with a particular audience in mind. I imagine that she is addressing a room filled with Hildas.

Beauty, meanwhile, speaks in a manner that is consistent with her usual conduct. With me, Beauty is always reserved. She does not reveal much, not about herself or the things that happen to her. When she does, her comments are simple and concise. I scan my notebooks for my first entry on Beauty, written three years previously. I find this: "Beauty returned to the shelter today. Her arm is bandaged from giving blood at the hospital. She expresses no interest in talking with me." My next profile is dated a few days after the Point Place eviction:

> *I sit down on a blanket beside Beauty. She is propped up on a pillow, inhaling glue. When Beauty finally notices me, she tries to conceal the plastic bottle by tucking it below her shirt. She appears more fragile than usual. The streetlight—muted by the drizzling rain—illuminates her face only partially. She is one of the smaller girls of the group, with big dark eyes and prominent cheekbones. Beauty dresses a bit like a tomboy, always wearing a baseball cap and androgynous clothes. Only her rubber bracelets stacked up along her right forearm indicate a feminine touch. A little boy approaches us. Beauty gives him some coins from her wallet. She tells me that she sometimes holds money for the younger kids. I look at her identification book and see that Beauty is seventeen years old. She tells me a bit more about her life, mainly that her mother passed away in 1999 and her aunt could not provide for her. She has three brothers who stay at home and go to school. She visits them occasionally, bringing them donated clothes. As we are talking, a little boy tries to hold my hand. Beauty shouts at him to go away. She explains that the younger kids have scabies, implying that I must not touch them.*

On the day we meet at the luncheonette, Beauty offers a more detailed account of her life on the streets:

Okay, I'll speak in Zulu. About me, I was chased out [of Thuthukani]. I went home. They [the care workers] took me home, I returned to Durban. I said I wanted to go back to Thuthukani. I was chased away [in 2000]. I went to stay at Pizza [Hut]. We slept during the day in the park [behind the Hilton Hotel]. At night we walked around, all over the beachfront. Boys were bothering us when we were sleeping during the day. The policeman with the gold teeth hit us. He hit us with a cane. He took the glue and spilled it on us. And then we went to stay with the grandmother [Nelly] at Marian Hill . . . She took us from the streets. She took us and every day she was telling us that we must come to the Point [Area] to find money.

Beauty laughs at this last part but then does not say much more, for she assumes I know everything else. Her narrative is typical of the way youth from Point Place discuss their past. It is highly descriptive of people, places, and events, but it remains up to me to connect these references to a broader chronology. I quickly learn the value of follow-up interviews.

*   *   *

In between my interviews, I continue to follow the movements of the Point Place youth. Their residence at Thuthukani is by no means a fixed thing. Within two weeks of their arrival, they are uprooted once again. The cited reason: deviant behavior. The scene is rather predictable. Rose arrives at Thuthukani as she always does, hurling commands and demands for order and discipline. While this generally works on the younger kids, the Point Place youth are not so compliant. Rose enters one of the bedrooms to discover a group of older boys smoking dagga and glue. Enraged, she demands their immediate expulsion. The boys merely laugh and jeer at her, bringing her to the edge of an apoplectic fit.

The next day Rose arranges for the SCF bus to transport all the Point Place youth to an unknown destination. Attitudes in the parking lot alternate between dismay and defiance. Ofentse blames the boys for their present predicament. They could hear Rose's rant long before she stormed into the room. They should have hidden their dagga and glue. Beauty and Angel are in agreement, voicing the common complaint "*Bayajwayela*" (They're disrespectful). Ofentse's annoyance is compounded by her worry over Musa's health. He is sleeping feverishly today and refuses to eat. Ofentse plans to take him to the hospital. She decides to wait until after the bus arrives, for she is worried about finding a safe place to store her bags. Khaya—Musa's father—is not with her at the moment. He works during the daytime sweeping the streets. As we wait, Mbali makes an unexpected appearance. A few days previously, she left Thuthukani to return home, presumably to dip into her granny's monthly pension. Sure enough, she enters the Thuthukani parking lot with new clothes. "So you're back," I greet Mbali, secretly glad to have another friend on the streets. "Whatever for?"

Mbali laughs a little, shrugs her shoulders, and responds, "You know I've always been naughty, even as a little girl." This I believe; it may be the only true thing Mbali has ever told me. Angel cuffs her friend with happy anticipation, imagining a turn at Mbali's new clothes.

Midafternoon the bus finally arrives. The Point Place youth load up with all of their possessions. This includes an array of items taken directly from Thuthukani's storeroom. They feel entitled to the stolen goods, rationalizing that donations are made possible by their presence.

"Where are we going?" the bus driver asks. A unanimous decision is reached: to the beachfront, to the Holiday Inn. Behind the Holiday Inn there is a small grassy park secluded from the streets by a rolling hill.

Upon their arrival, the Point Place youth make a concerted effort to transport everything from the street curb to the park as quickly as possible. Once they are set up, it will be difficult for the hotel security to intervene. A passing pedestrian remarks on the unfolding scene, comparing the cluttered layout to a burgeoning squatter settlement. The Point Place youth retort that they are not squatters. They are street kids. The pedestrian hurries along.

By now, dusk is approaching. Ofentse does not want to wait any longer for Musa to receive medical attention. I accompany her to the hospital, a short walk from the park. We pass the first barrier, a set of hospital guards. They let us in. Ofentse, familiar with the hospital routine, approaches the intake counter. She asks to receive a number for admittance. The screening matron looks up from her paperwork, sees Musa, and scowls. "The pediatricians have all gone home. It's emergency care only now. Why have you waited so long?"

Ofentse says nothing. Her face is expressionless. She just stands in front of the plastic window, looking downward with Musa in her arms. Exasperated, the matron hands Ofentse a number, motioning for us to step aside so the next patient can be seen. Several hours later, a doctor examines Musa and tells Ofentse to bring him back to the hospital in three days to receive his tuberculosis screening results. The doctor hands her a bottle of medicine, which she inspects before throwing it away. I attempt to retrieve the bottle. "Leave it," Ofentse instructs. "I know this medicine. It doesn't work." We step outside into the darkness. We decide to walk along the beachfront by the lights of the hotels. The municipal streetlamps are not working.

We reach the park. Blankets checker the grassy hill. Ofentse locates her bags and arranges a night pack for Musa. He will not be sleeping outside. Ofentse and Khaya have enough money to pay for an overnight shelter. Khaya will take Musa. He insists that Ofentse come with them, but she refuses, saying that she will not leave her friends now. She adds that she does not want to spend the extra money. I know Ofentse's explanations are only partial. She still has not forgiven Khaya for his repeated acts of infidelity, wanting to provoke him as much as possible by refusing to do anything that he asks of her. They shout at each other until Khaya gives up, taking Musa away with him. "You know," Ofentse tells me with satisfaction, "I'm not Khaya's wife. He never paid *ilobolo* [bridewealth], not even for Musa."

"You mean like *ihlawulo* [damages]?"

"Yeah, not even for the pregnancy. He has no claim to me." In other words, Ofentse does not feel indebted to Khaya or his kin since they never formally recognized her or Musa as part of their family. This means that she can renounce all expectations of acting like a submissive wife, including Khaya's demands that she follow him to the shelter.

Later in the night, Khaya returns to the park, insisting that Ofentse carry
the rest of their belongings to the shelter. She is incensed, because he has left
Musa alone, under the supervision of a stranger, in the shelter. Their arguing
escalates until Ofentse jumps up. She wants to go inside the Holiday Inn to
use the restroom. She knows that I will accompany her, because I am the only
one allowed to enter the hotel as a "tourist." The security personnel do not
presume that I am a vagabond or a prostitute. Just as we are about to cross
the street, Khaya cuts us off. He shakes his fist at Ofentse, and in response
she hides behind me. He tries to kick her between and around my legs. He
steps aside only after he realizes that she is not running away.

Later in the evening, just as he is about to return to the shelter, Khaya
seeks me out. "What happened to Ofentse?" he asks. "She never liked sleeping on the streets. Why now?" He is perplexed by her change of attitude. I
am beginning to understand, though. Ofentse depends on the other Point
Place youth, their safety in numbers. Only they can protect her from Khaya's
anger.

Early the next morning, security guards from the Holiday Inn venture into
the park. They notify the police about the makeshift settlement. They are
sympathetic to the plight of the Point Place youth but remain resolute that
everyone must clear out by afternoon. It is too unsightly, especially from the
upper floors of the Holiday Inn. By now the Point Place youth recognize the
severity of the situation. They cannot stay in the park. They cannot return
to Thuthukani. They have no place to store their possessions and no place
to sleep.

In this grim moment, something remarkable happens. A famous Zulu
television actress, Ruth Cele, crosses through the park on her way to the
beachfront. Intrigued by the unfolding scene, she stops and speaks to several
of the boys. Perhaps sensing a publicity stunt, or perhaps genuinely troubled
by their plight, Ms. Cele promises to help the Point Place youth. She pulls out
her cell phone and calls all the broadcast personnel she knows. Newspaper
journalists show up. Television cameras arrive. The Point Place youth, with
the elderly actress in front, march to City Hall and demand to meet with the
mayor. Ms. Cele proclaims that she also will sleep on the streets if the Point
Place youth are not provided with accommodations that very night.

Outside City Hall, everyone is left to stand except for Ms. Cele. Security
personnel allow her to enter the building. When she comes out again, she is
not quite as friendly as before. Apparently the mayor has informed her about
the criminal activities of the Point Place youth. Still, the mayor concedes to
her demands. He is tired of the publicity and negative press. All the youth
from Point Place are allowed to return to Thuthukani. It is too problematic

for them to remain in the park within view of the Holiday Inn. The Health Department transports a few of the younger kids. The rest are left to carry their belongings back to Thuthukani.

Although they have been granted a temporary respite, time is running out for the Point Place youth. Ofentse recognizes this perhaps more than anyone else. She is consumed with trying to find a job and safe, affordable accommodations. She knows that Rose will be back. It is becoming much harder to hide Musa now that he is learning how to walk and talk. One day Ofentse stops me outside the gates of Thuthukani. She takes a deep breath, turns to face me directly, and asks if she can be my maid. I am both dumbfounded and angered by the request. In that moment I recognize that no matter how much I may wish otherwise, my race and class standing will always define me as an outsider to the Point Place youth. More often than not, I will be looked upon as a wealthy white "missus." Within the space of a few seconds, my anger vanishes into sadness. I tell Ofentse that I do not need a maid. I can look after myself. Embarrassed, she pleads for me to forget the request. We silently pass through the gates of Thuthukani. I go home that evening to my own apartment on top of a hill overlooking the cityscape. I listen to some of my recorded interviews. It becomes so obvious to me. I start to draft a formal contract.

*   *   *

Angel is whispering into my minidisc recorder. She rests her chin on her hands, her brow furrowed in concentration. She treats the recorder as if it is a private confessional. I sit across from her. Ofentse, as always, is by my side. She listens intently to what Angel is saying. Every once in a while she holds a hand up, exclaims "Whoa," turns to me, and asks if I need clarification. Angel peers up at us in eager expectation, ready to continue. Ofentse and I do not need to look at each other to know that we are both smiling at Angel's earnest nature. Such interviewing becomes a regular feature of my fieldwork, my standard mode of operation. Ofentse participates as a translator and general facilitator. She is officially my research assistant, my cultural broker. She accompanies me on home visits, hospital visits, and prison visits, and to countless other places, showing me how to act and behave properly, what to eat and what to surreptitiously push to the side. Later on, she will sit next to me when I am at my computer; listening to every interview, she will painstakingly repeat each sentence so that I can type out every single conversation word for word. I do not trust professional transcribers: the slang is too specialized, the locale too specific; the references are too obscure, the voices too muted; and the background is too noisy. Most of all, I do not trust that anyone else will care enough. The stories that are told—the laughter, tears, pain, confusion, and anger—are all mediated through Ofentse. Countless times she protects me from both the physical and emotional pitfalls of engaging in this type of project. She tells me where I can and cannot go, whom I can trust and whom I should be wary of. By mere association, she dissuades pickpockets and potentially more serious assaults. She reassures me when I am confused, frustrated, and disheartened by the immense poverty, illnesses, and violence of the streets. She brings me into her network of friends, her family, and her life. In essence, Ofentse teaches me what it means to be a part of Point Place, to be hopping from shelter to shelter, to experience street life under a roof.

2 Standing (K)in

Yeah, I ran away from home. I found Nana there by the Durban beachfront. Nana said, "Do you want to be my baby?" I said, "Yeah." I was calling Nana my mother, saying "Ma." She came with the food, saying, "I can bring my baby. No one else can eat my food, only my baby." She gave me food. After eating the food, I'd go with her. I'd ask some 10 cents by the traffic light. Then we'd find a place to sleep. (Teeny, nineteen-year-old female)

In telling her story, Teeny mobilizes a paradigm of kinship to explain how she survived on the streets of Durban. Teeny had arrived in the city several years earlier, at the age of fifteen, having run away from an abusive home situation. Like many street youth, she first slept on the beachfront. There she met Nana. Although the two girls were of similar size and age, the contrast in their street stature was striking. Nana was familiar with city life and knew the territorial procedures of street begging. She assumed the role of a mother; Teeny became her baby. The two of them, according to several accounts, made a cute pair. Now, four years later, Teeny and Nana have grown up. They no longer beg by the traffic lights. Instead they have boyfriends who help support them. Something else has happened, too. Teeny lives inside Point Place, and Nana remains on the streets. From Teeny's point of view, they no longer are related: "I don't want to be Nana's baby because Nana sniffs glue. She does everything funny. She doesn't want to understand me. She doesn't want to solve my problems. That's why I want to forget Nana."

In this chapter I address the strategies of relatedness that make street survival a meaningful possibility for youth like Teeny. Here I refer to "relatedness" in terms of its reciprocal connectivity, noting the ties of commonality that bind individuals to one another vis-à-vis the constructed differences of others (Carsten 2004:82). For Teeny and Nana, this invocation of relatedness finds expression in the naming and claiming of kin. So does its revocation. Thus, this chapter addresses the various enactments of relatedness on the streets. It examines who is kin and who is not and under what circumstances. More specifically, it connects the material practices of the Point Place youth to an ideological framing of what it means to fit in and "stand" (*ukuma*) as kin in circumstances of extreme instability.

In isiZulu, *ukuma* refers to a set of bodily dispositions: to stand still, erect, or firm. It also means to stand consistently, predictably, or dependably (Doke et al. 1999:473). The linguistic affixes of *ukuma* put forth certain associations as well. "To stand in the way" (*ukumuma*) of someone, for example, refers to obstacles in life, not just physical but also emotional. "To stand for one another" (*ukumelana*) points to a reciprocal position, to a shared sense of encouragement and support. In this chapter I draw on both usages of *ukuma*. Sometimes street youth stand in the way of each other, while at other times they stand for one another. Their deployments of *ukuma* speak to the conflicts of daily survival as well as to the possibilities of cooperation and care. Hence, with *ukuma* at the forefront of its investigations, this chapter shows how street youth negotiate their standing in society precisely through their relationships with one another—as friends, kin, and lovers.

My discussion of *ukuma* fits into a well-established anthropological scholarship that examines the social continuums of belonging on the streets. Keith Hart (1988), for example, conducting research among street hustlers in Ghana, describes how friendships are built on feelings of trust, respect, and joint experiences. Frequently these individuated interests take on the shared expectations of kinship, an obligatory structuring of rights and duties. In the broader anthropological scholarship, the adjectival modifiers of "legal" kin (Maine 1861),[1] "ritual" kin (Mintz and Wolf 1950),[2] "adoptive" kin (Stack 1974), "fostered" kin (Goody 1982), and "fictive" kin (Weston 1991)[3] all highlight this blending of fellowships, the back-and-forth merging of achieved and ascribed associations.

This chapter draws on those previous studies, indebted to the anthropological modifiers that recognize the coalescence of choice and compulsion in social relationships. Yet in some respects it also departs from these designations, for those studies tend to focus on kinship as a bestowal of material, emotional, and spiritual support (Maddy 2001). Rather than looking to kinship as a direct conferral of benefits, my research with the Point Place youth emphasizes the contested and shifting configurations of their kin associations. It draws attention to the uncertainties of social belonging on the streets. My investigation of relatedness—of standing for and against one another—thus privileges the patterns of urban living that connect street youth in highly resourceful yet highly provisional ways.

*   *   *

> I remember that day. It was Sunday, it was raining, and we didn't have a place to go. This other friend of mine told me that there's a place where we can stay for free. At first I couldn't believe it. Here in town there's such a place like that? So he took me there. He took me to his friends. His friends showed me around. (Khaya, twenty-seven-year-old male)

> I was like, "This is the place?" It was dark, very dark. Gate. Stinks. Umm, I was like, "Gosh." I was walking with other girls. So I was like, "Girls, are you staying here?" And they were like, "Yeah, we do. You'll see. There's no problem. We clean up every morning 'cause there're so many of us. Other people come and go. So then it gets dirty." When I was staying a day I was like, "Okay, fine. If anyone else can stay, so do I." (Sally, nineteen-year-old female)

The youth who make use of Point Place do not just happen to walk in. Friends bring in friends, usually people they have met on the streets, in shelters, or in prison. These peer connections are critical for establishing preliminary introductions and asserting a residential claim to the building. The age and gender of a newcomer determines the success of this incorporation. Young boys tend to be at a disadvantage, as are unattached girls. Because of their small stature, young boys cannot secure their belongings, so they prefer to sleep outside on the beachfront, where they have a better chance of obtaining money, food, and blankets from sympathetic tourists and outreach workers. Similarly, a girl without the backup of a boyfriend or a strong female companion cannot secure her most vital assets—namely the clothes and toiletries that maintain her as an attractive sexual "catch" capable of acquiring additional resources. Still, while young boys and unattached girls may not command the achieved status of an older Point Place resident, they do have the ascribed advantage of cuteness and desirability, which may become the basis of a selective relationship: that of filiation.

Typically it is the older and often new or unattached girls who assume a mothering role toward the smaller boys. The older girls cultivate these relationships for two reasons: young boys have dependable access to disposable cash, usually from street begging, and they are unlikely to demand any immediate monetary or sexual remuneration. Small boys also evoke a quality of vulnerability that the older girls respond to with protective tendencies. For their part, the younger boys often look to older girls for cooked food, hygiene, and other demonstrative comforts that they associate with maternal dispositions. Roxanne, a newcomer to Point Place who befriends two small boys, explains this relationship of reciprocity:

> I give them food if I have money. But sometimes if they have R2 or R3 they'll bring it to me.[4] They'll say, "Hold this here." You'll fill up on food from the money. They give me then . . . If I have money I eat with my girlfriends, but I know that this one plate of food must be held aside for those young boys. Because they beg outside and when they've got money, they bring it. (Roxanne, nineteen-year-old female)

While material transactions are important to these relationships, they include less tangible concerns of devotion and dependency as well. It is not unusual for a younger boy to become so attached to an older girl that he assumes the position of a watchful guardian, making sure that she walks the streets safely, especially in the evenings:

> And Jimmy, he loves me because he knows me from Point Place. He loves me. If someone is going somewhere, he doesn't want to go with that person without his auntie Khulile. He knows me too much, and he loves me. He follows me even when I go to Bible College. He follows me into the prayer meeting. He goes every time. (Khulile, eighteen-year-old female)

In sum, sentiments of nurturance and mutual affection tend to frame relationships between older females and younger boys.

The older males take on a more authoritarian role. They expect deferential treatment from the younger boys, and when it is not forthcoming, they may threaten, curse, or beat the younger boys into subordination. Jabulani, who is twenty-four and a longtime resident of Point Place, explains: "You see, some of them don't respect me, but when I shout at them they start to respect me . . . I think they can respect me because they know I came first. They came after me—all of them." The older boys claim that enforced "respect" is necessary for establishing order and control within Point Place. Still, while at times abrasive, their interactions with the younger boys are not based solely on disciplinary tactics. Many of the older youth spend time with their younger counterparts in various forms of play, whether on the soccer field, on the beach, or hanging out on the streets. In their everyday activities, the older boys set themselves up as models of emulation, sometimes as patriarchal figureheads and other times as lighthearted, easygoing companions.

Generally speaking, the interpersonal relationships of the youth who live at Point Place reveal the age- and gender-based hierarchies of their homes. As a collectivity, though, they tend to emphasize their commonalities, which they articulate through imaginings of siblinghood. These sib relations are based on years of shared experiences on the streets and in institutional settings like Thuthukani. In calling one another "brother" and "sister," the youth of Point Place highlight the resilience and interdependence of their current living arrangement: "You see, I don't want to leave them because I've got years with them. They're like my brothers. I haven't got a family. They're my family, all of them, you see" (Themba, twenty-four-year-old male). Ordinary understandings of friendship do not capture the depth of emotion that many Point Place youth feel toward each other:

> Jerry is my home-line. I'll say my home-boy. He's like my brother . . . I'm always with him. Yes. You see, if I go and hustle, I go with him. Jerry, I can say that he's my brother. I don't know how to explain it. Jerry has never been my friend. He's my brother because of everything we did. (Xolani, twenty-one-year-old male)

> Sometimes when I go to Point Place, I go out to the roof. I'm always sitting there by myself. And then sometimes I cry while I'm sitting alone because now all these memories are coming back to me. I don't know how Bongi finds out. How she's always there. Sometimes I think, like, we are sisters. (Thabisa, eighteen-year-old female)

Through these testimonies, the youth of Point Place convey a type of companionship that is highly inclusive regardless of gender, age, or ethnic differences.[5] Such sib relations often form the basis of room membership, with peers sometimes residing together as brothers and sisters. Although these rooms generally remain single-sex dwellings, this does not detract from an overarching sense of complementary sibling unity:

> Most of the girls, they depend on us [boys]. Because there's no one who can just take the girls, like many girls, and stay with them, especially when you know about their past and things like that. We also come from the same place, and we have the same problems. We're in the same situation, so we can understand. (Shorty, twenty-two-year-old male)

> I treat them as a family. Even the boys over there, I treat them like my brothers. Sometimes I get naughty. I dance with them. I play with them, chasing them around. Sometimes I bully them. I say, "I'll hit you." Then they chase me around. It's fun, like a family. I treat them like a family. (Roxanne, nineteen-year-old female)

To summarize, the sib relationships of the Point Place youth demonstrate the possibilities of supportive peer connections. As siblings, they relate to one another on fairly equal terms.

The cross-complementarities of the Point Place sib relations are notably different from their sexual connections.[6] These relationships, while also formulated along intragenerational ties, are marked more by conflict and strife than by any collective sense of harmony or accord. Breakdowns occur frequently, with the most contentious disputes revolving around issues of trust, fidelity, and the control over productive and reproductive rights. To a large degree, these relationships reflect unfulfilled aspirations of a socially recognized adulthood: that of gainful employment, marriage, and the ability to provide consistently for others, including elders and children. As I describe in greater depth in chapter four, the Point Place males are unable to secure steady jobs, which limits their ability to support a long-term girlfriend, let alone afford the costs of bridewealth (*ilobolo*) and marriage. The Point Place females—in response to these material insecurities—maintain their daily subsistence through a rotating selection of boyfriends within and outside the building. This setup of multiple concurrent lovers, undertaken by both the males and females from Point Place, undermines their ability to maintain a stable domestic unit.

Hence, inside Point Place, boyfriend-girlfriend relationships rarely last for more than a few months, and oftentimes only a few days. Yet, while short-lived, these relationships are instrumental to the normative workings of a household (Wilk and Netting 1984): those residential activities defined respectively by production (the division of labor), distribution (exchange and transaction), transmission (rights to resources), and reproduction (socialization, enculturation, and sex). In the remainder of this chapter, I delineate the daily routines of the Point Place youth to show how their sexual partnerships make the sustainability and solidarity of their sib relationships possible. These sib relationships, in turn, present opportunities for household formations that facilitate sentiments of mutuality and practices of sharing within and between rooms.

Household Production

Inside Point Place, every room forms the nucleus of a peer group that revolves around the production of domestic labor. Residents within these rooms are responsible for the upkeep and maintenance of their living space. In single-sex dwellings, housekeeping duties are allocated through a flexible rotation of chores. Some of these daily tasks include sweeping the floors, making beds, fetching water, cooking, washing linens and clothes, disposing of waste, and repairing broken items—usually doors, windows, and beds. If there is a significant age hierarchy, younger boys and girls may be coerced into performing more unpleasant chores, like sanitizing the nonworking toilets. The boys typically clean the communal areas such as the hallways, stairwells, and front entrance. Here residential status is apparent, as newcomers are the ones who mop the floors, while more established boys oversee the work. To

Figure 9. A typical bedroom inside Point Place. The stereo to the right is powered by batteries and a portable generator, since the building has no working electricity.

Figure 10. A young man washing his clothes on the rooftop of Point Place. The water is fetched from the public toilets outside, since there is no running water inside the building.

ensure that these tasks are performed, an older boy will padlock the front gate to prevent anyone from entering or leaving the building.

Among residing couples, household activities are conceptualized through a gendered division of labor. Girlfriends expect their boyfriends to give them spending money, while boyfriends expect their girlfriends to cook, wash clothes, and maintain the room in an orderly fashion. In practice, though, these gender roles are not rigidly enforced, and occasionally the boyfriend will be the one cooking, cleaning, or washing clothes. Boyfriends also are more likely to fetch water outside from the public toilets, an arduous task that the girls avoid whenever possible. Yet, while these tasks may be evenly distributed, in the minds of the Point Place youth, any excessive deviation from the normative gender roles of domestic production may be grounds for speculation or even alarm:

> See, in Point Place they were surprised that Khaya was doing my washing and the baby's washing. They said that I gave him *umuthi* [occult substances]. Like for him to listen to whatever you want. For him to do my washing, it was something unusual, and for him to do the baby's washing, too, it was something unusual. (Ofentse, twenty-four-year-old female)

To account for these reversed gender roles, youth at Point Place often look to paranormal explanations. Accusations of *umuthi* and witchcraft, although perhaps made in jest, do reveal an underlying anxiety about the natural order of household formation. Transgressions from these ideals are acceptable only as long as somebody is willing to perform the domestic labor. When this is not the case, confrontations occur in which boyfriends make claims on their girlfriends' productive capabilities. While a girlfriend has recourse to a variety of responses, including a renunciation of her "wifely" position, most often she will concede to the domestic demands of her boyfriend as long as he also is willing to uphold his productive role: that of income earner.

Income-generating practices both inside and outside of Point Place generally are left to the boys. Typical jobs include car guarding; car washing; street sweeping; selling fruit, vegetables, candy, cigarettes, and joints; operating sidewalk phones; street performing; panhandling; and the occasional temporary work of cleaning stores, carrying boxes, and delivering goods. Among the Point Place youth, an occupational ambiguity exists between asking for something and taking something. This ambiguity is reflected in the commonly used isiZulu verb *phanda*, which on the streets of Durban has the double meaning to beg/to steal.[7] Those who steal generally limit their activities to petty crime—for example, the snatching of cell phones, cameras, purses, watches, and jewelry. All these sources of income at Point Place are highly irregular, and so the amount of disposable cash varies. On average the boys make between R15 and R40 a day; many days they may earn nothing, while on other days they earn in excess of R1000. instability

Whereas the boys engage in a variety of income-generating activities, the girls of Point Place do not have the same options. Occasionally they assist their boyfriends in small entrepreneurial jobs such as rolling joints. By and large, however, the girls remain inside the building performing domestic labor. Girls who venture out alone to the beachfront, clubs, or other apartments are stigmatized as "doing business." The females living inside Point Place exert a considerable amount of social pressure on anyone who they suspect is engaged in sex work. Although extremely condemnatory of prostitution, most of the Point Place females do have multiple sexual partners within and outside the building. Moreover, as evidenced in other parts of KwaZulu-Natal, they often view these relationships from a perspective that links romantic love to material desires (Hunter 2002, 2009).

Household Distribution

The widespread distribution or pooling of resources is the most effective strategy for ensuring that the Point Place youth have something to eat and smoke every day. Communal cooking and the sharing of food—either bought or donated—are of paramount importance for establishing social networks within Point Place. Such exchanges are not limited to room membership:

> Yeah, we were just used to each other. He liked me, Themba. Before he died, he used to come to my room, maybe asking for sugar. I'd give it to him. I used to give him 50 cents if he was short. He used to send me to the shop. He liked cabbage. He used to send me to go buy cabbage. There was a time that he came to my room, and I was eating *amasi* [curdled milk]. Other boys gave me the *amasi*. I only ate one spoon, and then Themba asked me for some. He said he was hungry. I took two spoons, and I gave him this *amasi*. (Angel, eighteen-year-old female)

To not share food or "to eat alone in the corners" is seen as a profoundly antisocial act that may lead to the rejection of a roommate. The distribution of food essentially marks relationships not only between friends—"I see my friend, if I'm hungry, we'll be hungry together. If she has something, she'll give to me, too" (Angel), but also between lovers—"Hey, I say no more *jola* [be in love with] Shorty because Shorty wants another girlfriend now. He forgot me, but never mind, I went and found my own food" (Teeny).

Perhaps more so than food, the distribution of clothes within Point Place signals a complex ranking of social relations and personal status, particularly for the girls:

> In the morning they decide that okay, you today are going to wear white pants
> and Liyanda will wear black pants. And then you'll take a bath in the afternoon.
> Then you'll wear those clothes, and she changes her mind. She'll just tell you
> to take them off. Even if you don't want to, you have to take them off and give
> them to her. (Ofentse)

The command a girl displays over the delegation of clothing usually is restricted to her own room. For example, if one girl borrows an item of clothing
from a girl in a different peer group, she is not expected to return the borrowed item until after it is worn. She is expected to wash it, however. To not
wash borrowed clothes indicates disrespect or personal animosity. Clothes
also may be instrumental in the acceptance of new girls:

> The first time that I came here, Sisi saw me. She saw me by Spar [the grocery
> store] and greeted me. We were wearing the same things, same T-shirts. She
> greeted me, saying, "Hi, how are you?" So I told her that I'm fine. She said,
> "What's your name?" I told her my name. She told me her name. She said,
> "Would you please come and visit me? I'd like to be your friend." (Unathi,
> eighteen-year-old female)

Befriending outside girls with nice clothes is a common recruitment strategy
among the Point Place females. Yet, while they are always on the lookout for
new outfits, accumulating too many clothes can lead to a girl's downfall. Other
girls will steal her clothes on the justification that she already has plenty of
items to wear. They will gossip that she is engaged in sex work, for how else
can she afford such nice ensembles? Or her boyfriend, if he is not the one
supplying the outfits, will begin to suspect that she has a new lover. Hence
it is in the best interests of the Point Place girls to distribute their clothes
widely, for it not only increases their own wardrobe selection but also acts as
a leveling device that defuses resentment and suspicious accusations.

Household Transmission

Whereas the distribution of food and clothing is a relatively straightforward
process—essentially anyone in need can lay claim to these resources—the
transfer of rooming rights is a more complicated affair. First, the constant
interference of the police disrupts any stable sense of residential rights. The
frequent mobility of the Point Place youth also inhibits clear demarcations
of proprietorship. Second, the continual rearrangement of space in itself
undermines the possibility of retaining a discrete enclosed room. Within a
single apartment unit, countless living configurations have emerged as every
available bedroom, bathroom, kitchen, closet, and three-cornered area has

been converted into multipurpose sleeping, bathing, eating, and working quarters. Inside Point Place, space is utilized to its maximal potential yet should not be regarded in purely functional terms (Lawrence and Low 1990). For in the packed composition of bedrooms—where up to four people may sleep on a single mattress, with another four sharing two blankets on the floor—particular relationships of authority, status, and companionship are made visible to all.

To a discerning observer, the most obvious indication of rooming privileges is the fact that the older youth have padlock keys. Yet not all the rooms inside Point Place have doors, and even fewer have functioning locks. Here, then, a person's physical presence signals room tenure. One might assume that the females would have an advantage because they spend the most time inside Point Place. But their dwelling spaces usually are referred to by their boyfriends' names. Only in instances of single-sex occupancy will a room be demarcated as belonging to a girl, and even in these arrangements rooms are designated by a general female collectivity—for example, *oMary* (the group of Mary). The same is not true for the males, who are more likely to assert possession of a living space through individual entitlement—for example, *indlu kaThomas* (the room of Thomas). Swifty explains how he claimed his room—a converted bathroom—inside Point Place:

> That room, Jacob and Amanda [a boyfriend-girlfriend couple] had an argument. Amanda left . . . They said I must go and stay in that room. Amanda told Pretty [my girlfriend] that when she comes, she must go and sleep there. Pretty used to come. It ended up being my room, like that. Because I saw that I must close the door, I bought that thing—a door lock. I put it there. I fixed the door nicely. I did it because I left my things inside. I closed it nicely. She came then, Pretty. She cleaned, cleaned, cleaned. I don't have time to clean. (Swifty, twenty-four-year-old male)

In the end, the males typically are the ones to secure a room as well as the ones to hold on to a room even after the dissolution of a sexual relationship.

Household Reproduction

Within the context of Point Place, reproduction refers to both sexual procreation and processes of socialization.[8] Sex is an everyday occurrence, and, correspondingly, the females become pregnant on a regular basis. In most cases expectant mothers designate their Point Place boyfriends as the fathers of their babies. While only one young man is recognized as the father, many people inside Point Place contribute to the maintenance of newborn babies.

This communal form of support includes formula, clothing, diapers, and blankets, as well as less tangible provisions of healthcare and babysitting services. Because boyfriends are routinely sent to prison, it is not uncommon for a close friend of the father to assume a special responsibility for the baby, akin to a godfather. As one young mother explains:

> I was staying with Lucky [my boyfriend's friend] . . . Lucky bought formula for the baby because the baby didn't want to breastfeed. The time that I gave birth, my milk didn't come out. The doctor said I mustn't breastfeed.[9] I must buy formula for him . . . Lucky bought it for the baby until the police came. (Amanda, eighteen-year-old female)

As living testimony to this invaluable assistance, the parents named their baby son Lucky in honor of their friend.

Along with the material and immaterial reproduction of bodies, the youth of Point Place are exposed to another, grimmer effect of sexual activity and procreation: death. Their household strategies, while at times highly imaginative, also make them vulnerable to choices that in the South African context of HIV/AIDS have bleak consequences for their reproductive health and interpersonal relationships. It is exactly at the site of the most precarious relationships within Point Place—those of lovers—where HIV/AIDS has its foothold. While most youth within Point Place have multiple sexual partners, only one will be recognized as the paramount love interest. The others remain secret affairs, rarely gaining the primary status of an open relationship. Partners who outwardly maintain an appearance of fidelity consequently pass on sexually transmitted infections. This fiction of fidelity is reinforced by not using condoms, which in the minds of lovers communicates an intimate degree of trust and faithfulness. The physical manifestations of HIV/AIDS are readily apparent inside Point Place. Nonetheless, among residing couples, there remains an extreme reluctance to talk about the virus in personalized terms. It is more likely that close friends—usually thought of as siblings—will be the ones to broach the topic as well as the ones to care for their ailing companions.[10] Thus, inside Point Place, prolonged forms of illness have the dual effect of signaling both the devastating demise and the enduring strength of reproductive kin relations.

*   *   *

To conclude this chapter, I present a court case between the residents of Point Place. I narrate this section as an extended ethnographic vignette to show how the youth who live there negotiate the lived associations of their everyday relatedness. They do so, moreover, with approval from state officials, who acknowledge the social relations of the Point Place youth and ask them to stand for one another (*ukumelana*) as kin, especially in times of difficulty and duress. Somewhat paradoxically, then, state officials—although engaged in projects to dismantle Point Place as a site of youth cohabitation—also uphold the basic premise of the building's existence—that of friends standing for one another as supportive kin and companions. A letter:

> Hello, Sisi my friend. I'm saying to you I miss you and you must know I will come there to see you, maybe on Thursday when I get the money. I'll come with your birthday present. I won't forget you. I have a problem with Amie. She doesn't want to give me the T-shirt, my T-shirt that I gave you.
>
> It's me your friend Thandisa,
I love you my friend.

Nineteen-year-old Thandisa hands me the above letter. She wants me to deliver it to her friend Sisi, who is awaiting trial for attempted murder. Sisi is being detained in prison. I agree to pass the letter on to her the next day, for by now it is too late to visit. By 10:00 A.M. the prison waiting room will already be full. Instead, I decide to go directly to the courthouse with Ofentse. We know that the bailiff will provide accurate details on Sisi's trial date.

Sisi's arrest is a convoluted affair, one that I piece together through interviews and conversations with key participants and bystanders. The incident began late one Saturday night after most of the Point Place females had returned from the clubs and bars. Drunk, they prepared themselves for bed, demarcating their sleeping spaces with blankets and sponge mattresses. One of the younger yet more assertive girls, Celiwe, claimed a dingy bathroom as her own. Not much later, she awakened to the presence of another girl, a newcomer to Point Place. The newcomer mistook the converted sleeping space—its linoleum floor and porcelain fixtures—as a real bathroom and relieved herself in the nonworking toilet. Enraged, Celiwe confronted her. "What do you want in my toilet!" she shouted, slapping the girl hard across the face.

Other youth, hearing the commotion, ushered the stunned newcomer back to the room of her boyfriend, Jabulani. Celiwe followed the crowd, swearing at the girl for her insolence and stupidity. Jabulani eventually tired of Celiwe's harangue and ordered her to shut up. He slapped her across the face to show that he, too, was serious. Celiwe vowed retaliation. She left the bedroom, grabbed a table knife, and returned to stand in front of Jabulani's door.

Knock! Knock! Knock! Jabulani ignored the pounding at his door, but it persisted. Suddenly the newcomer opened the door, kicked Celiwe in the shins, grabbed her wrist, and twisted the table knife out of her hand. Too drunk and surprised to defend herself, Celiwe turned away. The newcomer stabbed her with the knife, two rapid jabs above the shoulder blade. Celiwe fell to the floor, pretending that she had died. Alarmed, Jabulani hoisted her up and, with the help of several other boys, carried her to the hospital, where she received stitches in the emergency room.

Afterward, Jabulani and Celiwe returned to Point Place and to their respective rooms. Jabulani waited with his girlfriend and two other boys. They waited and waited and waited. Sure enough, Celiwe's friends came to the door and shouted to Jabulani: "Your girlfriend is undermining us!" They demanded that he open the door, but he refused. They start pushing it in, and Jabulani and his two friends pushed back. The door was rickety, and eventually it gave in to the force of the females. Four girls entered the room. Sisi was among them, carrying a pocketknife. She stabbed the newcomer four times on the buttock and once on the forearm. The attacking girls then ran away.

Jabulani phoned for help, and an ambulance arrived to take his girlfriend to the hospital. He also called the police, who apprehended the girls outside the gates of Point Place and transported them to a holding station. The following Monday, Jabulani attended a preliminary court hearing. The girls denied stabbing the newcomer, but Jabulani countered their protests with his own evidence. He told the magistrate that, yes, they indeed had stabbed his girlfriend. He claimed that they had nearly murdered her by slashing her in the stomach, causing her intestines to spill out. He produced a partial police statement and a crumpled doctor's note. Shaken by Jabulani's embellished story, the girls demanded to see a lawyer. The magistrate postponed the case for two more weeks and sent them back to prison. Bail was not an option.

Ofentse and I learn about Jabulani's dramatic court appearance from the bailiff. Because the accused girls are minors, we are not allowed to watch the proceedings. Only family members can attend juvenile court cases. After speaking to the bailiff, we decide to interview Jabulani. His decision to press charges is extremely unusual. Jabulani and Sisi have known each other for years, and up until now their interactions have been friendly.

"What do you think should happen to the girls?" I ask Jabulani.

"I'll be very happy," he responds, "if they feel the pain they caused. They can be poked [stabbed], or maybe they can stay in jail for two or three years. That would be fine with me."

"But," I continue, "you've resided together for so long. Why such problems now?"

"Yeah," Jabulani replies, "I stayed with them for a long time. I don't have a problem with them, but they showed that they have a problem with me because they poked someone I'm dating when I'm not dating any of them." In other words, Jabulani would have understood the girls' actions if he had been dating someone from their group. That would have justified the attack against his new girlfriend, but he never has dated any of them.

Most of the other youth from Point Place look unfavorably on Sisi's actions. Still, they view Jabulani's decision to call for legal intervention as excessive. They believe that internal disputes should be resolved within Point Place. Whenever a Point Place youth files formal charges against another youth, there is a considerable amount of pressure for the charges to be dropped. Invariably they always are. I have witnessed this countless times between boyfriends and girlfriends. But never have I seen a legal dispute between two established residents of Point Place who have regarded each other with mutual affection, like a brother and sister.

To elaborate: For the Point Place youth, the courthouse represents a site of solidarity, not division. Outside the courthouse doors, groups of youth wait for their friends and lovers who have been brought up on charges relating to theft, drug possession, disorderly conduct, suspicious activity, public intimidation, and the like. They pass on words of encouragement as well as more tangible provisions—usually small, portable items like fruit and tobacco. Occasionally they provide the requisite bail money. Colloquially speaking, the Point Place youth "stand" (*ukuma*) for the indicted, not as friends but as kin members. They tell the judges, prosecutors, and social workers that they are the brother, sister, aunt, uncle, or cousin of the accused. In doing so, they can sit in on juvenile cases. They also can sign off for their friends' release.

And so on the day of Sisi's court appearance, I am not surprised to encounter a group of Point Place youth waiting around for another unrelated case. When they see Ofentse, they ask her to be the aunt of the accused. They already have designated a young man to be the brother. The bailiff approves, allowing the "aunt" and "brother" to enter the courtroom. Echoing the words of my young interlocutors, the bailiff explains that these kids should be treated as family members. They "stand for one another" (*ukumelana*), she remarks, because they have no one else.

Among a throng of other Point Place youth, including Jabulani, I sit outside the juvenile courtroom waiting for Sisi's docket to be called. In the two weeks since the stabbing, Jabulani has concocted a new plan. He no longer wishes incarceration for Sisi and the other girls. He thinks back to their shared experiences. I ask him about his injured girlfriend, and much to his embarrassment, he cannot remember her name. In any case, she recovered and has gone back home. The bailiff calls Jabulani to step in. He enters the courtroom with a young woman named Rachel, also a longtime resident of

Point Place. About five minutes later, everyone, including Sisi, rushes out. I see Ofentse, who witnessed the proceedings firsthand (as the aunt for the previous case, she never left the courtroom). Rachel, quite convincingly, pretended to be Jabulani's injured girlfriend. She showed the judge an old stab wound on her arm and claimed that she suffered no other grievances. The judge, not wanting to ask Rachel to drop her pants to see the alleged buttock injuries, dismissed the case.

Everyone congratulates Rachel on her courtroom performance. They also tease her about her newfound relationship with Jabulani. They find the pairing humorous. Like most of the original Point Place inhabitants, they have known each other for a long time. A sexual relationship would be like a transgression of the brother-sister incest taboo.

*   *   *

The courtroom performance of Jabulani and Rachel attests to the imaginative constructions of relatedness that occur inside Point Place. Remarkably, even state agents partake in this production. They allow the Point Place youth to stand for one another (*ukumelana*) as kin. They value the framing of their urban connections. In many respects, the state's recognition of these attachments stems from a tacit acknowledgment of missing links. The Point Place youth lack supportive family members at home. Many of their parents are deceased, and their extended kin may not be willing to take on the responsibilities of helping them when they get in trouble. The youth also, to the frustration of social workers, prefer to keep their arrests a secret. They do not want to worry their kinsfolk or add to their shame or anger. In addition to not wanting their families to find out about their arrests, the Point Place youth obscure their ages. They prefer to be treated as minors, so if they are over the age of eighteen, they provide as little information about their personal lives as possible. They also tend to leave their identification books at home. Even if a social worker does manage to secure a phone number, this does not mean that it is a working number. The best solution, then, is a home visit, but this, too, is difficult because of limited resources. For example, a car might not be available. In sum, to pursue the kin ties of the home is a time-consuming, costly, and often futile endeavor, so state officials look to the fellowships of the streets. They privilege the intragenerational connections of the city over the intergenerational gaps of the home.

To focus on these horizontal ties of relatedness (e.g., on the intragenerational relationships of youth) presents a timely opportunity to consider the analytics of street belonging. Certainly the youth of Point Place reproduce the power asymmetries of their homes, most notably that of patriarchy. Yet they also imagine and enact more equal associations. Their sib relationships, in particular, reflect this sense of commonality. They are far and away the most inclusive and stable living arrangement inside Point Place. Summarily stated, the sib associations of the Point Place youth convey the core or "key" linkages of society, those relationships formed by the living and by the same generation (Peletz 1995:350). Indeed, this notion of relatedness, as created vis-à-vis one another and not as descending from others, extends to every relationship conducted within Point Place.

And here the case of Point Place offers valuable insight into the communities that older street youth establish for themselves, by themselves. Typically such communities receive very little public affirmation, particularly in the way of material support and resources. The youth who participate in them encounter the law enforcement arm of the state far more often than the assistance of social welfare (Samara 2005). To be sure, the youth from Point Place—like their counterparts in other street settings (Beazley 2003; De Boeck 2004; Diversi 2006; Hecht 1998; Kilbride et al. 2000; Magazine 2003; Taylor 2001)—engage in illicit undertakings. They impose on each other, too, sometimes forcefully. Yet, contrary to most expectations, they do not turn inward. They do not insulate or isolate themselves from connecting with others as domestic companions. With minimal introduction, anyone can enter the building. They can partake in the household activities and exchanges. They also can forsake these activities and leave without adverse effect. In other words, the Point Place youth look to extend their social attachments, not contract them. And they do so, more often than not, by standing for one another (*ukumelana*) as kin, friends, and lovers.

PART 2

Domesticities, Intimacies, and Reciprocities

3 Love, Betrayal, and Sexual Intimacy

"So, Zodwa, what exactly did you do to your boyfriend?"

Zodwa looks at me appreciatively. News travels fast inside Point Place, and she wants to set the record straight. "I burned Tau's clothes. I poured water on his bed. I poured paraffin. I poured soup. I poured *mealie-meal* [cornmeal] and rice on the bed, too. And then when I finished, I left Point Place."

"What made you think of doing this?" I ask, knowing full well why Zodwa destroyed Tau's room. She caught him sniffing glue with another girl in another room, his prolonged absence an indication of a more serious betrayal.

"Tau makes me stupid. He says he loves me, but he's lying. I wanted to see what he'd be wearing now. Hah! Just one pair of clothes."

I am not fooled by Zodwa's bravado. And so I ask a standard question, one I repeatedly pose to the Point Place females, attempting to understand why they end up returning to their boyfriends despite the heartache, despite the abuse. "Do you still love Tau?"

"Eh-heh." Yes, Zodwa answers without hesitation. Zodwa is sixteen years old. She envisions a long-term future with Tau. She does not yet know that she is HIV positive.

* * *

In many respects, HIV/AIDS forms the backdrop to love, betrayal, and sexual intimacy in South Africa. It is visibly present in the lives of the Point Place youth yet simultaneously invisible, seldom talked about or acknowledged, at least in self-referential terms. Because of this, I rarely approach it directly in my interviews with them. Rather, I follow their cues and tread carefully around it. I speak about it in the abstract: "So what do you think about HIV/

AIDS?"; as a hypothetical: "What would you do if you discovered that you were HIV positive?"; or as a technical intervention: "How do you protect yourself from HIV/AIDS?" Never do I engage with it openly, certainly not in an emotional or revelatory capacity. Never do I say, "Tell me about your experiences living with HIV/AIDS." Never do I inquire about the conversations that they hold with their sexual partners: "So have you told your lover that you're HIV positive?" Always HIV/AIDS remains a "thing" distant and removed. It is an integer or a percentage overwhelming in its immensity but reassuring in its anonymity.

To cite but a few facts specific to South Africa: In 2005, at the end of my two-year field stay, an estimated 5.3 million people between the ages of fifteen and forty-nine were living with HIV/AIDS (UNAIDS 2006:505). In 2006, 345,640 people died from AIDS-related illnesses over the course of the year, accounting for 47 percent of all deaths, 71 percent for those between the ages of fifteen and forty-nine (Dorrington et al. 2006).[1] In 2007, the number of AIDS-related deaths was greater than in previous years, claiming the lives of 350,000 people, nearly 1,000 a day (UNAIDS 2008:217). In 2008, when I returned to South Africa to conduct follow-up research, the estimated HIV prevalence had "stabilized" at 10.9 percent (HSRC 2009:79).[2] Such stabilizations, however, are not uniformly distributed among the South African population.

In KwaZulu-Natal, the HIV prevalence, incidence,[3] and mortality rates are the highest in the country.[4] In 2008, the HIV prevalence was 15.8 percent (HSRC 2009:79). In antenatal clinics it was much higher, with well over one in three pregnant women infected with HIV. The gendered disparities of HIV exist within certain age groups, too. At the end of my fieldwork stint, in 2005, the HIV prevalence for male youth between the ages of fifteen and twenty-four—essentially the age range of the Point Place youth—was 5.9 percent. For females it was 24.4 percent. This equates to 63,000 young men living with HIV/AIDS compared to 262,000 young women. Despite the increasing rollout of antiretroviral treatment, life expectancy at this time had dropped to forty-three years (Dorrington et al. 2006).[5]

How do such enumerations, the outward manifestations of HIV/AIDS, belie the internal experiences of those living with this virus? How is it possible to envision long-term commitments when everyday companionships—not just lovers but also kin and friends—are radically foreshortened even well before the age of forty-three? Why do the Point Place youth largely choose not to go to the HIV clinic, not to get tested, not to seek help from biomedical practitioners? Conversely, what is being revealed when girls like Zodwa begin to ask, "*Ungiphelezela emasokweni?*" (Will you accompany me to the place of the lovers?) Zodwa is not asking if I will be her lover, but rather if I will take her to the STI clinic—"the place of the lovers" (*emasokweni*)[6]—where she can receive an HIV test. What is this seemingly counterintuitive connection between love and HIV/AIDS? I aim to illustrate this association not through the distancing enumerations of statistics but through the up-close relationships of the Point Place females—relationships that are convoluted in their intimacies and heartbreaking in their betrayals, yet simultaneously, and perhaps paradoxically, life affirming in their yearnings for love.

* * *

> I was going with my friend, there inside Point Place, for the first time when Jerry saw me. He asked me my name, and I told him. He bought me food. He said that he loves me. I didn't answer him. I saw him two more times. Then I said that I loved him, too. (Amahle, seventeen-year-old female)

> He told me that he loved me. He said he wanted to date me. I asked him why. I asked him if he was dating other girls. He said no. I said I'd come back and answer him. Time went by. He was arrested. He got out. Then I told him that I loved him, too. (Amanda, eighteen-year-old female)

> He greeted me. I greeted him. Then he called me over. We talked. He said that he loved me. When I agreed to him, I didn't love him. Now I love him because there are things he helps me with. (Alice, twenty-year-old female)

> We met during New Year's outside on the streets. He called me over. He greeted me. He told me that he loved me. I said I'd think about it. The next day I told him that I loved him, too. (Simosihle, nineteen-year-old female)

To understand the connections between love and HIV/AIDS, I present the sexual relationships of the Point Place youth from the beginning: with the love proposal. My insights on the love proposal derive from the historical and ethnographic research of Mark Hunter (2002, 2010), who notes that these expressions of admiration follow a distinctly gendered pattern in KwaZulu-Natal. Young men propose love (in isiZulu, to *shela*), and young women accept love (in isiZulu, to *qoma*). To accept love, however, as Hunter explains, is a glossed understanding of *qoma*. To *qoma*, in its dictionary usage, means "to choose a lover" (Doke et al. 1999:710). It can be argued that a woman's ability to choose a lover thus signals a degree of personal agency, albeit one that for the Point Place females operates within particular structures of patriarchy and systematic poverty. They feel that it is necessary to *qoma*, as they have few alternatives for daily survival. They rely on boyfriends to maintain their basic needs while also selecting additional lovers to supplement their status-driven desires. Yet, while seemingly constrained, the terms and conditions of choosing boyfriends are not a foregone conclusion. Love, above all, remains a negotiated affair in declaration and practice.

To account for these negotiations, this chapter focuses on love as discursive praxis. It emphasizes the plurivocality—the numerous voices, interpretations, and significations—of sexual intimacy in the city. In isiZulu, "to love" and "to like" are not easily discernible. The word *thanda* refers to both. In my transcriptions I translate *thanda* as "love" to highlight the connections that link sex to everyday material and emotional desires. "Hey, baby, I love you, I buy you a cell phone, get into my car" is one example of the materiality of love.[7] Often heard on the streets of Durban, these drive-by proposals rarely are accepted by my companions, at least not openly. For they are extreme examples of love as a commodity transaction, in this case sex for a cell phone. These proposals differ from the narratives presented above in which the Point Place females, after some deliberation, accept their suitor by responding, "I told him that I loved him, too." The difference, I argue, lies not in the offer of material goods or even the expectation of sexual exchange. Rather, it lies in the possibility of love as mutual support and a lasting connection.[8]

Repeatedly the Point Place females cite *nakana*—a reciprocal verb meaning "to care about one another; to take notice of one another" (Doke et al. 1999:520)[9]—as the primary consideration of whether or not they accept love.[10] While love takes on many emotional and material forms for the young women who live in Point Place, *nakana* has a specific spatial and temporal dimension: that of proximity and familiarity. It requires closeness and often is associated with cohabitation.[11] Not infrequently, the Point Place females describe *nakana* in terms of domestic companionship. Zodwa, the young woman introduced at the beginning of this chapter, makes this connection in her discussion of the ideal boyfriend-girlfriend relationship: "You must sit with him. You must do everything that he wants you to do. You must wash [clothes] for him, but he also must wash for himself. You must do everything for him. If he takes care of you, you also must take care of him."[12] To sit with a lover and to wash his clothes conjures up an image of close domesticity. Somewhat problematically, though, Zodwa continues by saying, "You must do everything that he wants you to do," which seems rather submissive. Is it possible that *nakana*, while offering domestic support, reinforces gender inequalities? Does it promote normative gender roles and ideologies that situate boyfriends as providers and girlfriends as recipients? If *nakana* hinged solely on acts of giving and receiving, then, yes, this might be the case; however, *nakana* is not only about giving and receiving. More accurately, it is about the acknowledgment of care, of noticing one another. To elaborate on this distinction, I discuss *nakana* in relation to anthropological designations of "the gift."

In gift economies, as Marcel Mauss (1990) famously writes, exchanges feel both obligatory and voluntary. Gifts compel acts of reciprocity not through the logic of ownership, which typifies commodity exchanges, but through the logic of acceptance. To accept a gift is to recognize a relationship that already exists. The drive-by love proposal exemplifies the logic of a commodity exchange. It objectifies the body as a thing to own and thus something to control and dominate. The exchanges of *nakana*, meanwhile, point to the logic of the gift, to the logic of reciprocity. "If he takes care of you," as Zodwa narrates, "you also must take care of him."

Roger Magazine (2003), an anthropologist working among older street youth in Mexico City, draws on the analytical insights of Marilyn Strathern (1988) and her ethnography *The Gender of the Gift* to explain this reciprocal action. Girlfriends let boyfriends act on their behalf, yet girlfriends are not passive recipients of support, for boyfriends themselves do not author their own actions. They require girlfriends to make them appear as such—that is, as potential agents capable of being providers.[13] "Agency and cause," in the words of Strathern (1988:273), "are split." Hence, while a force of action, *nakana* is not necessarily a force of domination. For, like the gift, *nakana* occurs well before the act of (sexual) exchange. It occurs through an *a priori* recognition of others, which presents opportunities for mutual understanding and care.

The logic of the gift and, more specifically, the logic of sociality are key to my framing of love, betrayal, and sexual intimacy in KwaZulu-Natal. For, with the proximity and familiarity of *nakana*, the Point Place females are more likely to agree to the intimate exchanges of condom-less sex.[14] This in turn opens them up to the transmission of sexually transmitted infections, including HIV/AIDS. The Point Place females are aware of the risks of contracting HIV/AIDS, yet in their narratives the losses of love loom much larger than the losses of life itself. Why, given the immensity of HIV/AIDS, is this the case? Drawing on Zodwa's story, as well as those of her companions, I propose that the Point Place females equate love with life, not as self-protection but as an expression of social personhood shaped by the everyday sustenance of *nakana*. Hence, when discussing the intimacies of love and HIV/AIDS, my description of *nakana* is not limited to boyfriend-girlfriend couples. Friends, as I explain below, also contribute to the production and maintenance of *nakana* relationships, including a role in sexual partnerships.

Inside Point Place, friends are instrumental to the domestic partnerships of boyfriend-girlfriend couples.[15] Friends often arrange these matches, prodding their companions to take an interest in others. When these relationships fail, friends also are the first ones to step in with material and emotional support. This support is of particular importance for the Point Place females, who, in the absence of boyfriends, rely on each other for food, clothes, and a shared living space. These girls have two options for maintaining their daily subsistence: to reside in the all-female apartment or in the room of a boyfriend-girlfriend couple. In these instances, sympathetic girlfriends, and not boyfriends, typically extend the offer of cohabitation. Friends thus level the potential irregularities of *nakana*, the gains and losses of love.

Nonetheless, while friendships support a larger social collectivity, they remain secondary to the idealized status of boyfriend-girlfriend relationships. Given the domestic abuses of these partnerships, why is this the case? For the Point Place females, the answer lies with the sexual exchanges of *nakana*. Boyfriends offer the possibility of reproductive continuity, of noticing and acting on another's behalf indefinitely. Boyfriends offer the possibility of having babies and, as I elaborate in chapter six, the possibility of reuniting with their families' homes.

*   *   *

To illustrate the centrality of *nakana* to the relationships of the Point Place females, I discuss the ambiguous status of sexual partnerships in South Africa. I begin with an explanation of commercial sex before moving on to categorical understandings of transactional sex, also referred to in the epidemiological and anthropological scholarship as "survival sex" or "informal sex work." Within the category of transactional sex, I differentiate acts of popular consumption from those of subsistence. Admittedly there is crossover between the two, for consumptive desires are not always distinct from everyday needs. Still, at the risk of reifying categories of sexual exchange, I subscribe to these groupings mainly to follow the discernments of the Point Place females, who speak of "outside" and "inside" boyfriends. Outside boyfriends tend to fulfill consumptive pleasures, while inside boyfriends meet basic needs. Not inconsequentially, the Point Place females associate *nakana* with inside boyfriends. Much of my analysis discusses these spatial and temporal significations of *nakana* in relation to categories of sexual exchange. Ultimately, though, I move away from categorical understandings of sexual exchange to position *nakana* within a powerful dialectic of social forces: that of confrontation and concession, revenge and reconciliation, obligation and freewill.

Commercial Sex

As seen with the drive-by love proposal, the Point Place females scorn the direct exchange of sex-for-something. They associate drive-by love proposals with prostitution, which for them entails a particular set of attributes: (1) a predetermined payment, (2) open solicitation, usually in strip-show joints and at escort agencies, and (3) short skirts, thereby extending commercial sex work to the streets. The Point Place females are adamant that they are not prostitutes. They often make a distinction between themselves and the young women who live in surrounding apartments. Those women, they claim, are the ones who are *abaqwayizi* (winkers/prostitutes) and *izifebe* (bitches). To sell one's body as a commodity or to openly exchange sex for money is considered a shameful act. Seventeen-year-old Pinky sums up the sentiments of many Point Place youth: "You see, I hate a girl who sells her pussy. I hate that girl. Why? You see, because I'm also a girl. I'd rather eat from a dustbin. I'd rather eat in a dustbin than do that!" For the Point Place females, prostitution is more than an act of desperation. It is a sign of moral degeneracy:

> I made one big mistake in my life. I went to do a strip show. But I realized that was wrong. I stopped . . . I didn't feel it was right for me, like too many people go there. They see me naked. When I go outside, they think of me as something else. They'll never see the positive side of me. They'll always think the negative things. She's a bitch, she's a what-what. We know her, whatever. And what if my boyfriend finds out about that? (Thabisa, eighteen-year-old female)

> I remember when I came here [to Durban]. I thought I was not going to get a boyfriend. I was not going to have sexual intercourse. I thought I was going to keep to myself. But then it was impossible. But there's one thing I always tell myself, no matter how hungry I get, no matter how poor I get, I'm never going to sell my body. That is something I don't think I'd be able to do. Because when you see people who do that, they don't look good. Even the boys don't think good of them. You see, it's very good to walk past a boy, and he calls you. Just that call, it shows you have potential. (Lindi, nineteen-year-old female)

As evidenced in the above passages, Thabisa and Lindi associate prostitution with "negative things." It is not "good." It has no "potential." Both of them contrast prostitution with another form of intimacy: the boyfriend/girlfriend coupling. Lindi explicitly links her urban livelihood to sexual intercourse with boyfriends, yet she does not correlate this type of sexual exchange with prostitution. Bongi, a self-assured woman of nineteen, explains the difference: "A [boyfriend] relationship is when you love someone, and you're sharing the love that you're giving to each other. You can make love, but there's no need for you to pay me . . . Like you always have to make me happy, and I'll make you happy. You have to share the love." For Bongi, love—more precisely, shared love—is the distinguishing element of sexual encounters.

Inside Point Place, those who engage in commercial sex work face a considerable amount of social pressure from their companions. Bongi explains the procedures for dealing with girls who are suspected of being prostitutes and why they cannot remain inside Point Place: "We told them people are calling us prostitutes. They're calling every girl inside Point Place [a prostitute]. They say girls from Point Place are prostitutes. So we told them if they want to carry on, they must leave us. But if they don't want to [leave Point Place], they must stop. Then they can stay." As Bongi indicates, being labeled a prostitute has serious consequences for all the young women at Point Place. First, it exposes them to a higher incidence of unsolicited proposals from men, which may lead to sexual assault: "They chase you. They run and grab your hand. And every time that you tell them no, what do they say? They say, 'What, you think your pussy is special?' and all that stuff" (Pinky). Second, being labeled a prostitute makes it more difficult for the Point Place females to return home. Such is the case whenever Point Place is written up in the newspapers, mentioned on local radio broadcasts, or discussed in community meetings. Inevitably these public forums describe the Point Place females as prostitutes. Angel experienced this humiliation when a police officer transported her and five other girls to a rehabilitation center: "She [the police officer] swore at us. She said we were prostitutes. She wrote in the newspapers that she helped six girls from Point Place. She said we were doing drugs and selling our bodies." In direct opposition to these public pronouncements, neither Angel nor the other girls would ever self-identify as prostitutes. Like the rest of the Point Place youth, they view prostitution as a renunciation of love and life potentiality. Out of fifty-three formal interviews, only three young women revealed to me that they engaged in commercial sex work.[16] Their explanations of prostitution are strikingly similar. For them, engaging in commercial sex work equates to giving up on life: "I wanted to come here to the Point. I gave up on my life" (Nobuhle, nineteen-year-old female). "I gave up on my life" (Simphiwe, fifteen-year-old female). "If you're a prostitute you have to be more careful, because you're giving your life away. You give up with your life" (Roxanne, nineteen-year-old female).

Transactional Sex

Commercial sex work entails a particular set of expectations and identifications usually framed in the commoditized language of "client" relations. Transactional sex, on the other hand, takes on much more fluid associations.

Such relationships—also known as survival sex or informal sex work—differ from prostitution in five main ways (Wojcicki 2002a:340–346, 2002b:268): (1) Sex is exchanged for a nonspecified amount of money and goods, which may include food and drinks as well as other items of value such as clothing, jewelry, cell phones, and disco tickets. (2) The duration of the relationship is indeterminate; it may last for just one night or one week, or it may continue on indefinitely as sporadic encounters or in more enduring forms. (3) Women may offer additional provisions besides sex, such as domestic services. (4) Family members are more likely to be aware of the financial and personal benefits that derive from informal sex work, thus leading to less public stigmatization. And (5) informal sex work often fits into more culturally accepted norms of exchanging sex for "gifts," as it is regarded as a more intimate affair in which participants are not constructed as strangers or clients but as "boyfriends" and "girlfriends" (Hunter 2002:100–101; Kaufman and Stavrou 2004:377–380). To briefly summarize, then, informal sex work is a highly fluid and adaptable arrangement of exchanging sex for goods. It is a transaction not just of economic value but also of enduring social consequence (Verheijen 2013).

The variability and hence ambiguity of sexual exchange appears in the deployment of a commonly used street word, *phanda*.[17] The youth of Point Place frequently utilize this word. It emerges whenever I inquire about their income-generating practices. For example, among the males, an occupational ambiguity exists between asking for something and taking something. The obscure application of *phanda* expresses this ambiguity, which in different contexts means either to beg or to steal. Dingani, a seventeen-year-old male living inside Point Place, narrates just one of the many ways in which the word *phanda* is open to interpretation: "*Bengizula, uyabona nje. Sihambe siyophanda*" (I roamed around, you see. We went and begged/stole). In English usage, "to hustle" would be the closest equivalent. For the Point Place females, *phanda* takes on another meaning, one that has closer associations with informal sex work. Here *phanda* best translates as "trying to get," whereby the final word of the sentence (e.g., money) remains unspoken but is tacitly understood. Simphiwe, one of the three girls to openly acknowledge that she engages in sex work, has this to say about the other Point Place females: "*Abanye bayafihla ukuthi bayaphanda ePoint Place*" (Others at Point Place are hiding it, that they're trying to get [money]). Even in this case, *phanda* should not be regarded as a mere euphemism for sex work (Wojcicki 2002a:356). Rather, the indeterminacy of the word reflects the fluidity of the sexual relationships that the Point Place girls engage in. It shows the ways in which they parlay their affairs into many simultaneous configurations, involving status, pleasure, and necessity.

Sex as Consumption

The Point Place females, while disdainful of prostitution, are forthcoming about using sex or even just their sexual appeal as a means of acquiring outside lovers and hence material goods. They often refer to lovers, still constructed as boyfriends, as *amabunja*, or they use the shorthand "O" or "i.k."[18] Their designation of an outside boyfriend differs from their designation of a boyfriend living within the building. The girls typically refer to their Point Place boyfriends as *indoda yami* (my man) or *i-boyfriend yami* (my boyfriend). This difference in nomenclature reflects a difference in sexual strategies as well. Generally speaking, boyfriends from within the building are linked to subsistence needs, while outside boyfriends are linked to consumptive pleasures.[19] Both kinds of relationships convey a material component. This materiality is most pronounced with outside boyfriends, for they are likely to have disposable cash and can provide their girlfriends with money and gifts. The Point Place females derive a great deal of personal status from these relationships, as they are able to display and share their wares with friends. Such items of popular consumption include fashionable clothing and footwear, hair extensions, cell phones, takeout fast food (preferably KFC [Kentucky Fried Chicken]), and alcoholic beverages.

In the following conversations, Nobuhle and Angel discuss the material importance of securing relationships on the outside. Both conversations are revealing not only for their connections between love and the acquisition of goods but also for their framing of infidelity, which they connect to feelings of confidence and self-worth. The first conversation is with Nobuhle, one of the young women who revealed that they had engaged in commercial sex work prior to their arrival at Point Place. At the time of the interview, she was living inside Point Place with her boyfriend.

Nobuhle begins, "When I was not dating Bonginkosi, I was dating Raj. I also accepted love outside. When I first came to Point Place, I was just wearing ugly things."

"How did you meet this boyfriend outside?" I ask.

"I was going with Raj in the morning. He was selling stuff [dagga] at the beachfront. I saw this other person. He always wanted to talk to me. One day I gave him the chance. He told me that he loved me and would take care of me. You see how I'm wearing these nice things now? I'll say this other person that I also am seeing loves me. He can make me wear nice clothes."

In a similar conversation, Angel explains to me and Ofentse how she acquired a new tracksuit unbeknownst to her Point Place boyfriend, Zakes. I initiate the conversation by asking Angel who bought her new clothes. Angel responds, "These are my friend's shorts. The shirt I bought from the little boys for R5. But the tracksuit, Wandile [an outside lover] bought it for me. And he's still going to buy me clothes. I told Zakes lies. I said that I got it from home."

For my benefit, Ofentse interjects, "Angel lied. She said she went home."

To clarify this chronology as well as Angel's previous admissions of infidelity, I ask, "So the time Zakes was fooling around with that other girl . . . ?"

"Angel was also doing it," Ofentse confirms.

"You'll meet Wandile," Angel gleefully continues. "He's a nice boy. You see, he visited our room and bought cool drinks [sodas]. He didn't choose certain people. He bought for everyone in the room to share. He bought us take-away [food] and then he bought me my own take-away. He bought maybe three cool drinks. He has money. I love him. I really love him."

A clear instrumentality exists for Nobuhle and Angel when it comes to choosing outside boyfriends. Still, their sexual relationships consist of more than just an interest in consumptive pleasure. The girls express sentiments of love as well. For Nobuhle such sentiments are initiated through the courting rites of proposing (*shela*) and choosing (*qoma*) love. Nobuhle's eventual acceptance of an outside boyfriend reflects how the Point Place females view love not as a given sentiment but as a negotiated process of communication, interaction, and offering. Similarly, Angel equates love with material goods, yet she also highlights the affections of her outside affair. She loves Wandile not only because he has money but also because he exhibits generosity with her friends. The secrecy of the relationship provides pleasure for Angel, too, because it offsets the infidelities of Zakes, her Point Place boyfriend.

This subjective, experiential understanding of love—and subsequent betrayal—cannot be captured by purely categorical applications of sex-for-money or sex-for-gifts. Moreover, to focus solely on the materiality of transactional sex situates the Point Place females in a problematic gender dynamic. It posits them as passive actors unable to maneuver beyond a single field of sexual exploitation. By eliding love, such models reduce the negotiating capacities of the Point Place girls to a limited range of responses that fall between acquisitive want and bare-minimum survival. Sex linked to consumption locates the girls at the acquisitive end of the spectrum. Sex linked to subsistence places them at the other extreme. Both perspectives present only a partial view of the love affairs that take place within and outside of Point Place.

Sex as Subsistence

To maintain themselves on a day-to-day basis, the Point Place females rely on a choice of boyfriends from within the building. Compared to lovers taken from the outside, boyfriends from within Point Place are unlikely to provide their girlfriends with status goods, for they have less access to disposable income. Instead they tend to support their girlfriends with basic necessities. This includes staple food (bread, baloney, rice, beans, eggs, potatoes, and meat), secondhand clothes, toiletries (toothbrushes, soap, hair cream, and Vaseline), and, perhaps most important, a designated living space. These relationships also entail a set of domestic expectations. The males offer daily sustenance and shelter, while the females, in ideal terms, cook, clean, and do the laundry. Often the Point Place females refer to these arrangements through the reciprocal exchanges of *nakana*. For example, nineteen-year-old Simosihle expresses such sentiments when she explains why she chose to accept a Point Place boyfriend: "I saw that Jerry is right for me. We'll take care of each other okay."[20]

Along with the affirmations of love, the dissolution of sexual relationships inside Point Place illustrates expectations of *nakana* as well. Such occurrences underscore the negative example of *nakana*, the feelings of neglect and abandonment that accompany a breakup. As Unathi, an eighteen-year-old female, narrates, "One day I got a problem. Howie [my boyfriend] fell in love with one of my friends. He stopped supporting me. He used to support me at Point Place. We were staying together. The time that he fell in love with my friend, he stopped supporting me." This displacement of support, whether in the form of material goods or sleeping arrangements, is a continual source of anxiety for the Point Place females. In these situations, they have recourse to three options: (1) Confrontation: "I said to my boyfriend, 'Why is it that when you give me money, Laura also wants money? Are we fighting over you?' He stopped giving her money" (Bongi). (2) Acceptance: "First day this other girl came, hey, she was *jola* [in love] with Shorty. Hey, I say no more *jola* [be in love with] Shorty because Shorty wants another girlfriend now. He forgot me, but never mind, I went and found my own food" (Teeny, nineteen-year-old female). Or (3): An active search for a supplementary lover. The third option, as I explain below, is perhaps the riskiest, especially if a girl takes another lover inside Point Place.

While the Point Place females may accept a number of outside lovers, they recognize that having more than one internal lover is a bad idea, for the tight spaces and close interactions lead to more chances of detection and the possibility of physical retaliation. If a girl is known to have more than one boyfriend, a general "meeting" will be called, at which other youth, in the interest of collective harmony, will force her to choose among her internal boyfriends. Angel explains the procedures:

> When Chase came out of prison, he was dating Sisi. Then when Phumlani got out from jail, they said Sisi must choose. They had a meeting, and she chose

Phumlani. The other kids said that she was causing the boys to fight. The boys wanted to poke [stab] each other . . . They said that when you're seeing one boy, you always must have just one boy. You mustn't have two boys, like Sisi.

If a relationship fails, it is not uncommon for a Point Place boyfriend to demand that his ex-girlfriend return everything he has given to her. Such was the case with Chase, who asked Sisi to give back all the clothes that he had bought for her. Angel, too, faces this predicament when she discovers her Point Place boyfriend, Zakes, kissing another girl. Feeling hurt and betrayed as well as worrying about the allocation of their meager resources, she demands an immediate breakup. In response, Zakes tells her that she must leave the room and replace everything that he has given her, including items already consumed—food, drinks, and glue (for sniffing). The bedding and blankets are to remain with him as well. Zakes knows that this is an impossible request. Angel cannot give up her own subsistence. To all public appearances, the two still are dating, yet this does not mean that she accepts his infidelities or his ongoing neglect. She chooses the third option, the taking of supplementary lovers from within Point Place. Angel justifies her affairs by declaring: "They used to kiss in front of me. Back then I wanted to pay revenge. Even now I'm going to make him pay."

True to her vows of vengeance, Angel seeks out additional boyfriends. Still, she follows certain rules of conduct when negotiating her internal affairs. Generally speaking, secondary lovers must minimize any untoward displays of domesticity. They must not impinge on the productive and reproductive expectations of the primary or publicly acknowledged boyfriend. Such was the case with Sandlana, an eighteen-year-old male resident of Point Place, who spoke about his affair with Angel. Here Sandlana notes the terms of his love proposal (*shela*) as well as the conditions of Angel's eventual acceptance (*qoma*):

> You see, Angel was still in love with Zakes the time that I told her I loved her. She told me let's wait until tomorrow because she wants to think properly. She said maybe she loves me now, as we're speaking, but if she's going somewhere else, maybe this thing is going to give her a problem. I said, okay, it's fine because you want to think right; you want to think properly. When I met Angel the next day, she told me, "Okay, Sandlana, it's fine. There's no problem that I have with you so we can have the love. But I mustn't tell Zakes." She doesn't want everyone to know, you see.

Later on in the interview, when I ask whether Angel does his laundry or cooking, Sandlana responds by saying: "No, Angel is not washing my clothes. I don't like to take her as my wife, to give her my clothing." To clarify his position as a secondary lover, Sandlana reiterates: "I respect Angel. I see her boyfriend because she stays [in the same room] with him. That's why I respect her." In sum, when describing the boyfriend-girlfriend relationships of Point Place, the females largely focus on the presence or absence of *nakana*, which primarily takes on the form of domestic sustenance. Sandlana, too, notes the expectations of domesticity that come with a publicly acknowledged sexual relationship. This shared living space does not just encompass boyfriend-girlfriend couples. It includes friends as well.

Friends are integral to the collective survival strategies of the Point Place youth, as they make up the social networks that take over when boyfriend-girlfriend relationships fail. Quite often friends provide the most revealing and critical commentary on what happens in the intimate spaces of Point Place. In the following interview, two young women, Amie and Sisi, remark on the failure of one of their friends to secure a long-term relationship. Notable not just for its explicit talk about sex, the interview also reveals the implicit expectations of the Point Place females. Amie begins by saying:

> Tom and Laura slept on Beauty's mattress. Just imagine. They told Beauty to move over. I said, "*Hayi-bo*! Tom and Laura are having sex in front of us!" I was looking with [my boyfriend] Mandla. He closed my mouth. Mandla said that I must keep quiet. Beauty just got angry. She asked me to lift her up. I lifted her up. She went and sat on the other side of the room. She didn't want to argue because she was sick. I later told Laura, "My sister, the thing that you did is not right."

Sisi continues, "The following day, Tom wasn't interested in Laura. He just turned and wasn't interested in her anymore. He just left her like that."

"He turned on her," Amie corroborates. "He wasn't interested. He slept with her. He didn't even give her R10."

The expectation of receiving something—no matter how small, even R10—is integral to the continuation of boyfriend-girlfriend relationships inside Point Place. From the perspective of the females, it underscores the centrality of *nakana*, of couples taking care of one another. Stated another way, sexual exchanges inside Point Place highlight the shared sustenance and, oftentimes, the losses of love.

*   *   *

To discuss the themes of this chapter—love, betrayal, and sexual intimacy—in greater detail, I return to Zodwa's story. In some ways it is an atypical case study. She is one of the few girls to ask me to accompany her to the clinic for an HIV test, a procedure that I detail below.[21] Zodwa's relationship with Tau also proves to be one of the most enduring relationships inside Point

Place, lasting for nearly two years. Yet, while these factors set Zodwa apart, her experiences conform to the experiences of the other Point Place females, too. For Zodwa's love story is a story not only about romantic intimacies and betrayals but also about friends. Friends make it possible for her to leave home. Friends shape her sexual connections. They direct her choices, limiting and expanding the possibilities of *nakana* on the streets.

Zodwa attributes her arrival to Durban to her best friend, Celiwe, who comes from the same rural settlement in the Eastern Cape. As Zodwa dramatically narrates it, "Celiwe said to me that we must go to Durban. She stole two children."

"Ay," Celiwe admonishes, clearly not liking the direction of the interview. From their back-and-forth banter, I learn that Celiwe befriended two children in the Eastern Cape who were visiting their aunt's home. At the time, Celiwe and Zodwa were staying in a shack next door to the aunt. Celiwe offered to accompany the children, a boy and a girl ages nine and thirteen, to their parents' home in Durban. She convinced Zodwa to join them, explaining that the children had entrusted her with R300 for the transport. She also told Zodwa about a building where they could stay for free with other youth in the city center. Upon reaching Durban, however, Celiwe changed her plans. She decided that the money would go further if she were alone, so she tried to ditch Zodwa and the children at the *kombi* rank. Realizing Celiwe's intentions, Zodwa ran after her friend, leaving the boy and girl stranded without money or a guide to take them home.

When I ask Celiwe and Zodwa whether they know what happened to the children, they shake their heads no. This is why they cannot return to their homes. Zodwa worries about retribution from the aunt. Celiwe, on the other hand, dismisses such concerns. Authority figures barely register in her thoughts. Police officers, social workers, ministers, parents, teachers, and the elderly all receive the same irreverent treatment:

> *Celiwe, Zodwa, Ofentse, and I are making our way inside a large shopping center, cutting through it to reach the beachfront on the other side. The security guard stops us, not to prevent us from entering but to try and speak with Celiwe and Zodwa. Both girls draw appreciative glances from passing men. Their smooth, glowing skin, bright eyes, and lively demeanor attract nods from everyone. Even though Zodwa is younger than Celiwe by a year, people tend to assume that she is older, for her tall stature and proud bearing make her appear more mature. Because of this, social workers often overlook Zodwa, believing she is too old for "intervention." Celiwe,*

*on the other hand—through the nature of her forceful personality
and attention-seeking antics—receives numerous offers of help. Social workers constantly shuttle her back and forth between homes,
children's shelters, and rehabilitation programs. For now, though,
the two girls are not thinking about their immediate futures. They
merely want to enjoy a swim and a bite to eat outside. They laugh
at the amorous comments of the security guard, telling him that he
is much too old for them. I nudge the girls along, hoping to speed
up their leisurely pace.*

*We step onto the escalator; as usual, a mechanical failure causes
us to have to hike up the steps, our bodies bumping against shoppers who have decided to come down at the same time. Before we
reach the top, Celiwe notices a frail, timorous-looking lady clutching
her purse to her chest waiting for an opening on the landing. The
woman's pale face is painted with a liberal application of makeup:
blue eye shadow, rosy rouge, red lipstick. Celiwe laughs in delight at
the thought of this geriatric dressing up trying to look young again.
A pink ribbon is tied into the woman's curls, causing her to appear
even more precious, and sadly more comical. Celiwe greets the
lady in singsong English: "Hello, cutie! I like your outfit! So pretty!"
Confused, the woman regards us all with suspicion, clasps her purse
even tighter to her chest, and teeters her way down the escalator.
Still smiling, Celiwe skips up the remaining steps. Zodwa shakes
her head in mixed admiration and issues her standard response:
"Wena vele uyiskelemu, Celiwe" [You're a real gangster, Celiwe].*

Since the age of ten, Celiwe has been moving between the Eastern Cape and
Durban, staying with family members and friends, interspersed with stints
on the streets and in children's shelters. She first left her home in 1997; after
her mother passed away, relatives sent her to live with her aunt in Durban.
In 2001 her aunt, too, passed away, and Celiwe had to return to her father's
homestead. Only then did she learn that her father and mother had never
married; rather, she was his mistress, and he had another wife. To maintain
a respectable household, Celiwe's father dispatched her to the homes of his
older children. Eventually Celiwe tired of her father's pretense. She also wore
out her welcome with her half-siblings, nieces, nephews, aunts, and uncles.
And so without much fanfare, she decided to stay with friends her own age,
settling down in a shack in the Eastern Cape with eight other teenagers,
including Zodwa.

Zodwa had also resided in several different households prior to coming
to Durban. As a young child, she stayed with her mother in the Eastern

Cape. When she turned fourteen, her mother sent her to live with her father, who was working in Cape Town. Zodwa preferred this arrangement—the amusements of township life—to the isolation of her mother's homestead. She also enjoyed the household responsibilities that her father entrusted to her, which often included paying the bills. One day Zodwa spent the household money on herself. Afraid of her father's reaction, she hid underneath his bed. When he returned home that evening, he carried on with his usual household routines, as if Zodwa's absence did not mean anything to him. The following morning, Zodwa left her father's home. She moved to another house located in the same township just a section away.

A group of drifters, friends and strangers, occupied the house with Zodwa. The girls shoplifted clothes and cosmetics from nearby chain stores. Security guards eventually caught them but let them off because of their young age. After this incident, the girls decided to limit their illegal activities to stealing clothes off neighbors' clotheslines. Again they were caught, but this time it was a more serious matter, one taken up by a block of housing sections. The township residents presented Zodwa's father with two options: he could whip Zodwa, or he could chase her away. Not wanting to hurt his daughter, he opted for the latter. Zodwa returned to the Eastern Cape, but instead of residing with her mother, she chose to stay with school friends in a nearby informal settlement. There she reconnected with Celiwe, who by then had made her way through a series of homes not just of her own relatives but also of passing boyfriends.

Boyfriends make it possible for Celiwe and Zodwa to remain in Durban indefinitely. Celiwe has many boyfriends. She considers herself fortunate, as boyfriends fulfill more than her minimal needs. They offer something she wants yet in the end always renounces—a home: "I have luck to date boyfriends who take me to their homes." Zodwa, on the other hand, is more discerning when it comes to accepting love proposals. She prefers to follow the advice of her female companions. This is how, at the age of fifteen, she chose her first boyfriend, Tau, whom she met at Thuthukani.

"They [the other girls] forced me the day I arrived at Thuthukani. They said I must *qoma* Tau. I accepted him, and we started dating the same day that I arrived." Zodwa agreed to date Tau for another reason as well: "Tau hit me. He asked, why am I not choosing him? He hit me. I still was scared of him back then."

A few weeks after Celiwe and Zodwa arrived at Thuthukani, the gates of Point Place—previously closed because of a police eviction—reopened. Tau staked out a claim to a room, justified by his lengthy time on the streets, in shelters, and in prison. Zodwa did not join him immediately but visited him from Thuthukani until one day he asked her to stay with him. Zodwa agreed and, with another female friend, ended up cooking and cleaning for a small group of older boys living in adjoining rooms. "I woke up in the morning. I cooked for them. When I finished cooking, I cleaned." For a full year, Zodwa has stayed with Tau. She rarely goes out to the nightclubs or bars. She has little interest in socializing with other youth, including Celiwe. She shuts her bedroom door when she hears Celiwe coming.

Celiwe, for her part, often mocks Zodwa, laughing at her when she hears that Tau has "given up on crime" to sell oranges by the taxi stand. Tau's earnings, while small, still attract the attention of other girls. He begins to share his glue with Pinky. Zodwa notices and, as described at the beginning of this chapter, attacks the material bonds of their sexual union. She burns their domestic possessions and runs away from Point Place. It is not sustainable, however, for Zodwa to remain outside of Point Place. She does not have the same street savvy as Celiwe; nor is she as interested in acquiring other boyfriends. Her self-imposed isolation makes her too susceptible to the dangers of the streets, and so in the end she returns to Point Place.

Even though Zodwa has reunited with Tau, she has begun to think more about her family. She has not seen her mother in a long time. Tau gives her the fare to visit her family. Zodwa's mother is happy to see her but forces her to remain indoors, because the aunt of the two missing children still has not forgiven her. Not wanting to cause further problems, Zodwa decides to return to Point Place. Upon her arrival, she notices that some things are amiss. She suspects that someone may have been using her bed. A few clothing items and cosmetics are gone, too. Several months later, her suspicions are confirmed. She catches Tau having sex with another girl. This time Zodwa does not settle for material destruction. Her anger escalates to extreme violence. She stabs Tau with a kitchen knife, and in retaliation he stabs her, too. As Zodwa narrates it:

> Tau poked [stabbed] me painfully. The knife came in here [on one side of my wrist] and came out here [on the other side of my wrist]. He poked me. I found him with another girl. There were three boys. They were sticking their fingers inside of this girl. I first poked Tau because he was stamping on my bed with his feet. It happened on the twenty-first of last month. I was hiding in the room, underneath the table. I fell asleep. I didn't lock the door to the room. The other boys got in. I heard a noise. I woke up. The boys walked into the room with this girl. They said to Zakes, "You must go and look for condoms." Tau was going to go first, after him, another boy. Zakes was going to go last because he was guarding the door. They started with their fingers inside of this girl. I stood up. I took a knife. I started with Tau. I poked him here in the back. He was still sticking his fingers inside of this girl. I wanted to poke her, too, but the other boys held me back. They separated us.

I ask Zodwa what happened to the girl afterward, and Celiwe responds, "She's in a children's shelter now. An outreach worker took her."

"I was angry," Zodwa continues, "because she was stamping on *my* duvet with her legs." I prod Zodwa to continue with her story, and she provides a lengthy narrative, detailing not just the violence of her sexual relationship but also the gives and takes of friendship.

Tau found me. I was sleeping in the girls' room. I took my clothes from our room. I said we broke up. I was sleeping in the girls' room with Alice. We were sleeping on the floor, next to the wall. Tau came. He was holding a table knife this big. He said he wants revenge. I wasn't nervous. I wasn't concentrating. I just looked at him. He was standing above me. He opened my blanket, and he poked me here. I didn't cry. The blood didn't come out. I just held my wrist like this. I left the room and sat outside for a long time. Oh, I went to Tau's room first. I took his bed sheet. I wrapped it around my wrist. Blood, it was not coming out too much. I sat, sat, sat on the outside steps. Tau came. He said I must go to the hospital. I said how am I to go to the hospital? Am I going to walk? Tau gave me R4. He said I must take a *kombi* and go to the hospital. Instead, I took the money and compromised with the little boys for some glue [i.e., Zodwa used the money that Tau gave her to buy some glue from the younger street boys]. When I was high, I felt the pain. I was high off glue. I went to the hospital. I walked. I said to Celiwe that she must accompany me. She said no, she will not accompany me. She wanted to be with her own boyfriend.

Celiwe, recognizing Zodwa's dismay, explains her reasons for not helping her friend: "She was going to make my boyfriend angry with me. I was having an argument with my boyfriend then. He said I mustn't leave."

"I said you must accompany me. I was hurt, Celiwe. Accompany me."

Refusing to offer an apology, Celiwe explains, "You know, when I go to Zodwa's room, when she's sitting there with Tau, I'll knock on their door. Zodwa will say come in, but Tau will say that she's sleeping. I'm turned away. Now I also wanted to show her. I was angry."

In the end, Zodwa walks to the hospital alone. Afterward she returns to Tau's room. She puts all her clothes back into their small trunk, washes the duvet, and forgives Tau. Zodwa no longer worries about him becoming "clever." He already is clever. She accepts this. As long as Tau conducts his affairs with discretion, Zodwa will keep her anger in check. She believes he loves her best, which is made evident by their shared living space.

Still, Zodwa misses her mother and her home. She tells Tau that she would like to visit the Eastern Cape again. He fears she will not return. To reassure him, she announces her intention to become pregnant. A baby will connect her to Tau permanently. Zodwa tries to conceive a baby but is unsuccessful. She decides to go to the hospital to have her womb "scrubbed." Reflecting on Zodwa's desires, Celiwe announces that she, too, would like to go to the hospital, not because she wants a baby but because she wants to have an HIV test. She has been reading some of the health pamphlets lying around the children's shelters, spread out on the tables, and posted on bathroom doors. She knows that HIV can be transmitted through unprotected sex. She thinks back to all her boyfriends. There have been many.

> *I am standing inside Addington Hospital, in the hallway of the Sinothando clinic. The clinic consists of three rooms sectioned off for those who want to have an HIV test, for those who want to monitor their white blood cell count, and for those who hope to gain access to antiretroviral (ARV) treatment. It is so crowded today that everyone is pushed against the walls, trying to make space for the patients who are lying on the gurneys in the center of the corridor, lined up from one end of the hallway to the other. There is blood on the floor, smeared in streaks across the linoleum. I turn my feet sideways, trying to keep my flip-flops clean. One of the patients on the gurney is crying. Her collarbones protrude sharply from underneath her gown. Dark circles stain the paper-thin cloth. She mutters to herself incoherently. A nurse, looking especially harried, comes to change the patient's bedpan. The nurse exposes the woman's genitalia to everyone waiting in line. Celiwe stands next to me. She gazes at the exposed woman but does not say anything. Celiwe is unusually solemn today. Ofentse and Zodwa are here, too. They stare at the posters hanging on the walls opposite us. The cartoon drawings and bubble conversations are meant to be understood easily even by those who cannot read. The posters reinforce a national HIV/AIDS campaign, one that focuses on the ABCs of prevention: Abstain, Be safe, and Condomize. I hear Zodwa say quietly to Ofentse: "Eish, ngingakhathazeka uma kungathwi nginayo. Futhi ngiyamuzwela 'muntu onayo" [Eish, I can worry if they say that I have it. And I feel sorry for a person who does have it]. Zodwa, like Celiwe, has decided to take an HIV test. She makes this decision once she hears that pregnant mothers can receive prenatal ARV treatment (Neviraprine), which significantly reduces the chances of mother-to-child HIV transmission.*
>
> *I am not exactly sure why the girls want me—and, by extension, Ofentse—to accompany them to the Sinothando clinic. It may have to do with logistics. I know the way and the procedures. It may have to do with my perceived status. Bureaucratic figures in*

institutional settings—prisons, hospitals, shelters, welfare agencies, courthouses, and police stations—tend to be more considerate when I am around. It may have to do with trust, although this last reason I am much less certain of. In any case, I do not want to be there because I do not want to see the results. I have made the trip to Sinothando several times before. The outcome never has been easy. This time, in particular, I am worried. Up until a few days ago, neither Celiwe nor Zodwa seemed to have given much thought to the possibility of being HIV positive. The quick timeframe leaves me feeling anxious. In addition to asking for an HIV test, both girls want to go home the next day, mainly to pick up their ID books—a necessity if they want a job, a formal training certificate, access to social welfare grants, or in Zodwa's case prenatal care. Part of me wishes to postpone the trip, to give the girls more time to think about whether or not they would like to be tested for HIV. The other part of me wants them to take the test, knowing that their estranged families will be the ones to deal with the immediate consequences. In the end, I accompany the girls to the Sinothando clinic because it is their request. To ask for an HIV test is a momentous decision. The youth from Point Place rarely speak about HIV or AIDS in personal or direct terms. Even when friends die of AIDS-related complications, no one says so openly. Their cause of death usually is attributed to tuberculosis and always is discussed in hushed tones. For Celiwe and Zodwa to want to know their status signifies a departure from the usual procedures of evasion.

It is now late afternoon, and I know the girls will not have enough time for a counseling session and an HIV test before the Sinothando clinic closes. I ask Celiwe and Zodwa if they would be willing to go to the Hope Clinic, located in the Durban Christian Center (DCC) not too far away. I usually avoid this clinic, for the counselors tend to espouse moral messages of sexual abstinence. But the clinic does stay open later, and the HIV test is administered for free. Also, the Hope Clinic is not attached to a public hospital, so it tends to be cleaner and quieter than Sinothando. The girls agree, and we head out, navigating our way past the gurneys, smeared blood, and crying patients.

True to my previous experiences, the Hope Clinic is cleaner and quieter than Sinothando. It also is more orderly. When we enter, the receptionist immediately hands Celiwe and Zodwa an intake form to write down their personal information. Soon afterward the girls are ushered into separate rooms for their counseling sessions. Celiwe comes out quickly. Zodwa takes longer. She eventually comes out, too. The counselors ask the girls to wait outside until they are called in again for their HIV test. The clinic uses two types of testing methods: Rapid Oral and ELISA (enzyme-linked immunoassay). The first takes saliva from the gums; the second collects drops of blood from a pricked forefinger. The results take only a few minutes. As we are waiting, a short man—his head reaching no higher than the receptionist's table—starts making his rounds. He is wearing the dark suit and white collar of a minister. I assume that he comes from the DCC. The minister addresses Celiwe and Zodwa directly. The first part of his message is expected, the second part less so. The minister cautions them to stop having so much sex. Otherwise their vaginas will become too loose and nobody will marry them. The girls laugh at the minister's candor, slapping their hands against their thighs in delight. Even Ofentse smiles, grateful for the comic relief.

A counselor directs Celiwe and Zodwa into separate rooms to take their tests. As before, Celiwe returns to the reception room first. She drags her feet along the carpet, flops down on top of Ofentse, and whispers into her ear. Ofentse smacks Celiwe hard on the arm. I know this means that Celiwe is HIV negative. I am elated, and for a moment I forget about Zodwa. We all do. I then feel her by my side. Zodwa is smiling for Celiwe, too. Zodwa still does not know her own results. The counselor calls Zodwa back into the office. The door closes softly with a click. Bang! The door flies open and slams against the wall. Zodwa launches her entire body across the room, landing on the chair furthest away from the counselor's office. She screams at the counselor to shut up. The entire room is silent. Zodwa drops her voice. She keeps shaking her head, murmuring Tau's name, repeating to herself it is impossible. We all know what just transpired. The counselor tries to convince Zodwa to return to the testing room, but Zodwa refuses. Celiwe looks at me. She seems to be on the verge of laughter. Celiwe does not know how else to react.

I walk over to Zodwa and kneel in front of her chair. Even though it is not okay, I tell Zodwa that it is. I tell her that she still can have babies and a future with Tau. Zodwa responds by saying, "Quiet, don't talk too much now." We sit silently for a few more minutes, until Zodwa requests that we all return to the Point. We quickly gather our belongings, wait for Celiwe to collect her HIV-negative slip (proof), and then leave. On our way out, Celiwe asks Zodwa exactly what happened. She tells us that the counselor said some-thing along the lines of "What would you do if I told you that you were HIV positive?" From this statement, our conversation turns into: "So you don't really know your results, you still could be nega-tive?" Ofentse suggests that Zodwa return to the Sinothando clinic with Tau so professional healthcare workers can test both of them together. Zodwa agrees to the idea. Every step we take away from the Hope Clinic puts her in a better mood. By the time we reach the car, we all are smiling and chatting like nothing serious just happened. On our way back to the Point Area, I receive a call from the Hope Clinic. The girls wrote down my cell phone number in the contact details of their in-take forms. The counselor asks me to bring Zodwa to the Hope Clinic the next day. She regrets the way she informed Zodwa about her test results. I tell the counselor that I will try, but I know my attempt will be futile. Zodwa is in shock and denial. She never will agree to return to the clinic. Instead, the next day we make the five-hour drive to their homes in the Eastern Cape. Our journey is notable only for what is not said.

*   *   *

"The problem," Bongi declares, "is the boys. The guys are the ones who don't want to use condoms. Like, when we girls are all together in our room, we talk. We say, 'Eh, AIDS is really killing us. We have to use condoms.' Like yesterday we told one of my friends, Glory, the one who is sick, that she has to use a condom because she can get AIDS anytime, anywhere, because the disease is very bad."

"So," I prod, "the girls are talking about HIV/AIDS, just the boys don't want to use condoms?"

"Yeah," Bongi responds, "the boys are killing us."

The youth of Point Place experience the losses of AIDS on two fronts: with their families and with each other. Arguably, many of them reside in Point Place because of HIV/AIDS.[22] They may be classed as AIDS orphans.[23] They may not have a suitable home that will accept them as bereaved kin with all the obligations—monetary and otherwise—that accompany this designation. To bypass these kin dislocations, they often turn to each other to set up their own structures of family, love, and support. Their losses, however, continue. For, as Bongi notes, her friends are not using condoms.[24] The Point Place fe-males may not have the capacity to negotiate condom use with their sexual partners, especially if they rely on boyfriends for material provisions. Still, in our conversations, these limitations do not come to the fore. Rather, as seen with Zodwa, the Point Place females are more likely to envision a future of shared sustenance, including the possibility of children. Thus, to conclude this chapter, I return to the spatial and temporal significations of *nakana*, contrasting the intimacies of these encounters to the alienations of the streets.

"Do you know any Point Place girls who don't have boyfriends?" I ask Amie and her two best friends, Bongi and Sisi. "Or do girls always have boyfriends here?"

"Yeah, yeah," Amie responds to my question, without elaborating.

I try a follow-up: "What is the best type of boyfriend to have, one with money?"

"No," Amie answers. "Sometimes other girls do that, but me, I never."

Bongi glances sideways at her friend and counters, "Sometimes we do that, Amie. Don't deny it. We go after money."

"Me, I don't go after Mandla's money," Amie answers with a reference to her Point Place boyfriend.

Unconvinced, Bongi presses forward. "How did you choose Mandla? He had stolen money. You went after his money. Sometimes we do that, we follow the money."

To which Sisi pipes in, "We go after cases [of beer]."

"We go after money sometimes," Bongi reiterates.

Amie tries again: "I don't go after Mandla's money." The other girls laugh at her self-deception.

"When we're at the bars," Sisi counters, "we go after money."

"Okay, fine." Amie is defeated.

The desires of the Point Place females—as indicated by Bongi and Sisi—are strategic. Amie only concedes to this calculation after Sisi broadens the discussion to include a consideration of outside boyfriends, something Sisi refers to through cases of beer and bars. Why is Amie unwilling to situate her Point Place relationship within the consumptive realm of an outside relationship? Bongi and Sisi are upfront about going after money even within Point Place. Why not Amie? Perhaps because Amie does not want to situate her relationship as a one-way exchange that links love to exploitative desire.

Such is the case with Teeny, who gamely accepts offerings from an outside man. The conversation begins with my asking Teeny how she finds food when she is staying at Point Place:

Me, I keep another man. This man, hey, he tells me that he loves me. He always comes to Point Place. He gives me KFC. He gives me money. He thinks I'm a stupid girl! He thinks that I can love him with money and with KFC? I take the KFC. I say, "Thank you, I'll see you tomorrow." I walk over to the other side of the building. I eat and eat. Afterwards he calls me, asking if I'm full. I say, "Hey,

I'm coming," and then I run away. Every day he comes and does the same thing. I take the money. I take the KFC. I won't say that I don't want to take it. Take it! I didn't force him to give me these things. I take it, and then I run away.[25]

I ask Teeny about food, trying to determine how she maintains her daily subsistence inside Point Place. She responds to my inquiry in an unexpected way. She speaks of trickery and illusory love. This deception, as Teeny narrates it, begins with the suitor who tries to woo her with a fast-food transaction: "He thinks that I can love him with money and with KFC?" Note how this contrasts with one of her previous statements: "First day this other girl came, hey, she was *jola* [in love] with Shorty. Hey, I say no more *jola* with Shorty because Shorty wants another girlfriend now. He forgot me, but never mind, I went and found my own food." In the sexual context of Point Place, Teeny links love to personal subsistence, a subsistence that is maintained not with KFC but with everyday *nakana*, as evidenced through the sharing—or in her case the loss—of staple food.

Still, outside affairs have advantages, which cannot be replicated inside Point Place. Teeny takes the KFC from the man. She takes his money and runs away. Her mobility provides her with a degree of agency. Tricking outside men into a one-way exchange is a constant source of amusement for the Point Place girls. Such amusements are not without their risks, though. In another interview, Teeny relates the dangers of unwanted desire. She speaks of an attempted rape by an outside acquaintance:

I went outside with Joy. First, we went to Artie upstairs. He had stolen our blankets, our sleeping blankets. You see, Zodwa was bragging. She thinks that she can sleep with her boyfriend in front of us, have sex. I saw that there was nothing for us. We are old now. I said to Joy we must leave Zodwa and look for our blankets in Artie's room. He gave us our blankets, and we washed them. We went outside. Joy ran away. She left me. This guy grabbed me. He grabbed me from the back. Then he lifted my skirt like this. I said, "What's wrong?" He slapped me. I said, "What's wrong, why are you hitting me?" Then he slapped me for the third time. I hit him with a bottle. The police van stopped. Those guys living next door spoke for me. They said I was a child. They said they saw this guy hitting me.

Teeny's narratives reveal both the prospects and the perils of outside engagements. The prospects (consumptive pleasure) are fleeting, whereas the perils (the traumatic effects of sexual assault) endure long past a single encounter.

*   *   *

South Africa has one of the highest per capita incidences of rape in the world. The nongovernmental organization People Opposing Women Abuse reports that every twenty-six seconds, a woman in South Africa is sexually assaulted.[26] Over the duration of one year, from March 2005 to April 2006, nearly 55,000 cases of rape were reported to the police.[27] The Point Place females overwhelmingly cite rape as the greatest threat to their personal wellbeing.[28] Several of them mention sexual assault as the motivating factor that caused them to leave their homes. Yet, while these same girls fear being raped on the streets, in townships, and in their homes, they rarely mention this type of assault inside Point Place.[29] Presumably the vocal presence of females, particularly in the all-female room, prevents males from taking untoward advantage. The males, too, view rape inside Point Place as anathema. One young man even compares it to incest: "Rape a girl? I can't because this girl is my sister. She has stayed with me for a long time. Now she is my sister. She knows me. I know her" (Yogi, twenty-seven-year-old male).[30] Still, as another girl notes, when the Point Place males are smoking or drinking, "They don't take you like their sister anymore. But if they were girls, they wouldn't do that" (Memory, nineteen-year-old female).

The narratives of rape told by the Point Place youth focus primarily on an element of unfamiliarity, of being new to town, alone, and outside: "Maybe a girl just arrived in Durban. She doesn't know where to stay. She doesn't have friends. Maybe one boy will see her. He comes and fetches her. Then they all sleep with her. They'll make a train [i.e., gang-rape her]" (Dudu, seventeen-year-old female). When the Point Place females refer to rape, they frequently draw on the notion of being thrown away (*lahla*).[31] They link the violence of rape to an emotional and physical sense of violation: "*Usuka elele nawe ngenkani. Akulahle kude*" (He sleeps with you by force. He throws you far). To counter such vulnerability, the girls set up barriers of everyday protection. They walk in pairs, preferably threes. They familiarize themselves with the surrounding vendors, pedestrians, and lodgers. They watch the time of day. If a Point Place female travels alone in the evening, she may carry a pocketknife, a shard of glass, or a rusty nail. Always the girls are vigilant about their external surroundings, highly watchful. They extend this condition of circumspection to their outside affairs. The Point Place females may accept proposals of love. They may *phanda*. They may engage in the exchange of sex for goods or sex for money, yet they do so with a degree of self-consciousness that shows they are aware of the potentially abusive and exploitative dynamics of these relationships. Sometimes the girls even manage to change the direction of this exploitation. Mainly, though, they strive for something else in their sexual attachments: they do not want to be thrown away, abandoned, or forsaken; they do not want to be caught in a one-way exchange. Their differentiation of boyfriends shows this concern.

Outside boyfriends embody the risks of venturing beyond the familiar or the close. Such distancing stands in contrast to the relationships conducted within Point Place, to the proximity and professed sense of intimacy that accompany these internal affairs.

In the following conversation, nineteen-year-old Lindi attempts to explain the different feelings of love she experiences with her Point Place boyfriend, Mxhosa, and her outside boyfriend, Bandile. "I love Mxhosa and I love Bandile. I love them both. But I think it's in different ways. I don't have sexual intercourse with Bandile, only with Mxhosa."

"What made you decide not to have sex with Bandile?" I ask.

"I don't trust him," Lindi responds. "He's a dancer. And I know boys who dance."

"What are they like?"

"They've got a lot of girlfriends, all around the place. And he's well known. Girls talk about him and everything. So I was just afraid to have it."

"What made you decide to have sexual intercourse with Mxhosa?"

"I trust him," Lindi laughs. "I don't know. I really don't know. I feel free with him. I've never felt this way with a boy before."

Lindi differentiates the love she feels for her two boyfriends through a concept of trust. Among the Point Place females, "trust" has concrete social effects. It directly links up to practices of sexual intimacy. Lindi refrains from sex with her outside boyfriend because she does not trust him. She contrasts this with her feelings for her inside boyfriend, Mxhosa. Although she has known Mxhosa for only a few days, their brief acquaintance does not affect her decision to have sex with him. She trusts him. Or, more particularly, she trusts the qualities of *nakana* that he exhibits. He provides her with a room and food. As the other Point Place youth would say, Mxhosa "tries" for Lindi. In trying, he shows the potentiality of *nakana*, the possibility of a reciprocated commitment. Such assurance rarely develops in outside affairs. It requires the joint familiarity and perhaps even the joint suffering of living together inside Point Place.

To elaborate on this notion of "trust" and "trying," I include my conversation with eighteen-year-old Unathi. Here she explains the love she feels for her two Point Place boyfriends, and why she cannot renounce them. "I love Philani because anything I need, he tries his best to do it for me. But I can't leave Howie."

"Why can't you leave Howie?" I ask.

"I can't," Unathi repeats.

"Is he your first love? The one you love the most?"

"Yeah."

"Does Philani know about Howie?"

"Yeah, he knows."

"Is he jealous?"

"Actually," Unathi elaborates, "I can say he is, but Philani will not do any-thing because he knows the full story about me and Howie. You see, Philani and Howie were friends. Philani was trying to help us, me and Howie. So I told myself that I mustn't take somebody else that I do not trust. I must take Philani because I have known him for so long."

Philani supports Unathi in times of need; he tries his best for her; they have known each other for a long time. Unathi trusts Philani more than any other suitor, and so she accepts him as a boyfriend. The Point Place females repeatedly draw on this formulation of trust, premised on acts of *nakana*, to delineate the reasons why they love their Point Place boyfriends.

The girls also cite trust as the motivating logic for engaging in unprotected sex with their Point Place boyfriends. Condoms, from their perspective, re-duce the possibility of real intimacy, of fulfilling the reciprocated exchange of *nakana*. Thus, while they recognize the dangers of HIV/AIDS, they view this threat as inconsequential, at least compared to the constructed barriers of condom usage. The demands of boyfriends to not use condoms certainly impinge on the negotiating capacity of the Point Place females, yet they too make deliberate choices to engage in unprotected sex. This can be seen with Lindi, who admits to not using condoms with her Point Place boyfriend, Mxhosa.

"Do you use condoms every time you have sex or just sometimes?" I ask Lindi.

"Well," she responds, "I used condoms every time until the day before yesterday." She laughs sheepishly. "I don't know. It just slipped my mind."

"So you forgot?"

"I didn't forget," Lindi contemplates. "But then, I don't know. I don't know where my mind was. Yeah, I kind of remembered but then thought again, no. Nay, I don't know why. Maybe I trust him too much."

Most of the Point Place females are aware that their Point Place boyfriends have other sexual partners both inside and outside of the building. Along with this acknowledgment, they frequently refer to the discomforts of sexu-ally transmitted infections, such as chlamydia (*ixonsi*), gonorrhea (*i-drop*), genital warts (*i-cauliflower*), and pubic lice. Oftentimes, shamed by their STI, they do not visit the clinic—or the place of the lovers (*emasokweni*)—until they are in extreme pain or until their STI becomes too advanced to continue engaging in sex. The following conversation with Thandisa, an eighteen-year-old female, reveals her candid acceptance of her boyfriend's infidelities and, along with it, an STI. I begin by asking Thandisa whether she talks about HIV/AIDS with her Point Place boyfriend, Marco. She responds yes, and when I ask her to elaborate, she provides this story:

> Like, when he had a STD [sexually transmitted disease], I asked, where did you get it? He told me that he slept with somebody else. I asked if it was Joy because every time he saw her in the passage, he used to club her. When he saw Joy, he clubbed her. Then I'd argue with him, asking, "Why do you hit that girl?" He'd tell me that this girl is sleeping with other boys. He said he got a STD from this girl. She gave him drop. I asked, "How? How could you? Why didn't you use a condom?" He told me that he was not taught to use condoms. So I said, "That's why you got this." I accompanied him to the clinic. Then after we got back from the clinic, he slept with that same girl! He got a STD again. He didn't tell me that he got this thing. Then he slept with me, too [laughs exasperatedly]. When he finally decided to be honest, he showed me his clinic card. He said to me, "Thandisa, take this card." I asked why. He said he got drop again. I said to him, "You got drop again?" He said, "Yeah." I asked, "How? How could you do this to me? Because you know I don't have anything. You sleep with me and now you tell me that I have drop, too." For the sake of love, I went to the clinic. When I came back, I took my treatment. I finished my treatment.

While cognizant of Marco's infidelities, Thandisa continues to love him and regard him as her primary boyfriend. As with other boyfriend-girlfriend arrangements inside Point Place, Marco provides Thandisa with food, clothes, and a room. He also visits her in the hospital when she is recovering from a stab wound. Perhaps most telling, Marco promises Thandisa that one day they will visit his mother. His desire for her to meet his family highlights an important distinction between outside and inside affairs. The Point Place females generally do not visit the homes of their outside boyfriends. Such considerations remain the privilege of those who have known each other for a long time, of those who reside together inside Point Place.

*   *   *

Although not ideal, the boyfriend-girlfriend relationships that form within Point Place offer young women a vision of a hopeful future, one that includes home visits, the possibility of children, and ongoing material and emotional support. Nonetheless, by opening themselves up to the intimacies of *nakana*, the Point Place females also open themselves up to the risks of a foreshortened lifespan: to HIV/AIDS. Such risks they find acceptable, at least compared to the immediate perils of being forsaken or thrown away (*lahla*). Their assessment of *nakana* is by no means a naïve or unfounded dream, for the Point Place males—as I discuss in chapter four—also believe that their sexual attachments hold the possibility of domestic stability, companionship, and care. As Zakes, Angel's boyfriend, narrates, "We speak about our lives. Maybe one of us, when we're older, one of us is going to find work. We'll get married and have our own house. You see, all of that." In short, Zakes envisions a committed future of *nakana*, one that entails employment, marriage, and a house that he shares with his long-term girlfriend and rooming companion, Angel.

And here the sexual strategies enacted by the Point Place youth share commonalities with the "ties of dependence" that sociologists Ann Swidler and Susan Cotts Watkins (2007:157) describe as part of a broader ethic of reciprocity and redistribution in sub-Saharan Africa. Almost everyone—except the most unfortunate, those without kin, friends, or lovers—participates in these social networks, leveraging them to create opportunities to withstand the hardships of everyday life (Swidler and Watkins 2007:151). Similarly, the Point Place youth create "ties of dependence" by activating obligations from a wide network of friends, lovers, and, to a lesser extent, kin. These ties, as evidenced by the tactics of Zodwa and her companions, have the greatest efficacy when they live in close proximity with their lovers. For, as cohabitating residents, they can promote nakana in its most basic form, that of acknowledgment. This mutual recognition presents opportunities for ongoing sustenance and support, which in turn helps the Point Place females, as a collectivity, mitigate the uncertainties and inequalities of their urban poverty.

4 Love, Respect, and Masculinity

Complainant: Jabulani Shozi, employed by the city municipality
Occupation: Street Sweeper
On February 24th at 6:30am I was walking down Botanic Gardens Road and three African males came to me. One of them was carrying a bottle. He tried to hit me with the bottle. Others searched my pocket and they took my cellphone (an A50 Siemen). A bag with my lunch box was taken too. The matter was reported to the police.

This is the official report of how Jabulani's cell phone was stolen. In truth, his girlfriend, Busi, stole it from underneath his pillow while he was sleeping. The police refused to fill out a case report when they heard about Busi's involvement, so Jabulani fabricated the story about the three African men. He added the part about the missing lunchbox, thinking it would add to his credibility, as he hoped to collect insurance money for the phone. What he wanted most of all, however, was for Busi to return to him. Busi took more than just Jabulani's cell phone. She also ran away with a homemade gun, R33, and a duffel bag. Yet she stole something else as well, something Jabulani cannot reclaim from the insurance company. "No, it's not easy to love her again," he explains. "You know what Busi did to me? She killed me. Busi already killed me." Busi, in other words, dealt a blow to Jabulani's sense of dignity and respect on the streets.

This chapter is a companion piece to the previous one. It, too, begins with a love proposal and ends with a breakup, but this time from the perspective of young men. The setting remains the same: Point Place. The succession of love affairs within and outside of the building remains the same, too. The expectations and the stated ideals, hopes, and desires of the Point Place males parallel those of the females. They have the same wistful desires of *nakana*, of love, reciprocity, and mutual care. Yet whereas the females link *nakana* to material goods, a shared living space, and emotional support, the young men of Point Place conceptualize it through another ideological framework. They link *nakana* to the domestic production of patriarchal control: to obedience, discipline, and respect. For them, the organizing principles of *nakana* relate not to models of sexual exchange, but rather to models of masculinity, which they enact as strategies of meaningful survival on the streets.

In her book *Masculinities*, historian Raewyn Connell (1995) puts forth a sociological framing of gender inequality that accounts for the plurality and hierarchies of male domination. She presents multiple categories of masculinity—hegemonic, subordinate, complicit, and marginalized—to highlight the relationships that men have not just with women but also with other groups of men. Notably, Connell (1995:81) does not designate these masculinities as "fixed character types" but as "configurations of practice generated in particular situations in a changing structure of relationships." Hence, she emphasizes male domination as a cultural relation, subject to historical variability, contestation, and change (Connell and Messerschmidt 2005). With these insights, I trace the presence of two dominant masculinities[1]—the *isoka* and *umnumzana*—that take shape within Point Place.[2] In isiZulu, an *isoka* is a man who is popular with the ladies.[3] He is a successful lover who courts attraction through his money, charm, and good looks (Vilakazi 1962:47). An *umnumzana* is the head of a household, a man committed to marriage and the protection of the home (Hunter 2005:391). Both masculinities uphold patriarchy, not through the use of direct force, although this may be applied, but rather through the coercive powers of consent. In short, the *isoka* and *umnumzana* reflect hegemonic masculinities.

To examine the institutional convergence of the *isoka* (a masculinity that values the status of acquiring multiple sexual partners) and *umnumzana* (a masculinity that values the patriarchal ordering and protection of the domestic unit), this chapter looks to the everyday practices and living arrangements of the Point Place youth. Inside Point Place, the males set up the terms of their social belonging, which they link to their roles as providers and thus as entitled residents of the building. This can be seen in the organization of domestic labor as well as in the transmission of rooming rights.[4] In both situations the males delegate and their female companions accommodate.[5] The Point Place males justify these arrangements of domestic privilege as an extension of *nakana*, of protective and affirmative love.

Accordingly, in tracing the convergence of the *isoka* and *umnumzana* masculinities, this chapter focuses primarily on the sexual attachments of the Point Place males. As with the previous chapter, though, I do not want to diminish the importance of a wider network of friends. These friendships, often conceived as sib relationships, are integral to the survival strategies of those who live in Point Place. They also are instrumental to the socialization processes that occur within the building. Sib relationships, unlike boyfriend-girlfriend relationships, highlight the social unity of the Point Place youth. As brothers and sisters, they articulate a powerful paradigm of solidarity, which they have forged through their shared experiences on the streets and in children's shelters. Yet, while cross-sex sib relationships are central to the social formations within Point Place, the bonds of brotherhood supersede this collective accord. For as brothers, the Point Place males uphold the patriarchy of the *umnumzana/isoka* complex, even if it means, paradoxically, that they must attend to their own domestic upkeep.

*   *   *

You see, my mom was staying there in Joburg where Ofentse stays. I had friends there. One day, on a summer day, there was a dance function. It was the first time that I saw her. She had her hair like this. I still remember. It has been seven years, but I still remember. She was wearing a long red dress and black and white sandals. But I didn't have money to go inside. I was sitting outside. After that, I asked a friend where Ofentse was staying and stuff like that. (Khaya, twenty-seven-year-old male)

I saw Joy going to church. I knew her from Point Place. I saw that I must go to church, too. (Thabo, twenty-six-year-old male)

Angel used to stay at Pizza [Hut]. Then she came and stayed here inside of Point Place. Now we used to see each other inside of Point Place. (Zakes, twenty-year-old male)

I met her on a Friday. I just came back from a wedding at home. I found her at the bar next door. (Wonderboy, twenty-year-old male)

We met at the BAT [performance] center. I have talent. I'm a person who has talent to sing and gumboot dance. I can do everything. (Manelesi, twenty-year-old male)

When addressing the procedures of proposing love to a girl—in isiZulu, to *shela*—the young men of Point Place focus on the circumstances leading up to their proposition. They note the spatial context, the location of their first encounter, as well as their deft positioning. The young women, meanwhile, emphasize the temporality of the love proposal. They refer to their acceptance (*qoma*) as a drawn-out development. The males rarely remark or reflect on this protracted deferral, yet their persistence in wooing a girl exhibits a regular pattern. Enough so that Kwanele, a shy young man of twenty-one, does not miss a beat when narrating the customary procedures of the love proposal (*shela*):

"If a boy likes a girl," I ask Kwanele, "what does he say to her?"

"You tell her that you love her," he promptly answers.

"How is she supposed to respond?"

"She has to answer by saying that she agrees or she doesn't agree."

"If she doesn't agree, what does a boy say then?"

"You beg her."

To beg for a girl's affection is a common occurrence among the Point Place males. It is a rite of courtship whereby a girl's initial reluctance is taken not as a permanent rejection but as a negotiable condition open to further pursuit. The ubiquity and unremitting persistence of the *shela* is not particular to Point Place; it has cultural antecedents throughout KwaZulu-Natal. Nor is the *shela* merely an expression of sexual passion, or even love. As anthropologists have long noted, the *shela* is an affirmation of a socially valued personhood, a process of acceptance in which boys learn to become men (Reader 1966:178; Vilakazi 1962:50).

To trace some of these developments, this chapter investigates the *shela* through broader social processes that demarcate ideals of masculine youth-hood in KwaZulu-Natal. It begins with isiZulu classificatory systems, which mark youth not only by gender and age but also by their emergent sexualities. The *English-Zulu, Zulu-English Dictionary* refers to some of these character-istics in its designation of an *insizwa*, which is a young man. Notably, "vigor" is one of the attributes of an *insizwa*.[6] The secondary meaning of *insizwa*—a hornless ox or bull—also is revealing for its constructions of youth-hood. The hornless ox or bull draws attention to the undeveloped or unmarried status of the *insizwa* (Doke et al. 1999:599). Anthropologist Eileen Krige (1936:373), writing about Zulu courtship and marital practices in the early twentieth century, explains the significance of this association.[7] In the past, an *insizwa* would don a special head ring, symbolic of the horns of a bull, which indicated his transition to manhood or an *umnumzana* status. The conferral of the head ring, however, was contingent on the *insizwa*'s participation in the *amabutho* or age-set regiments.

To briefly elaborate, the Zulu *amabutho* system as a type of military organi-zation rose to prominence in the early nineteenth century. Scholars attribute its key innovations to King Shaka Zulu (r. 1816–1828), whose expansionary conquests are well known in South Africa. One of those innovations was to consolidate the *amabutho* into three main regiments, with the youngest set never having served in war before (Reader 1966:4). The conscription of young males into the *amabutho* was only part of Shaka's military strategy. He also delayed their exit. And this, as some scholars note, was the true tyranny of his rule. For without the king's permission, a young man could not leave the regiment and thus could not marry—or don the head ring of an *umnumzana*—until he was much older (Krige 1936:119).[8] He remained an *insizwa*, "undeveloped" and unmarried, yet full of "vigor."

By the late nineteenth century, the imposition of British colonial rule in Zululand had severely curtailed the military exploits of the *amabutho*, and the units were disbanded in the early twentieth century (Krige 1936:107). The pervasive influences of Christianity, school learning, wage labor, and urbanization also served as major forces of societal change, undercutting youth's participation in the Zulu regiments. Yet, while the *amabutho* ceased to exist in a formal sense, male subjects continued to hold on to the associated mindset, shaping a shared political-territorial imaginary of Zulu nationhood predicated on a shared cultural imaginary of Zulu warriorhood (Waetjen 2004).[9]

The naturalization of a dominant youth masculinity in KwaZulu-Natal thus has ties to the *amabutho* system and its age-set hierarchies. I contend, however, that this naturalization is linked less directly to the military field of combat and more to the playing field of courtship. The love proposals of young men speak to the celebration of a conquest-oriented masculinity (Hunter 2010). Accordingly, in the remainder of this chapter, I delineate the historical and cultural trajectory of the Zulu love proposal. I examine the *shela* not as an individual utterance but as a shared discursive form through which a male personhood is asserted, recognized, and reciprocated, by and large, through the corresponding *qoma* of females.

The ambiguous rendering of the *qoma* as somewhere between passive acceptance and willful choice attests to the constantly reworked articulations of the *shela*. Hence, to be truly successful, a young man—or *insizwa*—needs to adjust his avowals of love to the receptivity of females. He must engage in both offensive and defensive tactics. Ethnographic accounts of anthropologists from the mid-twentieth century capture this dualism. Their descriptions, as I detail below, provide an analytical basis for understanding the maintenance of a conquest-oriented youth masculinity in KwaZulu-Natal.

As a caveat to the descriptions presented below, the anthropologists I cite portray Zulu courtship in highly idealized terms. Furthermore, they locate these rites within a general framework of transition. They depict courtship as a rite of passage, a pleasurable pastime that prepares youth for the eventual commitment of a mature betrothal. They note that through the acceptance of love, youth can become adultlike, if only temporarily. As Absolom Vilakazi

(1962:50) writes, "The girl who accepts a young man as a lover, even for a short time, boosts his ego and gives him status. The Zulu way of putting it is *umenzi umuntu*, i.e. she has made a human being of him by recognizing him as an adult personality and as a man." Likewise, D. H. Reader (1966:178) remarks, "By recognizing and accepting him, the girl has made a man, a person, out of her sweetheart." Reader's use of the word "sweetheart" adds a final consideration to the anthropological treatment of Zulu courtship. Anthropologists do not typically use this descriptor to refer to the boyfriend-girlfriend relationships of Christian, educated, or urbanized youth.[10] Rather, their designation of "sweetheart" describes love affairs conducted among so-called traditional, pagan, or heathen youth. This differentiation in nomenclature reveals as much about the sexual mores of mid-twentieth-century ethnographers as it does about their subject of study: Zulu youth.

*   *   *

A RURAL LOVE PROPOSAL[11]

Zala abantu ziya ebantwini!
Akukho'ntombi yagana inyamazane sikhona!
Noseyishayile akakayidli!
Noseyidlile usedle icala!

For people go to the people!
No girl will marry the wild animals while we are here!
Even the one who has beaten it has not yet eaten it!
Even the one who has eaten it has eaten guilt!

As noted repeatedly by anthropologists of the mid-twentieth century, sweetheart relationships, although playful and enjoyable, do maintain an element of coercion and aggression (Reader 1966:175; Vilakazi 1962:47). These pursuits of conquest begin before the age of puberty and often include the most seemingly subjugated accomplice: the herdboy. A herdboy, in Zulu pastoral society, tends to his family's livestock, usually cattle, goats, and sheep. From an outsider's perspective, herdboys sit low on the totem pole of age hierarchies. Subject to the dictates of everyone older than them, including women, herdboys have little voice in matters beyond their age group. This changes, however, with the competitive realm of love and courtship, for as Vilakazi (1962:48) writes, the herdboy finds himself in the privileged position of an *isilomo*, an unofficial advisor or confidant.

The herdboy's special status as an *isilomo* derives from his extensive movement across the rural landscape. He familiarizes himself not just with the environment and the livestock but also with everyone who passes his way. He knows the daily activities and routine habits of all but the most distant girls. He knows when they go to the river to fetch water and to the forest to collect firewood. He knows their acquaintances, and how many suitors are in pursuit of their affections. Thus he is a mine of information, an asset for any young man seriously contemplating a sweetheart relationship. The herdboy, like most free agents, is a clever boy. He does not take any particular suitor into his confidence. Rather, as Vilakazi (1962:48) writes, he plays the suitors off one another, only helping those who offer enticing rewards.

Supporting Vilakazi's work, Reader (1966:175) also addresses the negotiations of sweetheart relationships in the mid-twentieth century. He describes how young boys learn to become impressive suitors. From their older brothers and friends, they observe the rites of *kila*: how to entrap a girl in speech. They also learn to counter unloveliness (*isidina*) by applying, ingesting, and steaming with special medicines. Yet, even before these concerns with cleanliness, boys engage in the intricate procedures of proposing love, although not for a sweetheart of their own. As Vilakazi (1962:47) explains, older boys employ the younger ones as messengers. They act as go-betweens who "throw" words of admiration at an unsuspecting girl. If the girl seems receptive, the suitor will approach her directly, often sneaking up behind her to announce his love. Colloquially speaking, the girl is "hit by apprehension"—in isiZulu, *ishaywa uvalo* (Vilakazi 1962:48).

The vocabulary—"entrap" a girl in speech, "throw" words of admiration, and "hit by apprehension"—underscores the aggressive constructions of the Zulu love proposal (*shela*). The following description, recounted by Krige (1936:104), illustrates this ritualized assertion of masculine courtship and is worth including at length:

> After her first menstruation, the young men begin to take notice of a girl, but she may not answer them when they speak to her, until she has been given permission to do so by the older girls who already have sweethearts (the *amaqhikiza*). A young man may talk to a girl as much as he likes at this stage, and he may even catch the girl and twist her arms to try to get her to speak, but she will not do so. She will not even say, "Leave me alone," but will simply keep quiet. To show how strictly this rule is kept, and how strong is the control of the elder girls, an informant gives the following instance: "When I was a boy, still herding cattle, I once saw a young man emptying to the ground a whole pot of water which a girl was carrying, in order to keep her at the river a little longer so that he could speak to her to his satisfaction. Even after such insulting behaviour on the part of the boy, the girl still remained quiet, for though she was old enough to have a sweetheart, she had not yet been given permission

to speak to her wooers. Strangely enough, this same girl afterwards accepted the man and to-day is his wife."

As revealed by the above narrative, girls also partake in the social production of an assertive youthful masculinity. Older girls exert a substantial amount of control over younger girls, closely monitoring their courtships and denying them the opportunity to address their suitors (Delius and Glaser 2002:33). In doing so, they set forth expectations of female acquiescence. The compliant dynamics of Zulu courtship change considerably, though, once the senior girls grant the younger girls permission to speak. The younger girls rebuff the amorous calls of their suitors with cleverly directed witticisms known as *izifenqo* (Vilakazi 1962:46). A suitor stands little chance of retaining his masculine dignity against this onslaught of ridicule and repartee. To deflect the barbs of the *izifenqo*, he hatches a staged appearance. He ponders the location and provenance of his love proposal (*shela*) with great care. He hopes that by sneaking up on a girl and entrapping her in speech, he will cause her to forget her routine word devices, at least temporarily (Vilakazi 1962:48). Only then might he secure a sweetheart relationship of his own.

To indicate her acceptance (*qoma*) of a sweetheart relationship, the girl will remove a string of red beads from her body. She presents them to the suitor, informing him that he must speak to the senior girls to determine the amount of the lover's fee—in isiZulu, *imali yokuqoma* (Vilakazi 1962:48). The lover's fee conveys the suitor's seriousness. Thereafter he may raise a flag in his kraal, publicly proclaiming his love intentions (Reader 1966:176). The girl, in response, may compose a Zulu love letter written in beads to show her affection for the suitor (Vilakazi 1962:49–50). This outward display of courtship differentiates sweetheart relationships of the mid-twentieth century from the more secretive note-passing rituals of school-attending Christian youth (Vilakazi 1962:52).

Upon the conferral of the lover's fee, the *qoma* ceremony commences. The senior age-mates of the sweethearts organize and regulate the proceedings, which involve serious decorum, despite the large amounts of sorghum beer consumed by the boys (Reader 1966:176–177). The *qoma* ceremony marks the sweethearts not just as committed participants in love but also as committed participants in Zulu society. Furthermore, it establishes a degree of social control over their sexual encounters, as everyone in the community recognizes the two as lovers (Vilakazi 1962:51). The consummation of this affair occurs through the act of *soma*[12] (sex between the thighs), which, in addition to its regulation of sexual activity, also means to joke or sport around (Doke et al. 1999:764; Reader 1966:175). The act of external intercourse thus links up to the everyday sparring wordplay of sweetheart relationships (Reader 1966:175).

*   *   *

A TOWNSHIP LOVE PROPOSAL[13]

Dudlu ntombi!
Nongenankomo uyayidla inyama!
Gegelagege ntombi!
Nongenabhasikidi uyangena emakethe!
Ayinamabele inyoka yini?
Oseyishayile akakayosi!
Oseyosile akakayidli!
Oseyidlile usedle icala!

[A call of admiration to a girl]
Even the one without a cow eats meat!
[A call of admiration to a girl]
Even the one without a basket enters the market!
If it doesn't have breasts, is it a snake?
The one who has beaten it has not yet *braaied* [barbecued] it!
The one who has *braaied* it has not yet eaten it!
The one who has eaten it has eaten guilt!

The twentieth-century anthropological treatment of sweetheart relation-ships—with its emphasis on tactical pursuit, back-and-forth banter, and unfulfilled fertility—offers a provisional view of Zulu youth-hood, one that is distinct from the long-term engagements of adulthood. From this per-spective, sweetheart relationships are unsustainable, for they are not an end product but a facilitator of a more desirable, socially productive outcome: the so-called mature betrothal. The difference between a mature betrothal and a sweetheart relationship, from an anthropological standpoint, relates to the issue of lineage. A mature betrothal involves the formal recognition and participation of descent groups (Reader 1966:175; Vilakazi 1962:50).[14] More specifically, it entails the patriarchal orchestration of bridewealth exchange (*ilobolo*), an ongoing process of payment whereby the groom's family com-pensates the bride's family for the loss of her productive and reproductive labor. In contrast to *ilobolo*, the lover's fee (*imali yokuqoma*) speaks to the relative autonomy of sweetheart relationships. The earnings of young men do not contribute to the homestead but instead support the sweetheart, her associates, and his closest companions (Vilakazi 1962:49). The *ilobolo*, mean-while, reflects the consolidated interests of an established gerontocracy, who in due course subordinate the sexual exploits of youth to the productive and reproductive integrity of the homestead economy.

*   *   *

A COLLEGE CAMPUS LOVE PROPOSAL[15]

Dudlu!
Angithuki wena kodwa ngithuka uthando!
Dudlu!
Engenamazinyo uyayidla inyama!
Dudlu!
Engenabhasikidi uyangena emakethe!

[A call of admiration to a girl]
I'm not swearing at you, but I'm swearing love!
[A call of admiration to a girl]
Without teeth he can eat meat!
[A call of admiration to a girl]
Without a basket he can enter the market!

Sweetheart relationships, while integral to the affirmations and contestations of a conquest-oriented masculinity, provide only a partial view of youth courtship in KwaZulu-Natal, for Christianity—in particular, the "civilizing" directives of missionaries—substantially shaped these ideals, too. In early twentieth-century Zululand, Christian missionaries equated the successive partnering of sweetheart relationships with sexual promiscuity. They decried the "pagan" practice of *soma* as evidence of sexual laxity (Vilakazi 1962:54). To counter this perceived immorality, missionaries espoused doctrines of salvation through self-restraint, which included prescriptions of sexual abstinence and ordinances against polygyny. For young Christian lovers, the promise of a mature betrothal helped mitigate the sin that they associated with their sexual encounters. Until then, their affairs remained clandestine, hidden from their parents, schoolteachers, and even peers (Vilakazi 1962:54). As a result, by the mid-twentieth century, the incidence of premarital pregnancy increased dramatically among school-attending girls. The diminished candidness about matters of sexual foreplay, along with the disparagement of *soma* as a dirty and shameful practice, ensured that Christian youth knew very little about the technicalities of sexual intercourse and thus the technicalities of contraception (Reader 1966:214).

Furthermore, once Christian girls became pregnant, they had little recourse to compensation in the form of either marriage or alimony, for the secretive nature of their affairs provided their boyfriends with ample opportunity to deny paternity. This differed from a sweetheart relationship, in which the older relatives and age-mates of the pregnant girl, en masse, would accost the offending *isoka*, forcing him to either pay for "damages" (*ihlawulo*) or commit to a mature betrothal (Gluckman 1950:181; Krige 1936:158). Christian male lovers, on the other hand, quite easily and without much sanction avoided such accountability by running away to larger towns and cities, leaving their girlfriends to face the social opprobrium of their families, schools, and congregation (Vilakazi 1962:57). Christianity, in effect, cultivated a new type of masculine personhood that advanced the love interests of young men through the retreat of sexual responsibility.

On par with Christian doctrines of progress through self-discipline and achievement, the rapid industrialization of the South African economy in the early twentieth century ensured that young men had plenty of opportunity to secure a livelihood outside the family homestead (Delius and Glaser 2002:40). Their wage earnings also significantly restructured the age-based hierarchies of the homestead economy. The mining sector, in particular, illustrates how young men used their labor power to subvert the household authority of the *umnumzana* (Moodie 1994). Wage earnings made it possible for young men to renounce the homestead, never to be heard from again.[16] Yet even within the homestead, the incomes of migrant workers significantly restructured generational relations of authority. They could afford *ilobolo* at a younger age, thereby weakening the regulatory control of their fathers and older patrikin. Wage earnings also made it possible for young men to select their own brides, a practice supported by Christian ideologies of romantic love and companionate marriage (Hunter 2002:107, 2010:44).

Similarly, in Durban, secondary industries such as the dockyards and textile factories played a significant role in the purchasing power of Zulu youth, particularly in the post–World War II era (Maylam 1996:15–16). To avoid the prohibitive costs of commuting long distances, young men established residences with women who were employed as domestic servants. These women lived on their employers' properties, a loophole in apartheid policies that denied Africans the right to reside permanently in town. Although young men saved money on room and board, their earnings—like those of the mine workers—often were directed toward new forms of expenditure, for their domestic living arrangements frequently led to illegitimate offspring. Increasingly the designation of "sweetheart relations," as Vilakazi (1962:35) notes, referred to the possibility of Zulu youth maintaining several unknown dependents in town. Thus, with the expansive forces of urbanization, the sweetheart relationships of Durban's youth—like the courtships of Christian youth—effectively usurped the rights of the *umnumzana* to broker and sanction marriages for the benefit of the patrilineage.

To summarize, by the later part of the twentieth century, the market economy—as opposed to the homestead economy—regulated sexual relationships. Still, up until the mid-1970s, young men continued to view marriage as a viable albeit expensive option (Hunter 2002:107). This changed in the 1980s with the stagnation of the South African economy. In Durban, those working in the manufacturing sector faced massive retrenchment, as did mine workers in other parts of South Africa. Changing gender norms and the lifting of influx-control laws in 1986 also made it easier for women to secure employment in urban centers, thus putting them in direct competition with men. Unable to find stable jobs, young men no longer could afford *ilobolo* payments. They could, however, afford a girlfriend, and not just one but many. Increasingly, young men celebrated their manhood not through marriage, as an *umnumzana*, but through the accrual of multiple sexual partners, as an *isoka*, which they linked to male prerogatives of polygyny (Hunter 2002:107). Only with the onset of HIV/AIDS have young men begun to question the feasibility of an *isoka* lifestyle and, along with it, the possibility of becoming an *umnumzana* as they age.

*   *   *

The historical and cultural legacies of these two masculinities—the *isoka* and *umnumzana*—are readily apparent inside Point Place. As Connell (1995:77) argues, however, "This is not to say that the most visible bearers of hegemonic masculinity are always the most powerful people." In other words, the *isoka* and *umnumzana* masculinities are ideal types for the Point Place youth to emulate. The ethnographic examples I provide below reveal the fragility of these enactments. The Point Place males struggle to secure the material backing that would legitimize their standing as providers and protectors, and so their female companions challenge their authority. In response, the males assert their dominance with physical force while also recognizing that the true attraction of their companionship resides with their ability to maintain the basic premise of *nakana*, of looking after each other.

The *Isoka*

Certainly good looks, charm, and wit help the *isoka* in attracting many girlfriends; so does a clever love proposal. Yet to be truly successful, the *isoka* needs to display his money and status items. Stylish clothing, cell phones, alcoholic beverages, and fast food all underscore the purchasing power of a highly desirable masculine personhood. Swifty, a twenty-four-year-old resident of Point Place, exemplifies the *isoka* persona. As he narrates:

> I was wearing my tracksuit and my vest. I was wearing my Nike *takkies* [shoes], the black ones, and a cap. An i52 [cell phone] was hanging here on my tracksuit. I had my key, my room keys. When I came here, I went past that bar . . . When I crossed here by the robots [traffic lights], it was like a movie. People at the Point were stopping and holding their waists.

Swifty is an exceptional case. Most of the Point Place youth do not have the means to partake in the hyper-materiality of an *isoka* lifestyle. They participate to the extent that they can, but when they do so, it is with a great deal of ingenuity and collective aplomb. Through a clothing rotation they sport Levi's jeans, Converse shoes, and Kangol caps. Their cell phones, while secondhand, sport a new ringtone and case every week. Likewise, even carrying a carton of KFC imparts a particular message of conspicuous consumption, as does the request to have pictures taken with Jack Daniels in hand.

The youth of Point Place have two options for maintaining themselves with style. Both fall under the indeterminate rubric of *phanda*, which, as I describe in chapter three, means to beg, to scratch around, to try to get, or to steal. The first option entails participation in the informal economy, where the males find casual work as car guards, street sweepers, and sidewalk vendors. Their earnings are reliable, though meager. The second option, "the fast life," enables the Point Place youth to secure money through irregular and illicit means. Themba, a longtime resident of Point Place, explains how he partakes in the pleasures of these commodity acquisitions:

"Yeah, we were living the fast life. You know fast life?" Themba asks me.

"What's a fast life?" I reply, wanting him to elaborate.

"You see, if I want a drink, I need money. I don't work. I need a drink. I don't have money. You see what I must do?"

Mindful of my recorder, he does not want to say that he steals. To keep the conversation going, I ask Themba what he used to buy when he had money. He laughingly replies, "Oh, maybe let's say it's R2000, I'd buy clothes, I'd buy *takkies*, then I'd go drink beer . . . Black Label, drink that, drink that, drink that. That's what happened most of the time . . . You see, I was a popular guy in the Point. Everybody knew me."

"The girls and the boys?" I prod.

"Girls and boys, everyone, you see, knew me. So now, hey, you're popular, everybody knows you, they say you drink here, you drink there, you do this, and you do that. But you have to change. So many of my friends have been arrested, ten years, fifteen years, twenty years, twenty-five years . . ."

Themba's description of the fast life—easy money, quick spending, excessive drinking, and extreme popularity—conveys the immediacy and immoderation of a consumptive persona. His account of the fast life corresponds with the testimony of Shorty, another longtime resident of Point Place and Thuthukani:

"At the end of '98, I decided no, hey, I can't be parking cars anymore. I was getting less money and things like that. So these boys used to come to the Point, you know. They'd get these cell phones or something and go back to Thuthukani. I started joining those guys. Then we used to come back, rob, and go back, you know, get money, rob, go back, and drink.

"How much could you get for a cell phone?" I ask.

"That time, it used to depend because cell phones were new, you know. So if you get maybe a 5110 [model], you have maybe R500 for the moment. For the moment you have R500. It was like, you know, easy come, easy go. You're just going to spend it because it came easy."

Although it is not stated outright, the fast life, with its excessive and immediate spending, includes easy accessibility to girls as well. In conversations with me, the Point Place males rarely flaunt their sexual encounters. The subdued telling of their love affairs differs substantially from the bravado they express in describing their economic exploits. In one interview, though, among five females, Swifty relates several daring escapades with reference to his sexual conquests:

> There was a party at Durban [train] station. Nobody could dance. I was the only one who could dance. I was number one. Then this boy came and said, "Can I talk to you?" I said, "You, a lad? You want to talk to me?" People were scared of me. What was wrong with this boy? I said to him, "Wait." I had girls all around me. They were asking me to give them sweets, this side and that side . . . I gave these things to these girls. I had many packets of sweets—sweets and chocolates. Then I went and kneeled down. I said, "What's wrong?" This lad was not scared. He said, "Justice and the others [a rival gang] want you." I wanted to get out. I went out this side. They were on the other side. I ran. I ran. Before I ran, I jumped. No, they didn't catch me. I went inside the park. No one could catch me . . . They were going to shoot me that day with my gun. I don't know what happened. No one knows what happened. When they saw me the following day, they didn't believe it. No one believed it. I was wearing overalls and a yellow T-shirt and *takkies* I was hurt on my heel. I stamped on my *takkies*, one side, like this. I was wearing white socks. I was so drunk. I was with this child. I was with this girl. It was the first time that I saw her, and it was the last time that I saw her.

At this juncture, Bongi, one of the girls listening to the story, clarifies, "You had sex." Then, in the same almost uninterrupted narration, Swifty continues to speak about the days following his unlikely escape from Justice:

Again, when I walked down the streets with Princess, no one believed it. I was holding a T10 [cell phone] in my hand. I opened it. And a 5150 [cell phone] was hanging here. Princess was holding a 3310 [cell phone]. She put it in her breasts. She had a 38 [revolver] special. She put inside her panties. Princess, she was Miss What-What that day.

"I know Princess," Bongi interrupts. "She was beautiful."

"Princess," Swifty continues, with noticeable pride, "was beautiful, and all the girls I dated at that time."

Swifty's candid narrative highlights the connections between street style, street status, and street consumption. It also draws attention to his popularity with females. On the dance floor and off, Swifty conveys the desirability of the *isoka* masculinity. His conquests come across not only during the hour-long telling of his escapades, but also in the banter that follows afterward.

With much amusement, the girls tease Swifty about his secret love affair with Simosihle, another girl living inside Point Place. The girls do not fault Swifty for cheating on his girlfriend, Pretty. They fault him for choosing Simosihle, as she has a boyfriend, Jerry. Amidst the ensuing clamor, the recorder picks up these singsong chants:

"We're going to tell Jerry! Jerry despises! We will hit you, the Lord protect!" And then in unison, "What do you want from her [Simosihle]?"

To which Swifty appeals, "But you're not happy to be with me? I have a good heart."

The girls respond, not by denying Swifty's inherent goodness, but by referring to Simosihle as "a bitch with scabies." Swifty remains quiet, and one of the girls, perhaps realizing they spoke too freely, announces in a tone of hilarity and obvious untruth: "Swifty's wife is Ma Hag!"—a reference to an old woman who sells Ecstasy tablets around the corner from Point Place. Swifty smiles; he concedes to her clever fabrication. A few weeks later, I learn that Swifty's primary girlfriend, Pretty, has gone back home. She discovered him sleeping with another girl—not Simosihle, but the one who accused him of being married to Ma Hag.

Certainly in comparison to the other youth, Swifty recounts his love affairs in a highly boastful manner. This is not to say, though, that his exploits are an anomaly within Point Place. The other boys, too, frequently and without much reflection remark on the presence of additional lovers. When questioned, "Do you have one girlfriend or many girlfriends?" the response may follow: "Only two" (Derrick, twenty-two-year-old male). While perhaps more reserved or circumspect about their sexual relationships than Swifty, the other Point Place males generally concede that they engage in numerous love affairs, provided they have the means to attract the girls. As one recently embittered suitor remarks, "A girl loves you when you have money. Or I'll say when you *phanda* a lot. A girl loves you for that thing, that you have your money. Not that she loves you. She loves the money" (Thabo, twenty-year-old male). Or as another rejected lover states more concisely, "You know in town, only money talks" (Bonginkosi, twenty-three-year-old male).

To summarize, the young men of Point Place harbor no illusions about the materiality of love. They know that money attracts girls, and they act accordingly, often through illicit undertakings. Yet, while they attach great symbolic capital to the fast life and hyper-consumption of an *isoka* persona, these same young men disparage females who, like them, pursue money for pleasure. These girls may be tolerated for casual affairs, but they rarely gain the standing of a primary girlfriend. They are considered too acquisitive and promiscuous. Seventeen-year-old Dingani, who earns money by begging, stealing, acting as a low-level drug runner, and roasting corn on the cob for street vendors, touches on this distinction when I ask him whether he has girlfriends inside Point Place:

"Yes," Dingani replies, "those who want my money only."

"Do you give them money?" I ask.

"Yeah, but not now. Let me tell you, Laura makes me a fool, and today, too, she made me a fool."

"What happened?" Ofentse inquires.

"She says that she loves me," Dingani responds. "She made me buy her a [meat] pie. Then I ate it."

"Are you seeing Laura now?" I ask Dingani.

"We had an argument, and I told her that there are girls who love me. Not her. And I told her to shut up, and then I left. The thing that made me not love her was because she was making me a fool."

Among the Point Place youth, to be made a fool implies infidelity of a very public kind. Dingani responds to this humiliation by asserting the supremacy of his material worth. He buys a meat pie and eats it himself. He also tells Laura that many other girls love him. Both acts affirm the dominance of the *isoka* masculinity, a type of personhood that acquires status through the manipulation of consumptive desire.

*   *   *

"It's the truth." Skora, a nineteen-year-old male living inside Point Place, is emphatic. "I'm telling you, I see things. The girls I stay with, I know them. They're sleeping with many boys, and they date many boys."

I am not easily convinced by this one-way indictment, and so I ask Skora, "But what about the boys in Point Place?"

"And the boys, too," Skora agrees. "But it's the boys' thing."

"What do you call a boy who sleeps around?" I ask.

"It's the same as the girls," Skora replies. "He's an *isifebe* [bitch]. In the olden days, too, our fathers, our great-grandfathers, they had *isithembu* [polygamy]."

"Did you call them *amasoka* [pl. of *isoka*]?" I inquire.

"Yeah!"

"Is it good to be an *isoka*?"

"No," Skora responds. "It's not right when a person is poor, because you're going to make the girl suffer."

In the above conversation, Skora draws attention to the sexual promiscuity of the Point Place females. He then concedes that the males, too, engage in numerous love affairs. He refers to the boys, like the girls, as bitches but justifies their behavior as being a male "thing," a prerogative passed down from their fathers and grandfathers, linked to the tradition of polygyny. Along these lines, Skora denounces the sexual exploits of the *isoka* as a problem not of gender inequality but of economic affordability. His explanation of why it is better not to have more than one girlfriend—or a girlfriend at all—is a common one among the Point Place males. They recognize that attracting a girlfriend for a day differs substantially from maintaining a girlfriend. Their insufficient earnings impede their ability to secure a long-lasting relationship. As Musikayisa, a twenty-one-year-old male, narrates, "I don't need a girlfriend because I'm barely surviving. Now if I get a girlfriend, what can I do with her? She'll want things. Now my money is too small to support her and me. Yeah, that's why."

To support a girlfriend requires more than a few drinks or a few rand. It requires ongoing sustenance and material provisions that the Point Place boys often refer to through the idiom of food—particularly staple food. Such maintenance can be tiring. Twenty-seven-year-old Khaya, for instance, feels obliged to "think" for his girlfriend. No matter how meager his provisions, he must share them equally. "You have to think for them [girlfriends]. Every time you get something small, you have to take it to her. Sometimes if it's two slices [of bread], you have to take it up there to her room." Although Khaya finds girlfriends wearisome, others, like eighteen-year-old Sandlana, take pleasure in the sustenance of these kinds of relationships: "I like to give that girl money, you see. If I give her money, she wants to eat that money with me, to share with me. And she, too, if she gives me money, I want to eat with her." The nourishment derived from these types of relationships reflects a broader conceptualization of *nakana*: of taking care of one another.

Like the Point Place females, the males also link *nakana* to acts of domesticity and shared reciprocity. This intimacy distinguishes the intentions of a "serious" or "good" boyfriend from the casual affairs of an *isoka*. Thus, while a Point Place male may have two girlfriends, his ability to support them and their ability to support him differentiates a relationship of *nakana* from one of pure acquisition. In the following interview, Derrick explains the love that he feels for his two girlfriends:

"How do you show your love?" I begin.

"You show it in many ways," Derrick responds. "I just had money. I bought her flip-flops. Now, that's when you show you love her. When I have money, I'm able to think that my girlfriend is hungry."

"How does she show her love for you?" I ask.

"She shows me. Maybe she takes my clothes and washes them."

I know Derrick has two girlfriends, and so I inquire, "Do you love both girlfriends the same, or do you love one more than the other?"

"I can say I love them the same because they're able to wash [clothes] for me," he replies.

"Do they ever get jealous?" I question.

"I can say that it might be so." He pauses for a moment and then continues, "But they don't know each other."

Through the conferral of food and flip-flops, Derrick shows that he is able to "think" for his girlfriends. In turn, they wash his clothes, an act of reciprocity that he links to love. These demonstrations of love rest on a pretense of fidelity. It is quite likely that if Derrick's girlfriends knew about each other, the domestic support would cease immediately. Such is the case with Ofentse, who learns about Khaya's outside affairs. They continue to reside together because they have a son who depends on their shared earnings. Everything else remains open to negotiation, often bitterly and violently so, as Ofentse narrates:

> On Sunday, when I woke up, Khaya asked me why I didn't cook the rice. I said, "No, you usually cook it yourself, why do you expect me to cook it for you now?" And he said that I don't want to cook. I don't want to do his washing. I don't want to do anything. I said to him, "But we agreed that I'm not going to do your washing, and I'm not going to cook. I'm only going to cook if I want to. If I don't want to, then I don't want to. Don't force me." I asked him if he agreed to those things just because he wanted me and Musa to stay with him. Then he started hitting me, and I hit him back.

For a girlfriend not to wash clothes or not to cook signals more than an act of neglect. It indicates a renunciation of *nakana*. The Point Place females usually attribute this renunciation to the competing presence of another girlfriend. The males, meanwhile, associate the loss of *nakana* with deliberate disrespect. Twenty-seven-year-old Yogi explains, "I was giving her everything, but now I'm not working. Things are bad, but I'm still trying to get [*phanda*] for that girl . . . Go inside there. Check my shirt. She never washed it. I'm a man here. Now she's trying to use me like a woman." A gendered division of labor exists inside Point Place, with males expected to earn money while females are expected to perform domestic chores. Yogi, however, cannot find work. His girlfriend, by refusing to wash his shirt, adds insult to an already imperiled masculinity. She treats him "like a woman," subverting normative gender roles and challenging his authority as a man with a room.

The *Umnumzana*

Whereas the *isoka* entices girls with promises of consumptive pleasure, the *umnumzana* entices girls with promises of *nakana*. He offers provision, protection, and—while marriage is unaffordable—the possibility of long-term stability. Inside Point Place, this means that an aspiring *umnumzana* commands respect through the organization of a room, which includes the companionship of a girlfriend. Provision and protection ideally equate to unconditional obedience, to the expectation of *"Yebo, baba"* [Yes, father]. When this is not forthcoming, the Point Place males use tactics of intimidation to enforce their girlfriends' compliance. Twenty-year-old George narrates these expectations:

> They were staying together inside Point Place. Everything he earned, he gave to his girlfriend. When he received R2 on the streets, he didn't say, "I'm going to buy a quarter [loaf of bread] and eat it myself." No, he'd get another R2 because he knew that he had a girlfriend staying inside his room. But that girlfriend was doing another boy. So he came and hit his girlfriend.

George highlights the generosity of a boyfriend who supplies his girlfriend with food and a room. For the girlfriend to cheat on her boyfriend constitutes an affront to their relationship as well as to the carefully constructed identity of an *umnumzana* personhood. To reaffirm his slighted masculinity, the boyfriend resorts to physical violence. These disciplinarian tactics are not limited to instances of infidelity. Among the Point Place youth, the frequently invoked phrase *"Uyajwayela"* (You're rude/undermining me) serves as a shorthand explanation for why girlfriends deserve beatings. The males justify these abuses as a necessary extension of *nakana*, an act of consideration that guides their girlfriends onto the "proper" and "right" path.

For example, in the following group interview, two young men, Thabo and Howie, attempt to understand why Ofentse no longer resides with her boyfriend, Khaya. They want her to forgive Khaya's misdemeanors, which they link to bad luck and occult forces. In response, Ofentse asks Thabo and Howie why they hit their girlfriends. Do they attribute their abusive actions to bad luck, too?

"Ofentse," Thabo commences, "during the days that you argued with Musa's father, what do you think was the problem? Was it bad luck?

Ofentse turns to me and explains, "They say I have bad luck."

Thabo continues, "Someone must have their back on you" (an implication of witchcraft by a jealous third party).

"Khaya doesn't worry me anymore," Ofentse replies.

"When did you last fight?" Thabo presses on.

"Last year," Ofentse responds.

"How do you feel when you don't stay together nicely?" Thabo is determined to solve the mystery of Ofentse's obstinacy. "What would make you satisfied in your heart?"

Annoyed by Thabo's persistence, Ofentse counters, "The time that you hit Joy, was it bad luck?"

"Joy's situation," Thabo explains, "made me hit her. She was drunk. That's when someone is asking for it."

Defending Thabo's point, Howie offers, "I only hit my girlfriend when she does something wrong."

Thabo and Howie beat their girlfriends when they act inappropriately. But rather than accuse Ofentse of bad behavior, they declare that she has bad luck. Later in the interview, the two young men leap up from their chairs when they learn that Ofentse has no intention of marrying Khaya.

"Ofentse, you want to raise your child alone?" Thabo is incredulous. "What if Musa sees you with another person?"

Howie adds, "What if he doesn't like that father?"

Not entirely joking, Thabo continues, "What if the father takes Musa and throws him under a bridge? What will you say?"

Thabo and Howie find it inconceivable that Ofentse would deprive Khaya of his right to fatherhood, which for the Point Place males also reflects the respected status of an *umnumzana* masculinity—someone who provides for his dependents. To dissuade Ofentse, Thabo and Howie bring up the possibility of child endangerment perpetuated at the hands of another jealous boyfriend. Such arguments, presented as a concern for Ofentse's and Musa's wellbeing, expose the daily coercion of upholding a dominant *umnumzana* masculinity.

Violence, both real and anticipated, enables the Point Place males to control their female companions. Yet in the end, their abusive acts reveal more about the insecurities of a threatened masculinity than about the wayward tendencies of girlfriends. Such beatings often produce the very outcome the Point Place males strive to avoid. As Shorty explains, "Sometimes you feel afraid, like maybe you'll end up losing her. That's why you hit her, just putting that fear, she may not think to leave you . . . But then if you hit her, you're actually taking her away from you." Shorty's insight that hitting a girlfriend ultimately will hurt the relationship reveals the real power of the *umnumzana*, which is conveyed not through the direct application of force, but rather, as with the *isoka*, through the use of manipulated desire. The transmission of rooming rights inside Point Place reflects this hegemonic production of masculine privilege. It is a symbolic entitlement unrecognized as such and therefore all the more powerful, as it naturalizes and consolidates the authority of the *umnumzana* into a dominion of material control.

The individual room, enclosed by four walls and protected by a door and lock, represents the greatest asset of an aspiring *umnumzana*. Securing the domestic productivity of a girlfriend requires a secure room. The regular dispensation of material items, like food and clothing, is important, too. Yet these items are portable and subject to removal. The room, however, remains the undisputed domain of the boyfriend. When a relationship fails, the girlfriend moves out with all her belongings, and the boyfriend stays. The naming of bedrooms reflects this masculine appropriation of living space.

Over the duration of my fieldwork, only one bedroom, "*indlu kaMary*" (the room of Mary), receives consistent recognition through the name of a female occupant. Mary, an eighteen-year-old female and longtime resident of Point Place, holds on to her bedroom despite the presence of male occupants. The respect accorded to her, by her own admission, derives from her ability to identify as a tomboy:

> Yeah, I talk to boys, but you know the type of person that I am. I live like the boys. Sometimes my mind, I use it like the boys. The boys are used to the way that I am. They know that when you *shela* [proposition] me, I'll tell you that I won't be able to *qoma* [accept]. I won't be able to date a boy. The others say that I'm a tomboy. It's okay because I get along with the boys, but I don't date them.

Mary constitutes an exceptional case. Only in instances of single-sex occupancy will a room be demarcated as belonging to a girl. The Point Place youth also tend to refer to these rooms through a general female collectivity, for example, "*oCeliwe*" (Celiwe and her friends). This differs from the individual entitlement accorded to the bedrooms of the Point Place males, which Swifty explains:

> That room, Jacob and Amanda had an argument. Amanda left . . . They said I must go and stay in that room. Amanda told Pretty [my girlfriend] that when she comes, she must go and sleep there. Pretty used to come. It ended up being my room, like that. Because I saw that I must close the door, I bought that thing—a door lock. I put it there. I fixed the door nicely. I did it because I left my things inside. I closed it nicely. She came then, Pretty. She cleaned, cleaned, cleaned. I don't have time to clean.

Swifty secures his bedroom upon the breakup of another couple. The presence of a door lock and a residing girlfriend who cleans solidifies his status as someone who has assets to protect. Not a mutually exclusive endeavor, then, it is possible to act as both an *umnumzana* and an *isoka*, although the latter tends to undo the former, as seen by Pretty's decision to return home when she learned about Swifty's other affairs.

*　*　*

Like the Point Place females, the males are aware of the dangers of HIV/ AIDS. They know the consequences of acquiring multiple sexual partners, not using condoms, and aspiring to an *isoka* lifestyle. Skora explains these dangers to me, explicitly linking sex to death:

> Me, there's only one girl that I'm dating. There's the possibility that maybe we'll break up because of her bad behavior. I'm not supposed to date a person who drinks. Also, I don't want to abuse many other girls. You see, maybe me being a bitch [*isifebe*], maybe me being an *isoka*, it will end up getting me into trouble. I'll kill many girls. In the end I'll be alone.

Generally the younger males, ages fifteen to twenty, are the ones who participate in the "fast life." This changes, though, as they mature through various institutions. The threat of an extended prison sentence dampens their enthusiasm for illegal undertakings.[17] So does the possibility of imminent death. By the time they reach the age of twenty, all of the Point Place youth have seen and experienced, either themselves or through others, the debilitating effects of HIV/AIDS.

The protracted suffering of HIV/AIDS differs substantially from the accidents caused by speeding cars, the deaths resulting from jealous rivalries, or the risks involved in illegal activities. All those deaths occur quickly and usually without warning. Furthermore, such deaths tend to highlight the valued attributes of living life on the edge, of going out with style. HIV/AIDS, on the other hand, is excruciating to watch, especially in its advanced stages. The bodily depredations of AIDS make it impossible for the Point Place males to maintain even the pretense of an *isoka* identity, of a coveted desirability. Thus Themba, once a proponent of the fast life, finds himself in the position of forsaking all these previous pleasures: "So, if I got something, maybe R3, I don't go out for Black Label [beer] now. I go to Spar [the grocery store] and buy rice, soup, and things like that. I put it all in the house [room] where I stay so I can order tomorrow. I have food. I can't go out and search [*phanda*] for money, you see." Although nobody says it outright, Themba displays the ravages of AIDS—the emaciation, the sores, the bright pink receded gums, the haunted look. Rather than succumb to the disheartening associations of AIDS and admit defeat, Themba relinquishes the *isoka* identity to draw on another valued masculinity, the *umnumzana*: a figure of respect, discipline, and stability, a person who organizes his day through staple food and foresight rather than through beer and excessive self-indulgence.

Certainly, as they age, the Point Place males ponder the perils of the fast life with greater frequency. As Shorty muses, "You know as you get older, you start realizing you need to change and check things like that." Still, while they are willing to modify their desires, they refuse to accept personal accountability in the transmission of HIV/AIDS. For example, when describing the AIDS-related death of a friend, Shorty remarks: "In the hospital, he told me how he became sick, through this other girl." When asked whether the girl continues to reside at Point Place, Shorty comments, "No, because she was hurt by people saying, 'Eh, you killed my brother,' and things like that. You know, it affected her, and she didn't want to come back with a disgrace like that." Such stigmatization contributes not only to a pervasive silence about HIV/AIDS, especially around those who are sick, but also to an extreme reluctance to be tested for HIV. In the following interview, two young men, George and Delani, reflect on why it is better not to know their HIV status. I begin the conversation by asking them if they are scared of HIV/AIDS.

"Ay," Delani responds. "If I had it, hey, I don't know what I'd do."

"Perhaps you'd go to Addington Hospital," I respond, "and get treatment? But first they'd test you."

"No." Delani is adamant. "I don't want a test, even a test I don't want."

George confirms his friend's refusal. "It's better not to be tested because then you'll know that you've got HIV/AIDS."

"You're going to be stressed, more stressed, you see," Delani explains.

"Stress," George adds, "more stress."

"You'll be thinking too much," Delani continues.

"Sometimes at the end of the day," George elaborates, "you might find yourself trying to kill yourself because you know that you have HIV."

"But if you knew, though," I ask, "wouldn't you change your life? Wouldn't you start living better? Maybe you'd stop smoking, start eating better . . ."

George is not optimistic. "To eat better, to stop smoking, it's a waste of time."

"You know that you're going to die," Delani confirms.

I persist, "But you could still live longer."

"Ay." Delani is unconvinced. "It's better not to know if you got this."

"But what if you have a girlfriend?" I ask. "If you don't know, then maybe you'll infect your girlfriend?"

"Yeah," Delani agrees, "but you must do safe thing."

"Do you use condoms, then?" I inquire.

"Yeah," Delani responds.

"Sometimes or all the time?" I ask.

"Sometimes," Delani elaborates. "If I don't trust the girl, I use it."

"What makes you trust a girl?" I question, thinking of how the Point Place females also use notions of trust to decide whether they will use condoms or not.

"Hey!" Delani exclaims.

To which George elaborates, "You look at the behavior of the girl, then you trust her. When a girl comes here maybe for the first time in town, right, you're going to look at this girl. You actually can see how the girl behaves. That's why sometimes you don't use a condom. But when you stay with somebody and you already know her history [like the Point Place females], *eish*."

I'm perplexed. "But isn't the girl who comes to town, the one whom you don't know, isn't she very dangerous? Because you don't know her, maybe she's infected? She might look perfectly healthy, she might be beautiful and young, but she still can be HIV positive."

"Yeah," George explains, "you don't know her history, but now when you look at her, you've got that feeling. You can trust her. I know it's dangerous, but when you look at her, the thing that comes to your mind is that she's not HIV positive."

In the second half of the conversation, George and Delani touch on an important distinction of trust, again showing the gendered differentials of *nakana*. The Point Place females trust their Point Place boyfriends more than their boyfriends on the outside. Thus they often agree to unprotected sex within Point Place—something they try to avoid when engaging in sexual relationships with outside boyfriends.

The Point Place males, meanwhile, find the close proximity of their female companions more worrisome than reassuring. They frequently remark on the promiscuous behavior of the Point Place females and so strive to find sexual partners on the outside. They believe that those girls, especially the ones who are new to Durban, make better girlfriends. They often bring their new girlfriends into Point Place as rooming companions. In doing so, they set up a paradoxical living arrangement: the outside girlfriend becomes an inside girlfriend, and so a figure to be distrusted. To protect themselves, the Point Place males resort to disciplinarian tactics meant to control the behavior of their girlfriends. They assume the role of an *umnumzana*, always on the lookout for an intruding *isoka*. Condoms, from their perspective, indicate failure, for their girlfriends—deemed trustworthy before entering Point Place—should remain HIV free. In this context, unprotected sex is an affirmation of fidelity as well as a successful, dominant masculinity.

* * *

I'm sitting on the concrete floor of Jabulani's kitchen, located in an informal settlement on the outskirts of Durban. Jabulani's home is a recently constructed two-story cinderblock structure. Only the windows need to be set; as of now the panes are empty, leaving the upper level exposed to a gust of gray ash brought in from outside. When the breeze settles, Jabulani wipes the windowsill with the palm of his hand. He turns his palm upward, inspects the sooty residue, and dips his hand into a plastic bin of soapy water. The bin holds a pile of dirty dishes still soaking from the night before. Busi, Jabulani's girlfriend, will scrub them shortly. Along with Busi, Jabulani shares the upper floor with Siphiwe, a friend he knows from Point Place. They split the rent, R500 a month. Both Jabulani and Siphiwe work for the city municipality. They're gone for most of the day, and so their girlfriends, Busi and Liyanda, watch the house while they're away. I'm here with Ofentse and her son, Musa, at Jabulani's request, an invitation for us to visit anytime. I met Jabulani on the rooftop of Point Place three weeks previously, the day the police evicted everyone from the building. When I took a photograph of him on that day, he smiled widely at the thought of having his own home.

Today Jabulani smiles widely again, this time anticipating the chicken dinner Busi will serve him. The centerpiece is squawking in front of us. Liyanda just released the bird from its cardboard box.

A scene of cacophony commences: Musa—scared of the chicken, its aggressive stance and clucking sounds—screams and cries. He tries to climb up Ofentse's legs. In response to Musa's contorted body and frantic shouts, the chicken puffs its feathers up even more, causing Musa to howl louder. The liveliness appeals to Busi's sense of amusement. She picks up a kitchen knife and runs after the chicken. Sensing danger, the chicken makes a dash toward the bright light of the open door. Siphiwe anticipates its escape route and slams the front door shut. Musa, terrified of the noise, cries even harder. To avoid Busi's long strides and swinging knife, I scoot my way into the corner of the room. Unfortunately, the defecating chicken notices my movement and charges. The chicken, just about to reach me, swerves upward. I close my eyes, expecting sharp talons to pierce my face, but I feel none. A single feather grazes my nose. When I open my eyes again, I see that the chicken has settled above me, on top of the concrete partition that divides the room into two separate halves. The chicken appears to be roosting, temporarily safe from Busi's glinting blade.

I brought the chicken as a housewarming gift for Jabulani and his companions. Jabulani once told me that he and his housemates consumed sixty eggs in one sitting, yet they do not intend for this chicken to live long enough to lay even one egg. They want to kill it before somebody else steals it or, even worse, before a dog devours the bird—bones, beak, claws, and all. Such losses are a common occurrence, especially in this informal settlement where they do not know their neighbors. Even so, Jabulani is not overly worried. He informs me about his cache of weaponry: tear gas, a wooden cane, a sjambok [whip], a kitchen knife, and his most prized possession of all, his homemade gun. I think that Jabulani may be joking. I'm not certain, but as with the story of the sixty eggs, I decide not to inquire further. Instead we watch Busi begin preparations for a late afternoon supper. She starts with the dirty dishes.

"How did you meet Siphiwe?" Ofentse directs this question to Jabulani.

"Okay," Jabulani responds, happy with the turn of conversation. "The story of how I met Siphiwe. This man here, I was scared of him."

"Why?" I ask.

"Because, on my side," Jabulani continues, "I thought maybe he's a killer. Because you see, in fact, he was really robbing people, a lot of people. So whatever I had in my pocket, to keep it safe, I'd have to run, right. Then we went to prison, and he became my friend. He was the one who sent me to prison. From prison, he started to be my friend 'til now. Now he's my friend forever. Once you touch him, you touch me. Once you touch me, you touch him. I even got his family phone numbers. I know them, yes."

"Do you work together?" Ofentse inquires.

"Yes, we work together, we're living together. Whatever we do, we're doing together as brothers."

"Do you sleep together?" Ofentse mischievously asks.

"Yes." Jabulani's response to her question is amicable. "We sleep together. I can say that we sleep together, not in the same bed but in the same room. We eat from the same pot. Now I take him like my brother, my real brother, yes."

"And you, Siphiwe?" Ofentse hopes to engage him as well.

"Yeah." Siphiwe issues his standard short response.

"But he's rude." Jabulani tries to provoke Siphiwe into conversation. "Very rude."

"When are you going to get married?" Ofentse abruptly switches topics. The question brings laughter from Siphiwe.

"I'd like to get married," Jabulani responds, "but I don't know when. I can't say when. Only God knows when I'll get married."

"Maybe next year?" Ofentse knows this is not a real possibility because he cannot afford it.

"Maybe," Jabulani replies. "If God likes me to get married next year, I will."

"Are you going to marry Busi?" Ofentse asks.

"Of course, of course, of course," Jabulani laughs.

"Because you love her?" I add.

"Yes, yes," he agrees.

Feeling left out, Ofentse poses a question to Jabulani: "Do you love me?"

Without hesitation, he answers, "At the moment I can say yes because you're my sister."

Jabulani has a special friendship with many of the youth from Point Place. He is viewed as a brother to all those who have spent a significant amount of time living inside the building. This is true for Ofentse, whom Jabulani regards as his sister. It is through Ofentse that I, too, become close to Jabulani. I met him on my own, but his subsequent openness and willingness to talk about matters of the heart stem from his close friendship with Ofentse. He trusts and protects her, and by extension he trusts and protects me as well. With Jabulani, I am able to broach topics like domestic violence and express opinions on gender equality. While he does not always agree with me, he contemplates my questions in an open manner that shows a willingness to engage with many points of view. This is less true of Siphiwe, whom I never interview individually. Siphiwe and I remain friendly with one another, yet we both recognize that there are issues too sensitive for us to speak about across a male-female divide. Instead Siphiwe sits in on some of my group interviews, occasionally adding comments, but for the most part keeping his opinions private. Jabulani's narration of how he and Siphiwe became friends illustrates this dynamic. As Jabulani mentions above, he knows Siphiwe from Point Place. They did not become brothers, however, until both of them were sent to prison: Siphiwe for robbery, public intimidation, and carrying a concealed weapon, and Jabulani for guilt by association.

*   *   *

It was early in the morning on a quiet summer day when Siphiwe asked Jabulani to accompany him to the public toilets near the beachfront. Jabulani, with not much else to do, agreed. He has always enjoyed strolling the streets, greeting women on their way to the beach. Many go to bathe at the pools, while others carry large canvas bags on their heads, hoping to sell beaded trinkets to the tourists. Jabulani appreciates everything about these women— their chatty banter, feminine looks, entrepreneurial spirit, and productive activity. As is often the case, he greeted all the women with an affable "Hello!" while Siphiwe, by contrast, stared straight ahead, observing everything but saying nothing. On that day Siphiwe was carrying a concealed weapon, a switchblade in his pocket. Jabulani did not know this.

The boys entered the public toilets and went into their respective stalls. In the midst of attending to his business, Jabulani heard a commotion. It was Siphiwe ordering two younger boys to hand over their money. Siphiwe's switchblade was open, his "fire was on." One of the boys gave him R40. The other boy managed to escape and returned a few minutes later accompanied by a police officer. The police officer saw Jabulani standing next to Siphiwe, laughing with him, and arrested them. Jabulani was sent to prison for six months for guilt by association.

To my amazement, Jabulani holds no grudge against Siphiwe. Instead he invites Siphiwe to live with him when he is released from prison. Siphiwe agrees. They stay together at Point Place initially, and then later on in Jabulani's cinderblock home. Siphiwe does not come alone. He brings Liyanda, his girlfriend of several weeks.

Siphiwe believes the new accommodations will be a good change for Liyanda. She is lazy at Point Place, sitting around all day waiting for food and clothing donations. She will have to work hard in Jabulani's home—fetching water, preparing food, and washing clothes. Busi will be a positive influence as well. Unlike Liyanda, Busi is a diligent worker, the first to wake up in the

morning, sweep the floors, make the bed, and prepare breakfast—a full meal
of porridge, fried eggs, and buttered bread. With Busi, the kettle remains
full of water, ready to be boiled at a moment's notice. Not surprisingly, the
Point Place girls often refer to her as "auntie," a term of endearment as well
as derision, for in some circles it implies an element of despotic control. This
does not bother Siphiwe. He only has one concern. Busi tends to monitor
Jabulani's purse strings. She often dissuades him from drinking beer with his
friends. Siphiwe vows not to let Liyanda interfere in such matters. Liyanda
will not "pull him by the nose."

Siphiwe is incorrect in his assessment of Busi's ability to reform Liyanda. Liyanda continues to sit around most of the day, only occasionally helping Busi
with the household chores. But Busi does not mind, for she never adjusted to
the "fast life" of Point Place. She is relieved to be out of the building. Liyanda
feels differently. She misses the nightclubs, the bars, and the beachfront. As
she explains, "We smoked. We ate cakes and *biryani* and leftover food from
the nightclub below . . . We were not going to leave Point Place if the police
didn't force us to go." At this remark, Busi slaps her hands together, swiping
them as if she would like to throw Liyanda's comment away.

Busi counters, "Even if the police didn't come, I was going to leave." But
then she quickly concedes, "I went into Point Place with Jabulani. I said I
was going to leave. I ended up staying for good."

Like many of the females, Busi learned about Point Place by agreeing to
love. Jabulani and Busi first met on the streets, near the public toilets and
water tap. Even then, Jabulani could see Busi's efficiency of manner, reflected
in the way she fetched water, lifting the plastic jug to her shoulders and head
without spilling a drop. He proposed to her right there, without hesitation.
She declined. He persisted, though, learning where she preferred to hang
out (outside the supermarket), where she walked along the beachfront (near
South Beach), and where she stayed (in one of the nightly paying shelters).
Jabulani rarely saw Busi in the bars or clubs, but when he did, she would be
dancing or standing among friends shouting to be heard. Busi, as everyone
knows, never sits quietly. Finally, one day, to everyone's astonishment, she
accepted Jabulani's love proposal. She found his clever banter and attentive
demeanor appealing. His municipal identification badge—showing that he
had a real job and a steady income—did not hurt his prospects, either. So at
the age of seventeen, Busi entered Point Place believing that she would stay
only temporarily, but she remained with Jabulani for nearly a year.

The details of Busi's personal background are unclear to me and Ofentse,
and even to Jabulani. We know she grew up in a rural area, and that her
mother passed away when she was seven and her father when she was fourteen. We know she received very little formal education. She cannot read or

write in isiZulu and cannot speak or understand English. We know she prefers to follow traditional healing practices and, to Jabulani's despair, does not like to attend church. Everything else remains obscure, perhaps deliberately so. Busi, unlike most of the other Point Place youth, never slept on the streets. Nor did she participate in the common street youth experience of shelter hopping. Essentially, we do not know how she survived between the ages of fourteen and seventeen.

*   *   *

Even though Busi has little formal education, her memory for detail and her passion for talking lend her the attributes of an impressive narrator. She speaks in a steady, uninterrupted rhythm that is easy to follow. Her stories, while not always chronological, reveal keen powers of social observation. From Busi I learn what happens behind closed doors. I am able to probe Jabulani and ask questions about things that he would not volunteer without my knowledge of what happened previously. Through Busi I come closer to domestic violence from the perspective not just of young women but also of young men. Such is the case when I ask her why Siphiwe and Liyanda no longer reside together. Siphiwe is back inside Point Place, and Liyanda has gone back home.

Busi explains, "Siphiwe hit Liyanda. They were fighting because Liyanda accepted another boyfriend. Siphiwe said she must go back home."

"Did you know about the other boyfriend?" I inquire.

"I only knew of one other." Busi elaborates, "She said it was her friend. He used to come to the house. They would smoke cigarettes together. Oh, and there was another one from that side [of the informal settlement], and this other one with the red car. There were four of them including Siphiwe."

I am surprised by this number and ask Busi, "How did she meet her other boyfriends?" Busi responds:

> One of them was going to work in the morning. He'd come at two o'clock in the afternoon to see her. The other one, from that side, was always here. She'd ask cigarettes from him. Other times she went to his shack. This last one, the one with the red car, we'd see him when we'd go to the phones or when we'd go buy popsicles. It was on a Sunday, we were washing [clothes outside]. He chatted with Liyanda. On Monday, Jabulani and Siphiwe went to work. He [the outside boyfriend] fetched Liyanda at twelve o'clock. She left. She came back to the house at three o'clock.

"What happened when Liyanda went with the man in the red car?" I ask.

"I stayed behind," Busi continues. "I slept. When she came back, Liyanda was crying. I asked, 'Why are you crying?' She didn't say. She carried money,

R30. She didn't say how she got it. She said we must go to town. We left. There was blood coming out."

"Where was she bleeding?"

"Below."

"Did she say how she was hurt?"

"I don't know what happened." Busi pauses. "They were dating, really."

"Could she walk?" I still do not understand why Liyanda was bleeding, but Busi does not explain further. Instead she presents a lengthy narrative about what happened afterward:

> Yeah, she just walked like we are walking. We returned home. I told Jabulani in the afternoon what happened. He kept quiet. That Sunday Jabulani didn't go to church. Siphiwe and Jabulani locked themselves inside the house. I left with another friend. I don't remember where we went. We came back. The boys locked Liyanda inside the room. Siphiwe was standing at the door holding knives. Jabulani was holding a *sjambok*. The boys spoke to her. They first said, "Why are you eating *umcako* [a mineral that is thought to prevent pregnancy]? She said she just eats *umcako*. They said, "Why are you making yourself sterile?" She admitted it. They hit her. The boys didn't hear us. We tiptoed. We tiptoed. We hid. We were hiding outside. The boys talked and talked. We were listening. Liyanda mentioned my name. I went inside. I knocked first. They said I must sit with Liyanda. They said, "Why have you accepted [*qoma*]?" I asked, "Who did I accept [*qoma*]?" I laughed at them. Jabulani slapped me because I was laughing. I said, "Even if you hit me, I don't know a thing." He hit me and hit me. He said, "You'll admit it." He left me. He saw that no, I don't admit it. Liyanda ended up admitting to this man of hers. Siphiwe told my friend to take all of Liyanda's clothes. My friend threw all of Liyanda's clothes on the floor. The boys opened the door. They said go out. Siphiwe said he wanted to poke [stab] Liyanda here. He missed her. I went to the old man below. I told him what happened. The old man came upstairs. He told the boys about the red car. He asked Liyanda, "Why did you accept [*qoma*]?" She didn't know. She said that she was just being naughty. The boys said go, then. They said we both must leave. I said, "I'm going nowhere." They said we all must go. Jabulani told us to go and stay at Thuthukani for two days. I said, "You're drunk. I'm not going anywhere." Jabulani chased me with tear gas. He grabbed me. He threw me on the floor. I stood up. I hit Liyanda. She said that she was just playing around. She wanted to be hit with me. I hit her again then. The old man returned. He asked Siphiwe and Liyanda to go because they have caused a lot of noise. Siphiwe said, "I hear you, old man." He took his bag and he put in his clothes. He held Liyanda. He said that he'll get her. He left. He returned. They slept. Siphiwe slept alone. Liyanda slept alone. They chatted at night. Liyanda slept with Siphiwe. They did their thing at night [i.e., had sex]. They forgave each other.

The next day, Siphiwe and Liyanda leave Jabulani's home. Busi remains. I interview Jabulani a few days later, wanting to know why he hit the girls.

"I was angry," he explains. "My heart was sore."

"Did you ever think you'd hit them?" I ask, knowing that Jabulani left his own home because his mother hit him when he was a child.

"Uh-uh. No."

"Do you regret hitting them?" I inquire.

"No," he states.

I am surprised by his honesty. "You're glad you hit them?"

"Yes, I'm happy," he affirms.

"You're happy?" I repeat.

"Yes."

"Why?" I ask.

"Yeah," he elaborates, "because I was putting them on the right way, not the wrong way. So I'm happy if they're doing the right thing now."

"Why do you feel responsible?" I inquire.

"You see, I was with them in a bad situation. Now Busi still wants to live with me, so you see, I have to be responsible for her." Jabulani believes that he has justified his abusive actions, but I press on.

"Do you think it's okay for men to hit women?"

"Oh, well, I don't think it's okay," he explains. "But if we hit them, maybe they'll change their mind. They'll leave all those wrong things and will do the right things. Yes."

Later in the conversation, I ask Jabulani, "Are you afraid that when you hit Busi, she might leave you?"

"Yeah," he responds, "I'm scared. But I tell myself if she leaves, maybe she'll come back again."

"Why do you choose a *sjambok* [whip]?" I inquire.

"A *sjambok*, it's because I know Busi is scared of it. And also Liyanda is scared of it. So now I know that they're scared of the *sjambok*, both of them. When I hit them with it, they'll leave everything that they're doing. When I take a stick, they're going to feel like I'm playing. When I take a *sjambok*, they know that I'm not playing."

In this conversation, Jabulani explains his actions by taking on the disciplinarian role of an *umnumzana*. He feels "responsible" for the girls and hits them to show them the "right way." He does not view his tactics as excessive, especially since Busi continues to reside with him. Yet Jabulani underestimates his control over Busi. He errs not on the side of a patriarchal *umnumzana* but on the side of an incorrigible *isoka*.

Busi is unable to conceive a baby, so Jabulani starts to look for another girlfriend. He stays away in the evenings, usually after payday. Busi learns about his infidelities from the other youth at Point Place. She confronts him, and in response he tells her that he plans to find a new girlfriend with fewer "rules." That same evening Busi waits for Jabulani to fall asleep. Then she stealthily takes his cell phone, his gun, his R33, and a duffel bag. In the morning, Jabulani awakens to this momentous loss. Over the next several weeks, he searches the streets for Busi, hoping to recover the stolen items. His quest becomes an obsession. He stops going to work and loses his job. When he cannot pay rent, the landlord kicks him out of the house. With nowhere else to go, he returns to Point Place.

Here Jabulani picks up the pieces of a broken dream. He moves in with friends and eventually manages to stake a claim to a pantry, determining once again who can and cannot reside with him. With a bent nail, he secures the door to his new room. He decides that he would like to be an *umnumzana* from here on, not an *isoka*. Several years pass, and still Jabulani searches for Busi. He refers to her as his *umakoti* [bride], as his real love. He believes that nothing has gone quite right since she left him.

*   *   *

In this chapter, I address the historical and cultural trajectory of two dominant masculinities in KwaZulu-Natal: the *isoka* and the *umnumzana*. I note their persuasive appeal, showing how the youth of Point Place look to both personas as figures of desirable emulation. The *isoka* acquires self-worth through the accrual of multiple sexual partners; the *umnumzana* acquires self-worth through the productive and reproductive capabilities of a residing girlfriend. Both figures find affirmation in the deployment of the love proposal (*shela*). The *shela* outwardly demonstrates the discursive dominion of the Point Place males. It highlights the material status of the *isoka* and the domestic stability of the *umnumzana*. Essentially, through the *shela*, the Point Place males structure the conditions of their sexual attachments. They are providers and protectors, while their female companions are the beneficiaries of their support.

As such, the *isoka* and *umnumzana* masculinities reflect a continuum of male privilege and patriarchy. These two identities operate in tandem with one another as well in opposition. The sexual exploits of the *isoka* often undermine the domestic authority of the *umnumzana*. This can be seen in the breakups of the Point Place youth. The Point Place females are willing to accept the infidelities of their boyfriends as long as they conduct their external affairs in an inconspicuous manner. Yet the *isoka* figure is far from discreet. The *umnumzana*, meanwhile, has difficulty supporting more than one girlfriend. Apart from his room, an aspiring *umnumzana* has few material resources, and those cannot be diverted without the primary girlfriend feeling the effects. Conflicts with girlfriends thus occur on a regular basis for the *isoka* and *umnumzana*.

The debilitations of HIV/AIDS also pose particular challenges for the Point Place males. As they acquire bodily afflictions, it is difficult for them to maintain the outward desirability of an *isoka* figure, and so they tend to assume the identity of an *umnumzana*. Here, too, they face problems as they attempt to assert control over their female companions through tactics of intimidation and physical violence. Such actions rarely bring the desired outcome of respect, for in the end the Point Place males recognize that their self-worth stems from the mutual support of *nakana*, and not from fear or abuse. Ultimately, then, it is more likely that the Point Place males derive *nakana* from each other, as loyal brothers, than from their love affairs and cohabitations with girlfriends.

PART 3

The Power of Home

5 Residing with the Spectral

Dusk was approaching in Durban, and pedestrians hurried to the taxi lines, eager not to be caught in the descending dark. Yogi walked at a leisurely pace. He was not overly concerned with the emptying sidewalks, nightfall, or brisk winter chill, for Point Place was quite near. Along the way, he came to a cemetery with its gate ajar. Curious, he entered. Small memorials to the deceased—flowers and votives—dotted the ground. Yogi happened upon a particularly attractive candle: a red one, decorated with fanciful moons and stars. Pleased with his unexpected find, he picked up the candle and hid it beneath his shirt.[1] He slipped outside the cemetery, walking slowly and deliberately, not wanting to arouse undue suspicion. Without further incident, he entered Point Place. He set the candle on his windowsill, intending to light it later in the evening. Everything continued on as usual, seemingly normal. By midnight Yogi was a changed person. So was his girlfriend, Sisi.

The clock struck twelve. Yogi burst forth from his room. His eyes blazed red; his teeth were elongated into sharpened points. He was bellowing in pain, in unsuppressed rage. Thousands of invisible needles were piercing his flesh. Sisi was not with him. She was in the bedroom flailing on the ground, possessed by something only she could see. The youth next door, hearing the commotion, pushed past Yogi and ran into the room. They found Sisi clutching at her throat, gasping for breath, pleading for a woman named uGogo to stop strangling her.[2] "I'm sorry, Gogo!"[3] Sisi cried over and over again. "I'm sorry!" uGogo seemed to neither hear nor care. Menstrual blood stained Sisi's skirt and legs, leaving dark streaks on the floor.

The candle had burned low. Its melted wax congealed on the sill; in the flickering light it looked like thickened, coagulated blood. One of the boys picked up the candle and flung it through the open window into the night sky. Yogi's eyes began to focus. The redness faded away. His teeth reduced in size. The pain subsided. Yogi crouched down next to Sisi. He pulled out a R1 coin and told Sisi that as long as she held on to the silver coin, she would be safe from uGogo. The convulsions gradually ceased. Sisi's friends wiped away her tears. They washed the blood from her thighs and carried her back to bed.

The next day, the same thing happened. Sisi continued to have seizures. Her period flowed uncontrollably. She only stopped convulsing and bleeding when given something to hold on to, something shiny or reflective—a coin, a spoon, or a broken piece of mirror. Yogi also encountered uGogo. Yet rather than falling to the floor, he underwent another type of catharsis, one of hyper-verbosity. He cornered unsuspecting youth in the hallways and stairwells and on the rooftop of Point Place. He exposed their secrets, revealing their darkest fears to everyone. What Yogi knew was seemingly impossible. He accused certain girls of being negligent mothers, leaving their babies at home, abandoning them to enjoy the pleasures of town. Others he denounced as fat freeloaders undeserving of sympathy or help. They clearly came from prosperous families. Still others he condemned as too thin, harbingers of hidden STIs. He pointed out the murderers, thieves, and rapists. They all were guilty. They all must leave Point Place. Yogi's disclosures were devastating, private knowledge made painfully public. Nobody blamed him, though. It was uGogo speaking, not him.

Other kids started to see uGogo, too. They met her late at night, a floating misty figure dressed in long, flowing robes, her face and hair concealed by gossamer scarves. uGogo beckoned to these youth, encouraging them to join her outside the windows. Some, like Sisi, fell to the ground convulsing, their eyes rolled back, imploring uGogo to leave them alone. Others feverishly searched for red candles. When they came back with white ones, bruises and cuts appeared on their faces and bodies. They said that uGogo was hurting them, vengeful for blood, demanding her red candles. A foggy haze enveloped the building. Large numbers of youth were smoking dagga and Mandrax incessantly, all pushed to the edges of sanity—even the nonbelievers. Then it happened, what uGogo seemed to want.

Yogi leapt onto the windowsill like a cat, ready to jump.[4] A few of the older boys perceived his suicidal intentions. They rushed toward him, but they were too late, and he slipped outside. One boy managed to grab on to his arm and tried to pull him back inside. Yogi did not resist. Dangling three stories above the pavement, he had returned to his senses. A fall would mean broken bones, possibly death. The other boys joined in and slowly raised

Yogi upward, straining not to fall out the window themselves. But then the Nigerians from the nightclub below interfered. They heard the ensuing chaos, leaned out the first-floor window, grabbed on to Yogi's legs, and yanked him down. Instead of catching him, they let him drop.

Yogi landed headfirst on the sidewalk. Some pedestrians who had witnessed the fall called an ambulance, and the paramedics arrived to take him to the hospital. An hour later, he limped his way back inside Point Place. uGogo, he announced, did not want him to receive medical treatment. He climbed the stairs. The white gauze wrapped around his head loosened and trailed behind him, skipping along the stairs and darting around the corner. The other kids whistled in disbelief. Yogi looked like a zombie, an unraveling mummy. He was overcome by something that was not quite of this world.

The next day the police arrested Yogi for housebreaking. They sent him to prison. Although he was gone, uGogo remained. Kids continued to see her. Sisi continued to fall ill. Finally, on a Sunday, some of the churchgoing youth told their Zionist priest what was happening.[5] He arranged for members of his congregation, the Twelve Apostles, to enter Point Place. They flicked holy water in the darkened corridors, in the elevator shaft, and in Yogi's room. They called Sisi forward and prayed for her, marking a cross on her forehead. They encouraged her to attend church and follow the teachings of the Bible. Sisi agreed. She went to a few prayer meetings, recited a couple of hymns, ate the sandwiches, drank the juice, and gratefully accepted the donated clothes. A week later, she stopped attending church. uGogo had left her along with everyone else, at least for the time being.

*   *   *

All these sightings of uGogo—which I have compiled from twenty-seven different accounts—occurred several months before I entered Point Place. I glean the first account, rather fortuitously, during an interview with Ofentse. At the time we are discussing her recent breakup with Khaya. She attributes the split to Khaya's repeated infidelity. Yet he is not entirely responsible for his actions. Other forces, she tells me, are at work, too.

Not so long ago, Ofentse became extremely sick, rapidly losing weight, incapable of even drinking tea. She assumed it was the flu. The other Point Place girls thought differently. They warned Ofentse to be mindful of her rivals, encouraging her to empty all her bags, sort through all her clothes, and wash all her linens. Sure enough, they found a packet of *umuthi*—strange herbal substances—tucked in the fold of a shirt.[6] With this discovery, Ofentse quickly recovered. Today she is not entirely convinced that somebody wishes her ill will, enough to use *umuthi* to force her breakup with Khaya. Still, she is not taking any chances with their baby son, making sure that all of Musa's clothes and bedding are *umuthi*-free. As Ofentse notes, regardless of her own upbringing as a Catholic (who now occasionally attends Anglican and Zionist services), witchcraft is still alive in South Africa, especially among the Zulus.

I ask Ofentse about other examples of witchcraft. She brings up uGogo. I am fascinated by the story and its implications, she noticeably less so. She wants me to recognize that only the kids who smoke and drink saw uGogo; she wants me to recognize that uGogo is not really real. "How could she be?"

"Yes," I counter, "but I am not so concerned with the *how* but rather the *why*. Why does uGogo take on the bodily form of a grandmother? Why does she come at that particular moment in time? Why to Yogi? Why to Sisi? Why not before? And why not after?"

Ofentse begins to understand what I am looking for: the metaphysical possibility of uGogo, the underlying meaning of her presence. "Okay," Ofentse concedes, "we'll ask them. We'll start with Sisi. Yogi is still in jail."

* * *

Ofentse and I are sitting at a small luncheonette with Sisi. Our interview with her progresses quickly, for her answers are limited to a few monosyllabic words, "Yes" and "No" being the most common response. She is shy in front of the recorder, in front of me. Ofentse claims that this is not like Sisi at all. Sisi has an assertive personality. She commands the respect of the other girls, quick to show her displeasure with a swift slap from her hand, a sudden poke with a knife. I never see this. With me, Sisi always is polite and restrained. Occasionally I sense her underlying humor, a coyness that she displays around the Point Place males:

> I am with the girls watching the busy exchange of clothes. Their flat has become a whirlwind of trading apparel—jeans for a pair of shoes, a halter top for a skirt, a purse for a mended jersey. Sisi skips around the common area, elated by her recent swap. Boys mill about as well, scoping out the scene, deciding whether or not to partake in the activity. Sisi bounces in front of them. She lifts up her skirt and flashes her ruffled underwear, teasing them about a tradeoff they'll never see. Ofentse shrieks in feigned dismay and tries to smack Sisi into proper ladylike behavior. Sisi is too quick for Ofentse, though, too quick for anyone. She hops away, grinning delightedly, along with the laughing boys.

Ofentse and Sisi have a close friendship, a mutual understanding. Sisi—for reasons unknown to Ofentse—has taken an interest in Ofentse's relationship with Khaya, beating up other girls who might lead him astray. Ofentse speculates that it may have something to do with their baby. Perhaps Sisi wants him to grow up with parents who are in a stable relationship? Ofentse reciprocates in kind.

Sisi has a younger sister, Tombi, who frequents Point Place. Sisi wants her sister to return home and not become susceptible to the vices she might encounter on the streets. Ofentse helps out, keeping a close eye on Tombi, consoling her when she is upset, encouraging her to return to school, to stop sniffing glue, and to delay having boyfriends. Neither Ofentse's nor Sisi's tactics are particularly successful. Their interventions largely go unheeded. This does not deter them from trying, though, assisting one another when they can. Even now Sisi is helping Ofentse. She has agreed to the interview.

Toward the end of our interview, Sisi begins to open up. She expresses concern about a pending court case involving the murder of her brother. She is scared of the defendant. He has threatened to kill her if she testifies against him. Over the course of this conversation, Sisi mentions a recent nightmare: "I dreamt about Yogi. He wasn't in jail anymore. He was here. He came to Point Place, he came to me, and his eyes were hanging out."

Ofentse and I prod her to speak more about the dream, what it might mean. We bring up uGogo. Sisi does not seem to remember her. She becomes noticeably quieter, saying that she will go home if Yogi is released from prison. Ofentse changes the topic of discussion. We talk about the Durban nightlife, the clubbing scene, and the Mariah Carey poster hanging on the wall behind us. Later I ask Ofentse, "What happened?"

"Sisi stopped blinking," she replies. "uGogo may come back."

*   *   *

Two months after my interview with Sisi, Yogi is released from prison. I am stunned to see him. I have known Yogi for many years, but by a different name. It is Thomas—the young man who first took me to Point Place promising me safe passage from Thuthukani. He rushes toward me in delighted recognition and shakes my hand in enthusiastic greeting. "I no longer know you!" he laughingly calls out. And indeed he looks different, too, paler and heavier than I remember, a telltale sign of a prolonged prison sentence. We briefly catch up, agreeing to talk later. For now, Yogi is much too preoccupied. With a wink and a wave he dashes off, intent on securing a room inside Point Place.

Several weeks pass before Ofentse and I have the chance to formally interview Yogi. He treats it as a special occasion. Overjoyed by the "party" we have arranged for him, he performs to his utmost capabilities. He wipes down the chairs with a dramatic sweep of the hand; arranges the table so it does not tilt; pours the liter of Coke with exaggerated care. When our plates of food arrive, he talks and eats at the same time, his spoon a utensil of animated punctuation. Grains of rice soar into the air and land back on the table, the chairs, and the floor below, effectively nullifying all previous attention to order and tidiness.

Yogi, I notice, has lost weight since his release from prison. His skin is much darker. He has been sitting outside in the sun, sniffing glue, forgetting to eat and bathe. All this I expect. Yet he has a smell that even I cannot fathom. It transcends the usual perils of body odor and unwashed clothes. Something is rotten, pungently so. Ofentse and I discreetly sit back in our chairs, leaning away from the table, away from Yogi. Ofentse thinks that he may have an untreated STI. Along these lines, he tells us about a painful sore, an *imvilapho*. Usually this type of sore is an external lesion that can be seen. In Yogi's case it remains hidden. He feels its presence, though, a throbbing ache in his groin.

I ask Yogi if he has sought help either from the clinic or through more traditional means, like an *inyanga* (a healer) or *isangoma* (a diviner). He responds that he and Sisi recently returned from the hospital. They had their blood taken. It came out black, thick as oil. They were poisoned, he claims, most likely by the Nigerians. I take a chance and inquire about uGogo. Yogi expresses surprise at my line of questioning. He pauses, enough so that I think he may not answer. But then he replies, "I was relaxing in my room. I was smoking a cigarette. The cigarette went out! *Voo!* I didn't know what was happening. After that, I was getting hot. Somebody was pulling me. I was crying. I was being forced out of the room. Then I went to the hospital; after that, prison."

Ofentse asks Yogi for clarification: "You threw yourself out of the window?"

Yogi shifts in his seat and corrects Ofentse: "Somebody called me, called me down. I never saw her face. She was wearing an *iduku* [a kerchief covering the head]. uGogo was calling me. I'm coming. Somebody is pulling me. That's Yogi falling down the window!" As he tells it, he did not jump out the window on his own accord. He wanted to meet uGogo and see her up close. Also, technically speaking, the Nigerians pulled him down.

Ofentse proceeds with the interview, determined to solve the mystery of Yogi's red eyes. "How did they change color?" Yogi remains silent. He withdraws from the conversation. He does not hear Ofentse anymore. I am incapable of adding anything. I am scared. Perhaps we pushed him too far? Perhaps uGogo has returned? Ofentse, too, is startled by the silence, but then in a smooth transition asks Yogi, "Hey, what type of job would you like to find?"

Yogi snaps out of it and begins to talk again. "It doesn't matter, any job. Only money I need." The interview continues. None of us mention uGogo again. Afterward Ofentse teases me, saying that I looked absolutely white, rather ghostly myself, when Yogi stopped talking. Since when did I become afraid of uGogo?

"No," I hedge, "I'm not frightened of uGogo. I was worried that Yogi might jump. You see, we were sitting on the second floor of an open terrace."

∗   ∗   ∗

In his ethnography *Zulu Thought-Patterns and Symbolism*, anthropologist Axel-Ivar Berglund (1976:79) notes that in isiZulu a linguistic distinction exists between timely and untimely departures. Zulu speakers describe a timely death as *goduka* (to return home), *dlula* (to pass), *hamba* (to travel), *shona* (to set, as in the sun), and *qhubeka* (to proceed), an untimely death as *fa* (to come to an end), *buba* (to perish), and *gqibuka* (to snap off). As used in Berglund's work, a timely death imparts a notion of continuity. An untimely death expresses the opposite, the breaking off of life. These understandings of death—as timely or untimely—apply to the afterlife as well. For with proper burial and decomposition, the deceased enter into another realm of existence: that of the *amadlozi*, the ancestors/shades.[7]

The *amadlozi* are a deep continuation,[8] a profound extension of the living spirit. To elaborate a bit further, the body and spirit—according to Berglund's respondents (1976:82–83)—are not entirely separate. This differs from Christian doctrines that posit a clear external/internal dichotomy. Rather, as Berglund (1976:87) explains, the living spirit has an observable presence. Like the body, it can be seen as a person's shadow, an image in a mirror, or a reflection off water. All three are referred to in isiZulu as *isithunzi*.[9] The disassociation of the living spirit (*isithunzi*) from the body occurs with death. The body—the corpse—remains on earth. The living spirit departs for another place. The shadow, in other words, becomes one of the shades.

The *amadlozi*, while from the place below, reappear on earth as omens, in visions, and in dreams. They are white, casting white shadows, and so are viewed most clearly in the dark of night (Berglund 1976:89–90; Ngubane 1977:50–51). They protect their descendants from malicious intent and thus are treated with deferential respect. If neglected, they are capable of inflict- ing illness, yet death is not their ultimate objective (Berglund 1976:28, 269). Rather, the relationship between them and the living is one of mutual interdependence. The *amadlozi* are interested in the perpetuation of the lineage. A timely death highlights this desirable progression. The passing of elders may be mourned but is not considered tragic, for they have children who will perform the necessary work to honor them as *amadlozi* (Berglund 1976:79–81). An untimely death is another matter altogether.

Untimely deaths are associated with the young, those who have not yet reached their full potential (Berglund 1976:79). Such deaths are tragic occurrences, for they threaten the continuity of the entire lineage, from the ancestors to the unborn descendants. First, an untimely death denies the possibility of honoring the *amadlozi*, as their descendants are responsible for these ritual undertakings. Second, it precludes the possibility of extending generations further down the line; it essentially cuts off the (unborn) children of the children. An untimely death is therefore regarded with extreme suspicion and anxiety, for it may signal the demise of an entire lineage. Such deaths are not readily accepted as a natural progression of life events but rather suggest a different type of order, a perversion of everything good, moral, and upright in society, a perversion that follows its own murderous, nonproductive logic—that of witchcraft.

The ultimate objective of witchcraft is to kill and annihilate a person completely (Berglund 1976:81, 266, 385). The actual physical death is the first murder. The second murder involves the taking of the life spirit, preventing the shadow from becoming a shade. The stealing of the life spirit—the *isithunzi*—typically occurs at the burial site. The deceased, not yet fully decomposed, is dug up and treated with noxious substances. The corpse is violated, the *isithunzi* appropriated. As anthropologist Harriet Ngubane (1977:31) describes, such desecration differentiates witches from common murderers. Both destroy life, but only witches know how to transform it, how to mold and shape the *isithunzi* for their own nefarious purposes. Witches are the personification of evilness itself. They are the annihilators of the life spirit and as such are the annihilators of the *amadlozi*.

The youth of Point Place are familiar with murder. They are familiar with untimely departures. Young people frequently die inside the building. They become ill and weak, wasting away from a sickness that nobody will name outright (HIV/AIDS). Outside, within blocks of Point Place, they die as well. They are stabbed, shot, beaten to death, and run over by speeding cars. Yet what uGogo does is something different, not consistent with these recognizable everyday forms of death and murder. uGogo demands red candles; she causes seizures; she strangles kids; she entices them outside their windows. uGogo wants something in particular, something that is reflective, that can be projected onto a shiny coin, a broken piece of mirror, or a spoon. uGogo, I believe, is after the *isithunzi*—the very life spirit of the Point Place youth.

*   *   *

METRObeat: When Days Are Dark, Friends Are Few

By Nomsa Nyawo (2005:22)

> Life is not easy if you are homeless, especially if you are a teenager. Living on
> the streets without shelter, clothes or food is a grim experience. METRObeat
> visited an abandoned block of flats on Point Road [. . .] to speak to the street
> children who take shelter in this derelict shell. The building is a nightmare,
> smelling of accumulated filth. It is pitch dark, even in daylight, with defaced
> walls and broken windows. There is no electricity or water supply.
>
> METRObeat spoke to Wiseman, who guided us around the building. [It]
> consists of just twelve units, but accommodates more than 120 street kids. As
> forbidding as the structure is, it is the closest thing to home for these "lost"
> children. Rats and cockroaches swarm in every corner, competing with the
> children for existence. Some of the kids even sleep in a toilet and bathroom.
> Many have lost their parents to violence or AIDS, and find themselves without
> a support network in a harsh world.

Point Place, as discussed in previous chapters, is an urban dwelling set in
the heart of Durban's metropolis, directly in between the beachfront and
the central business district. Its location makes the building an ideal place
of residence. It is close to everything that makes up a bustling cityscape:
stores, markets, nightclubs, transportation hubs, clinics, hospitals, municipal
agencies, recreational and educational facilities, as well as countless other
amenities visible to any passing pedestrian: streetlights, water fountains, and
sanitation services. To not have running water, then, to not have electricity,
to not have a working infrastructure, is seen as something that is distinctly
non-urban, an anomaly within the city comparable to living in the countryside. Like many of those living in the rural areas, the Point Place youth fetch
water from outside taps, light candles instead of switching on lamps, and at
night, when the public toilets are closed, deposit their excrement in plastic
containers to be thrown out the next day.

The youth of Point Place frequently remark on this juxtaposition between
the urban and the rural. They commonly invoke dichotomies of what is done
"here" in the city and what is done "there" on the homestead. Yet, while living
in a seemingly modern urban environment, the Point Place youth continu-
ally come up against the very distinctions that they describe as the other, the
rural, or the traditional. uGogo herself embodies such contradictions. She
is an elderly grandmother living in a building occupied primarily by youth.
She is a figure from the past yet inhabits the present. She demands obedience
and conformity from those who desire self-autonomy and defy authority.
She brings darkness and destruction to where there is light and life. She is,

in short, a force of irreconcilable oppositions, inchoate and indistinct yet simultaneously real and terrifyingly clear—even to those who cannot see her and do not believe in her.

"I never saw uGogo," Jabulani tries to explain. "I only heard her once, like somebody was walking in the passageway. I heard some noise, but I couldn't see that lady. I don't know where this ghost came from. I heard her, but I couldn't see her."

"He's wrong," scoffs his friend Shorty, who is nineteen. "Jabulani's wrong. You know, sometimes you can see a ghost on the farms, but not here in town. There is no way to see one in town. Maybe in one year ten thousand people will die in town. But I've never seen such a thing like a ghost."

"True, you can't see them," Jabulani concedes.

"Because there's electricity," Shorty offers.

"Okay, you can't see them in town. But you can see them in Point Place. Why?" We wait expectantly for Jabulani's answer: "Because there's no electricity!"[10] To our laughter Jabulani adds, "There is darkness, and in darkness you can *see*."

To see inside of Point Place, to see uGogo, is to see darkness as Jabulani proposes. But such darkness does not merely refer to unlit corridors. It also refers to states of despondency, fear, and loss.

Again Jabulani elaborates: "Many people have died inside Point Place. Since we've been there, nothing has been working. The elevator, it's stuck. Sometimes if you're stuck your heart will stop. You're scared of things. So you can die just like that. *Snap!* Especially if your family doesn't know where you are, where you went—so now they can't come and take you."

Ofentse joins in, explaining that family members must collect the spirit of the deceased.

"Otherwise," Jabulani concludes, "you'll be an uGogo from here onwards."

To die far away from home without receiving a proper burial or being collected by a family member is a common anxiety among the Point Place youth. uGogo, as Jabulani implies, relates to these trepidations, to the very real possibility of becoming an unsettled, unfetched spirit.

In a similar conversation, Liyanda and Busi contemplate the internal degradations of Point Place. Through uGogo the two young women address what usually is left unsaid: the mysterious afflictions and illnesses of their friends as well as the ignominious departures of the unclaimed dead:

"I remember that day," Liyanda recounts, "when Yogi walked into the girls' room. He went straight to Sisi, and he touched her. She was still sick. She had uGogo. He touched her, and they went outside. Sisi was crying. She came back inside the room. She covered herself with a blanket. Yogi turned into an animal. He had pointed teeth. We were crying. The boys came up from downstairs. They asked us, why are we crying? We told them what happened. They said no, there's no such thing."

"Do you remember that girl who died in the morning?" Busi interjects. "She was sick when she came."

Liyanda presses on: "And one of the boys said he saw a fireball. It was going down the stairs . . ."

Busi's comment about the sick girl who died seems unrelated at first. Liyanda is recounting uGogo's appearance directly, the up-close chaos of her existence. Busi has touched on something else, another trauma that she witnessed inside Point Place. I learn about the circumstances of this particular death from Ofentse:

"She came to Point Place. She came when the HIV was, what do you call it?"

"AIDS?" I prod.

"Yeah, it was AIDS. Like a week before she died, she couldn't stand up. She couldn't go to the toilet. She couldn't do anything."

"Why did she come to Point Place?"

"Someone dumped her there."

"Who looked after her?"

"We did, we tried, but she was violent. She was weak, but she was violent. And she died there in the girls' room with her eyes open."

"The girls saw this?" I am incredulous.

"Yeah, and we were scared to sleep in that room for about a week."

"Who took the woman out?"

"The police. Oh, it was heartbreaking. They put her in a plastic bag. It was like an animal died."

This illness, then—far from being unrelated to uGogo—is intimately connected to the same suffering and distress, to the same sense of panic and fright, to the same feeling of being stuck and broken, dumped and bagged, unclaimed and unfetched from Point Place.

Significance

* * *

Ofentse and I are sitting at our usual luncheonette, this time with Sisi's younger sister, Tombi, beside us. Tombi and Sisi are close as sisters and regard each other as protective companions, yet they are not at all similar in temperament or appearance. Whereas Sisi is reserved and contained, short and compact, Tombi is loud and gregarious, tall and gangly. She happily chats away about anything and everything, and quite often nothing, her outspokenness a noticeable contrast to Sisi's taciturn nature. The interview

setting, the formalities of obtaining participatory consent, and the recording device do not detract from Tombi's candor. She continues to reveal all,
speaking with total abandon. We learn inadvertently from her why uGogo
visits Sisi, the thing that Sisi did at home. Ofentse and I are not prepared for
Tombi's disclosure. Tombi herself seems surprised at her own indiscretion,
widening her eyes and covering her mouth as if she would like to take back
what has been said. Her explanation of uGogo confirms what many youth
at Point Place already have speculated: uGogo appears most vividly to the
guilty, to those who have committed terrible offenses.

*   *   *

In isiZulu, the power of anger—again to refer to Berglund's (1976:255) work—
sits in the soft palate of the mouth, called *ililaka*. Anger, wrath, and passion
all are known as *ulaka*; the plural form, *amalaka*, also refers to the inner
throat and tonsils, which form part of *ililaka*, too. Anger, in other words,
resides in the throat. To choke a person and smother all breath thus signals
more than an act of bodily violence. Symbolically it suggests the crushing of
passion, the suppression of procreative life in its most elemental form. Such
strangulated, twisted destruction evokes significations of a certain kind. To
clarify these significations, I turn to the physical placements of anger, to the
legitimate and illegitimate holdings of the throat.

According to Berglund (1976:255), legitimate and illegitimate anger rest
in different parts of the throat. Legitimate anger occupies the interior of the
throat, the site of eloquent speech and song; illegitimate anger occupies the
upper throat and nasal passages, the site of obstinate talk. The first promotes
order and discipline, adherence to a good and moral life. The *amadlozi*, for
example, are capable of inflicting illness and misfortune. Their wrath, while at
times implacable, is justified, a retributive measure meant to enforce proper
respect. Illegitimate anger is quite different. It leads to disorder and destruction. The wrath of witches typifies the wrath of illegitimate anger, for it is
counterproductive and unjustifiable (Berglund 1976:255–256).

The Point Place youth do not distinguish legitimate and illegitimate anger
in Berglund's terms, yet they do recognize uGogo's homicidal fury. To strangle
a person, even in a nightmare, as Ofentse explains, is an attack that is more
intimate and, arguably, more devastating than a stabbing or shooting, because
it invokes associations of evil spirits. Berglund's (1976:256) respondents offer similar explanations, correlating this type of assault to witches and to a
deliberate attack on one's life and dignity. They also note that strangulation
entails a particular kind of action. It means that talking—and the possibility
of reconciliation—is over.

*   *   *

"*ePoint Place indawo yokufa! Kungcono nibuyela emakini kunokuthi nife nje nge'ntutwani!*" (Point Place is a place of death! It's better if you return home than die like ants!) Yogi screamed his despair to everyone and to no one in particular: to the bustling city traffic, to the thronging pedestrians, to the paramedics who arrived forty minutes too late. A young boy had just died on the streets. He bled out first from his nose and then his mouth. It became a torrent of blood clots and vomit, soaking his clothes, spilling onto the sidewalk, leaving an indelible puddle. The boy died from untreated tuberculosis. The week before, another boy from Point Place had passed away. He was eating a donut while crossing the road, licking the grease from the waxy paper, when a truck ran the traffic light and mowed him down. His intestines spilled out onto the pavement, his arms and legs contorted into strange positions. He, too, died in front of everyone.

Shortly after Yogi's outburst, shortly after the deaths of his two young companions, uGogo returned to Point Place. Ofentse sensed it a few hours beforehand. She felt an electric shock when she touched Yogi. Her hair stood on end. Concerned, she cornered Sisi and gazed into her eyes. They were clear. Even so, Ofentse warned her friends about the possible coming. To protect her son, she burned *impepho*—a dried plant of everlasting flowers meant to cleanse the air and appease the *amadlozi*. That same evening, Yogi tore up his bed, overturned the cupboards, smashed the dishes, and broke down the door. uGogo had been gone for nearly a year but then reappeared again during the early winter months of my field stay to renew another cold season of death and destruction—to Yogi, to Sisi, and to many others living inside Point Place.

*   *   *

"You know that Yogi? How he is when he has that thing of his? He said something is choking him. He woke up, and he fought with the tables." Liyanda shakes her head as she speaks, contemplating the disturbances in her bedroom the night before.

Shoo! Nineteen-year-old Chester slides off his chair, settling closer to Liyanda, who is sitting on the floor. "What did you do?"

"I held my boyfriend tight. Ha! I held him tight. Yogi had his thing. He was hitting the tables, just here he flipped the table."

Chester nods knowingly. He heard Liyanda's boyfriend speaking about it earlier on.

"We reminded Yogi of it in the morning. He laughed at us."

"Hmm," Chester muses, "why do all these boys see uGogo? I haven't seen uGogo. There's no uGogo that's coming to Chester!"

Yogi and Sisi figure as the catalysts of uGogo, but their stories are not the only ones. Other narratives intersect, the significations of uGogo extending to all those who reside within Point Place. Thus I look to the recurring patterns of uGogo, to the R1 coin and strangulation, to the mediating symbols of life and death. To this I add the red candle. Although it was brought in and ignited by Yogi, its flame flickers on many, even on the disbelieving. For irrespective of the hand that lit it, the red candle imparts certain associations of malicious activity. Thus even Chester, who is skeptical of uGogo, prefers white candles to red, because, as he explains, their pearly reflections offer better protection from the darkness and the unknown.

*　　*　　*

The witch, by most South African accounts, is typically older, female, and childless. She wants to cause suffering and enjoys it immensely, wreaking havoc on everything that is considered good, decent, and upright in society.[11] She usually operates at night and, according to the Point Place youth, conducts her nefarious work by the light of red candles, not white. Yet, while alienated from daily society, the witch does not necessarily act alone. Often she employs others—"familiars"—to carry out her evil intentions. In the rural areas, a horde of familiars—baboons, owls, dogs, cats, and snakes—fall under the witch's dominion. In the urban areas, a special familiar, the *tikoloshe*, predominates. The *tikoloshe* is a hypersexual being renowned for its excessive body hair, short stature, and massive penis. The witch not only dispatches *tikoloshe* to perform wicked deeds, she also utilizes them for her own sexual purposes. Such depraved, immoral passion sets the witch apart yet again. Her sexuality is not productive or naturally generative; it is manipulative and abnormal. Like her sterile womb, it is entirely perverse.

To control her familiars, the witch utilizes *umuthi*. Not inconsequentially for the Point Place youth, the rural areas—with their strange, traditional ways—feature as the preeminent site of *umuthi*-making. As Jabulani explains, "You see, here in town you'll find *umuthi*. But you're not going to find strong *umuthi*. You'll just find weak. Because why? Here in town they buy it. In the farms they make it for themselves." Still, even in the cities, the allure of quick money and instant gratification—always at the expense of others—provides plenty of fodder for occult activity.[12] To illustrate these gains, Jabulani calls for an impromptu display.

"You see if I'm a witch." Jabulani looks around and zeroes in on Shorty sitting on the bed. "I'll want to use him." Jabulani deftly raises Shorty's shirt and presses his fingers against Shorty's stomach. "I'll cut him here and here. I'll put *umuthi* all over his body so he'll listen to me."

Laughing nervously, Shorty leans back.

Undeterred, Jabulani pushes Shorty forward. "He'll be my uGogo now." Jabulani emphasizes his say-so with a small jab to Shorty's arm. "He'll go into town. If I send him to kill somebody, he'll go. I even can send him to steal money from a bank."

As Jabulani speaks, another friend—who has been quiet up until then—enters the fray. "Zulu witch, *tikoloshe*!" he spontaneously exclaims.

Laughter erupts from us all, for Shorty, much to our amusement and to his chagrin, has been transformed into a sexually manipulated, profit-seeking *tikoloshe*.[13] To clarify this hirsute association, I ask if uGogo is related to a *tikoloshe*, if they somehow are the same.

"Yes," Jabulani responds, "I think uGogo is like a *tikoloshe* because you can't see her but she can see you. Yes, and like a *tikoloshe*, you can't see it but it can see you." For Jabulani, the simultaneous invisibility and presence of uGogo conjures up features comparable to a *tikoloshe*.

Although Jabulani readily accepts uGogo as being similar to a *tikoloshe*, other respondents reject this line of questioning. For example, Vusi, a seventeen-year-old male, prefers to compare uGogo to a ghost. "Eh, that thing, uGogo, she was like a miracle or something, like a ghost getting you, controlling you, shaking you."

Meanwhile, Bongi, who is nineteen and a self-professed Christian, describes uGogo as something closer to an ancestor. "See, I don't believe in ghosts," she says. "I really don't, but I was scared even though I don't believe in ghosts."

"So you think uGogo was a ghost?" I ask, hoping for clarification.

"Yeah, sort of," Bongi replies. "Like the *amadlozi*."

Twenty-three-year-old Andile represents another point of view. His understanding of uGogo changes numerous times even within the same interview. "uGogo," he begins, "I can say that she's a zombie, something of the night. She died inside." Sometime later he adds, "uGogo was not a *tikoloshe*. She was a ghost." And then again on further reflection, "You see a thing of the night, like a zombie, it can't come to a place that has electricity. uGogo was somebody's thing. That's why she was able to come to Point Place—she was sent by another person. There are people who want to destroy you. They use *umuthi*. A person just cries, cries, cries."

Andile's narrative, which is difficult to follow, adds to the mystical aura of uGogo. She is an elusive figure, impossible to grasp or fully comprehend. Andile's statement "uGogo was somebody's thing" reflects this ambiguity,

the uncertainties of her presence: Is uGogo a thing of the night? A familiar
sent by a witch? Or is she a personal thing? Something specifically related to
Sisi and Yogi? Andile's free-floating associations make it difficult to tell. Still,
while apprehensive of uGogo, he also cautions, "You mustn't take the things
that are not the truth because it happens that it's there. It's the things from
their homes." In other words, we should not believe in uGogo too much, for
she relates to matters beyond our experiential perceptions.

Andile, I subsequently learn, will not encounter uGogo for two other
reasons as well. One, he has the protection of his *amadlozi*: "Yeah, *amadlozi*,
they're here next to me." And two, he holds on to something that many of the
other Point Place youth have long since relinquished: "The way that uGogo
came, I can say it's combined with a certain type of witchcraft. Not really
strong, though. There's another thing, too. You must have hope. The thing
that causes uGogo not to come to me . . . I trust in God."

Andile's discussion of the supernatural is typical of the Point Place youth.
Despite different religious backgrounds and personal upbringings—from the
rural areas and from the townships, as Christians and as traditional faith fol-
lowers, as Zulus, Xhosas, and Sotho—they share a common recognition that
some forces are beyond their control. And so they act accordingly, drawing
on many different cosmologies and practices to protect themselves as much
as possible from illness, harm, and misfortune. uGogo is the fractured com-
posite of such cosmologies. She relates to the collective experiences of the
Point Place youth, to the untimely deaths and joint suffering. She also relates
to the setting of Point Place, to its internal degradations and disconnections.
Just as significantly, uGogo—as a grandmother figure—relates to the homes of
the Point Place youth. I thus conclude this chapter with the untimely passing
of Sisi. Her death reveals the immense violence and insecurity of everyday
living, not only on the streets but also in the home.[14]

*   *   *

"Cockroaches! Look, cockroaches!" A burnished insect, its legs protruding
upward, is moving in my mutton gravy. My appetite gone, I push my plate
away. "Cockroaches!" Tombi gleefully declares, this time swiveling in her
chair so that all the surrounding patrons can hear.

"Shhh!" Ofentse hisses. Tombi flashes her a lopsided grin, revealing two
crooked front teeth and matching dimples. Neither Ofentse nor I can resist
Tombi's charm, a liveliness that flickers most unexpectedly. We laugh and
contemplate our old haunt, the luncheonette, now—three years later—gone
horribly wrong. Still, meat is meat, and in due course Tombi rescues our
fare, scraping the contents of our plates into a takeout container. Spoonful

by spoonful, she sloshes up the gravy, dribbling it on our leftovers. She hums a familiar chant. Suddenly I have a memory of Sisi: *A tradeoff you'll never see!* The tune dwindles. Tombi's movements slow, then stop altogether. She is quiet, uncharacteristically so.

"Are you stressed?" Ofentse gently asks. Tombi looks at us unable to respond. "You miss your mother?" Tombi nods yes. Her mother passed away six months previously. "And Sisi?" Tombi's hand quivers. The spoon, dripping with gravy, dangles in midair and drops. It lands with a splattering thud on the floor. Tombi bursts into tears. The serving ladies glance our way questioningly.

*   *   *

"How did it happen?" I later ask Ofentse. "How did Sisi die?"

"It wasn't easy, not easy at all. Remember I called you?"

"I know, but I was back in the U.S. then."

"Yeah, you were far. But me, I was close to everything—Sisi and Tombi, their mother. I saw it all."

"How so?"

"I went to Sisi's home the day before she died."

"Can you tell me about the visit?"

"It's hard."

"Oh."

"No, it's not what you think. I made promises. Promises I couldn't keep."

"To Tombi?"

"No, to her grandmother."

I am confused. "There's an uGogo, a grandmother, in the home? How can that be?" And then it dawns on me. The thing Sisi did at home—not at the home of her mother, but at the home of her father, a father whom Sisi and Tombi do not share. Sisi, in a fit of rage, set the house ablaze. She left her uGogo asleep there, to asphyxiate from smoke inhalation, to burn unaware.

"Imagine," Ofentse echoes my thoughts. "Imagine."

"And the promise?"

"I will tell you."

*   *   *

Ofentse gazes at me steadily. She takes a deep breath. "I didn't see Sisi, not at first."

"You didn't see her?"

"No, not *see*, like recognize, I didn't recognize her. She looked so old, so very old."

"Is this when you went to her home?"

"No, this was at the hospital. I took Sisi there—at the mother's request."

"How did the mother know you?"

"She called me. Sisi or Tombi must have given her my number. She asked me to visit them."

"And you did?"

"Yeah. You know, I didn't expect it, but their home is nice. Four rooms, I'd say. Still, I could tell something was wrong, something besides Sisi's illness."

"Like what?"

"It was so quiet there. Usually if somebody is sick, really sick, neighbors will help out. You know, with the cooking and housework, stuff like that."

"How did the mother and grandmother receive you?"

"They were happy to see me, asked me how I knew Sisi and Tombi. When I told them, they didn't look at me funny, you know, the way folks sometimes do when they hear kids are staying alone in town."

"Because they think it's wrong?"

"Yeah, especially if you're a girl. But they understood. The situation. We can't stay at home. The grandmother wanted to know more about town, about Point Place. How we get food, if there's work, if anyone helps us, that sort of thing. That's when Tombi left the room."

"Why?"

"She knew what was coming next. She went outside to cry."

"Because of Sisi, of her illness?"

"Because of what they couldn't do for her—the burial. They couldn't afford it."

"But you said the house was nice, well kept?"

"Yeah, but they never applied for Sisi's ID. And so later when she got sick, they couldn't include her in their coverage, their funeral policy. The father's family wanted no part of it, refused to help with the costs."

"So how was she buried? Without a service?"

"That's when I made my promise. I told them I could take Sisi to the hospital."

"The hospital doesn't give out coffins, does it?"

"No."

"They incinerate?"

"Yeah, and if the body is unclaimed . . ."

"A mass grave?"

"The bodies, the ashes, they're all mixed up."

"Did Sisi hear any of this?"

"No, she was in the far corner of the room, sleeping."

* * *

I scour my field notes looking for a special entry, a phone call in the middle of the night from Ofentse telling me of Sisi's untimely passing. I find it—a testimony, a skeletal memory that I flesh out years later at our luncheonette.

Sisi stirs. Ofentse stands up to attend to her ailing friend. Sunken eyes gaze at the ceiling unseeingly, then focus, flash with recognition. Sisi smiles, her lips cracking with the effort. She wants to show Ofentse something. The blanket, Ofentse helps Sisi fold it down, revealing protruding collarbones, emaciated arms, and jutting ribs. Lower still she folds the blanket. Sisi moves her fingers to the hem of her dressing gown. She twists it to the side, exposing her thighs, her private parts. Rooted near her groin, a lump rests. It shines brightly, tightly. It covers the entirety of her pudenda.

"What is it?" Sisi wonders.

Ofentse does not have a ready answer. Later she asks me.

I do not know, either. But I think back to Yogi's imvilapho, to his hidden sore now visible for everyone to see. uGogo's tradeoff: uncompromising and unstoppable.

"Touch it," Sisi asks of Ofentse. "Touch it."

"But it might burst."

"I think we should let it."

6 Homecomings

Thulile did not die inside Point Place. She was murdered inside another building a few blocks away. That building, a gutted store, is similar to Point Place: no running water, electricity, or sanitation services. It too is occupied by street youth, although they are fewer in number because the space is smaller and the security tighter. That particular night the security was lax, the guard asleep in his chair, oblivious to the transpiring events.

Thulile entered the store discreetly, accompanied by another boy from the streets. Both of them were unaware that they were being watched. Like most of the younger adolescents, Thulile split her time between the streets, children's shelters, and her home. She often stayed at Point Place to visit her boyfriend, Hlanyo, an older youth known for his jealousy. Thulile thought she had slipped away from Hlanyo's domineering control, but she was wrong. He followed the couple inside the building and waited for them at the bottom of the stairs. Thulile's lover descended first, perceived Hlanyo's homicidal intent, and jumped out the window. Thulile was not so quick. Hlanyo stabbed her in the stomach and dragged her down the remaining stairs, depositing her body on the floor. Shortly thereafter, her lover returned with his friends, but they were too late. Thulile was dead.

I learn about Thulile's death the next day. Yogi tells me first, then Ofentse, then several other kids. Their stories are the same: Hlanyo murdered Thulile. Her funeral will be held the following Saturday. Many of the Point Place youth would like to attend, and I agree to help with the transportation costs. I am told, though, that I must visit Thulile's family on my own beforehand. I need to make sure that the youth from Point Place are welcome. Hlanyo was one of them, and they may be blamed for Thulile's death.

By this juncture in my field stay, I am familiar with home visits. I know what to expect from the family members: a great deal of perplexity and pain. To leave home at a young age, either by choice or by force, is a shameful thing. To return home, especially after an extended period of time, brings up these memories in a raw way. My foreign presence adds to this anxiety, for the family does not understand my involvement or interest in their child. Am I a social worker, a police officer, or a girlfriend? Am I responsible for their leaving home, for their staying inside Point Place? How am I connected? The prospect of encountering these questions—with the added despair of a murder—is daunting. It also is why I am sent ahead before the arrival of an entire congregation of runaway youth. I know enough not to go alone. I take Ofentse and a young woman named Alice who grew up next door to Thulile.

We let Alice lead the way. She directs us to a township outside the city center. During the journey, she shows us the homes of other youth we know from Point Place. Their dwellings, perched on craggy hills, are modest; some are wattle and daub shacks, while others are constructed from cinderblock and plaster. Thulile's family is better off than most. Their home has several independent structures arranged around a well-swept courtyard. Ofentse and Alice urge me to straighten my skirt and cover my shoulders with a sweater before I enter the main house. An older man opens the door for us, motioning for us to sit down on the couch. A woman sits on a mattress in the far corner of the room, a single white candle lit by her side. She keeps her back to us and does not speak. I assume that she is Thulile's mother. Alice expresses her sorrow to the elderly couple. She talks softly, her eyes gazing downward. The older man accepts her condolences and asks whether she will accompany them to the site of Thulile's death. The family needs to collect Thulile's spirit; otherwise their *amadlozi* (ancestors) will be restless. Alice agrees to his request. As we leave, more neighbors enter the house, a steady stream of sympathetic mourners.

On the day of Thulile's funeral, thirty-two youth from Point Place cram into two *kombis*. Our initial reception at the funeral is welcoming. An older man ushers us underneath a tent and encourages us to sit in the fold-back chairs. This treatment changes once the other mourners arrive. Family members ask the youth from Point Place to rise. They are directed to a space outside the tent, and I join them. About twenty minutes into the service, the same older man offers me a chair in the shade. I gratefully accept and leave my companions, who now are crouching in the dirt, talking among themselves. I sit next to Themba, the only Point Place youth who is seated, for he is too weak to stand.

From the chairs, I have a different vantage point. I can see the disapproving looks of the mourners. They are upset by the Point Place youth's noisy chatter and disregard for the sermon and gospel songs. The young people's attire offends them as well. Most of the females are wearing short skirts; a few are dressed in pants. I hear whispered comments about respectable appearances. Later, after the funeral, some of the girls express their sense of shame. Others are angry, saying that they would wear nice outfits if they could afford them. In between the low murmurings, I listen to the sermon. The minister speaks in a pure isiZulu, which I understand quite well compared to the mixed slang often spoken on the streets. It also helps that the minister's litany is repetitive and predictable: Young people should stay at home and respect their elders. They should attend school and help with household chores. They should work hard so they can become proud and prosperous adults one day. Those seated in chairs nod in agreement, sending directed glances at the Point Place youth. I do not think my companions notice, though, for they are preoccupied with the rising dust, overhead sun, and biting bugs. Most of them have left anyway, walking behind the hill to talk to one another and smoke without interruption.

*   *   *

In many respects, Thulile's funeral can be seen as an example of the intergenerational rifts between youth and adults in post-apartheid South Africa (Ashforth 2005; Comaroff and Comaroff 1999a). From the perspective of the elderly mourners, the Point Place youth fail to uphold the duties and obligations of a normatively "proper" filial subject: one who is law-abiding; tightly integrated into the collectivities of the household and community; aware of status hierarchies, including those of gender and age; and respectful of authority figures. The minister's sermon espouses many of these ideals and responsibilities, which he connects to the home as a site of nurturance and discipline. In contrast to the home, the street is a site of danger and depravity, a place where youth perpetuate lawlessness and fall victim to crime. These constructs are not unique to the minister's sermon; in South African popular culture, too, commentators often express the moralities of the home through the perceived immoralities of the streets.

The 2003 film *Beat the Drum* illustrates this dichotomy most vividly with its coming-of-age story about a young boy, Musa, who leaves his homestead in KwaZulu-Natal to look for a job in the city of Johannesburg. The movie presents a classic South African tale of rural-urban migration, in which Musa refuses to compromise the values of his home for the vices of the streets—crime, drugs, sex, and violence. Hence, we never see him without his school uniform, which remains amazingly well pressed throughout the film, or his cowhide drum—both symbols of youthful industriousness. The film ends with Musa unable to return home, for his grandmother already is overburdened with children who have experienced the loss of their parents due to HIV/AIDS. Instead Musa goes to an orphanage and reunites with other youth in similarly vulnerable circumstances.

The film thus presents the home and the street as incompatible social worlds. Musa cannot remain in either and finds himself in the position of accepting welfare assistance from the state and its benevolent benefactors. He is lucky to have a way out. The Point Place youth rarely, if ever, have such options once they reach the age of sixteen. Rather, in order to survive, they constantly move back and forth between the home and the street. This chapter looks to the cultural salience of these oppositional categories while also recognizing that their boundaries, even as spatial constructs, are far from clear-cut. For the residents of Point Place, home life is not so different from street life, and street life is not so different from home life.

*   *   *

To the question "Why do you reside on the streets?" the Point Place youth invariably respond, "Because of the situation." "The situation" refers to a number of difficulties in their homes. It refers to poverty and unemployment, to familial illnesses and deaths, to substance addictions and physical and emotional abuse. Broadly speaking, it refers to material constraints and traumas, to societal and economic inequalities that, from an individual standpoint, cannot be overcome. Taken as a whole, "the situation" provides a compelling explanation for why youth live on the streets instead of in their homes. On closer inspection, however, it accounts for very little internal variation. It does not explain why, within the same household, one child leaves and another remains. It does not differentiate the moments of disaffection, when the street becomes not just a viable but a desirable alternative to the home.

Certainly many youth stay on the street to support the home.[1] Those who come from the surrounding townships of Durban often visit their family homes, bringing back part of their earnings from the city as well as food and clothing donations from charitable organizations. They impart knowledge, too, for they are familiar with the welfare services of the state. Yet, while offering many advantages, the departures of these youth never rest easy with their kinsfolk. Their absences challenge the ideological constructs of the home as a site of nurturance, obedience, and respect. Just as worrisome, their departures make the estrangements within the home visible to everyone who sees them living, seemingly unsupervised and unwanted, on the streets.

In the remainder of this chapter, I address the estrangements of the home through extended ethnographic vignettes that detail the life stories of four Point Place youth: Angel and Chester, who come from the surrounding townships of Durban, and Jabulani and Liyanda, who come from the rural areas of KwaZulu-Natal. In each case, their families struggle to maintain a basic level of subsistence; they also struggle to maintain control over their children. This chapter focuses on these intrahousehold conflicts; it details the problems of the home from the perspective of the Point Place youth and their kinsfolk. While often contentious, in some cases these perspectives converge as youth and their elders share a common understanding of "the situation." It is an understanding that links the material deprivations of the home to the profound insecurities of kinship—to incomplete marital alliances, inactive lineages, and unfulfilled filial obligations. Thus, this chapter focuses not only on the living but also on the deceased—that is, the *amadlozi*.

*   *   *

Angel's Home Situation

Angel and Chester are the best of friends. While they are longtime companions, they have never dated each other, which possibly explains the resilience of their friendship. Chester, like many of the older males, takes a protective attitude toward Angel. On the streets he shields her from bullies. Inside Point Place he shares his food, dagga, and glue with her. When Angel is sick, Chester accompanies her to the tuberculosis clinic. When she needs transport fare, he gives what he can spare. Angel trusts Chester wholeheartedly. She even introduces him to her family, a decision that she does not extend to her boyfriend, Zakes, claiming that he is too ugly to take home.

> *Several of us are searching for Angel. Her father, Mr. Shangase, has come to Thuthukani to speak with her. He wants his daughter to return home for the Christmas holidays. We look everywhere but cannot find Angel, for she is in hiding, her body pressed flat against the rooftop above us. Once, in passing, Angel described her father to me as a stern man with a pointed beard. Mr. Shangase does not appear stern to me, merely sad and beleaguered.*
> *The care workers inform Mr. Shangase about Angel's illness, her constant coughing and rapid weight loss. They also remark on her changing skin color, a splotchy yellow. Angel has tuberculosis but refuses to seek treatment at the FOSA clinic, which is located outside*

the city center. She knows the nurses will keep her there and not allow her to participate in the holiday festivities. Angel promises to go to the clinic after the New Year's celebrations. For now, she does not want her father to see her looking so sickly. Unable to find his daughter, Mr. Shangase leaves Thuthukani, a dejected, solitary figure.

Nearly six months later, Angel, Chester, and I are sitting on a wooden bench inside Angel's home—a three-room shack perched on the side of an eroded hill. Angel wants me to speak with her father, and her mother, too, if she happens to be home. I am curious to meet Angel's family. The Point Place females often taunt Angel, saying that her mother is a bag lady. Because of this, Angel prefers to keep company with the boys. They are less likely to torment her. They also are less likely to steal her clothes. Today, though, she is not thinking about taunts or thefts. She recently has been released from the tuberculosis clinic and looks happy, healthy, and well fed. To atone for her behavior from last Christmas, she has decided to spend the Easter weekend with her family.

"Will my daughter remain at home now?" Mr. Shangase directs this question to me. He thinks I am a social worker (because Angel told him so). I reply uneasily that Angel must decide for herself. Mr. Shangase looks expectantly at his daughter. Angel explains, rather convincingly, that it is better for her to remain in the city so that she can pick up her medication. Traveling back and forth from home would be too expensive. Mr. Shangase's face falls in disappointment, but then, contemplating the pragmatism of her words, he nods his head in agreement. Angel, I know, is lying. The nurses instructed her to return home. She can pick up the tuberculosis pills from a number of clinics nearby.

To redirect the conversation, Angel opens the parcels of food we brought from the city center. Mr. Shangase flashes a smile at the display of sausage, rice, and canned fruit sitting on the floor. I am not sure where else we can put the bags, because the kitchen table, chairs, and counter already are covered with piles of mismatched shoes, many of which have fallen to the floor. Mr. Shangase tells me that he is a shoemaker. He has a small business in town, a wooden stall erected on the side of a busy road. Because it is not a secure location, he often brings his wares home.

As we contemplate the crowded arrangements, Angel's mother appears in the doorway. The resemblance between Angel and her mother is uncanny, leaving little doubt about their biological connection. The marital status of Angel's parents, however, is ambiguous. At times they claim to be married, and

Figure 11. The kitchen in Angel's home.

at other times not. The house belongs to Mr. Shangase. The five children—an older sister who passed away, Angel, a younger sister, and twin brothers—took Mr. Shangase's surname, while their mother, Ms. Ngcobo, retains the surname of her own patrilineage.

After greeting us, Ms. Ngcobo flits from room to room, searching for something to show us. "Ah-ha!" She plucks a card out from a stack of papers shoved above the doorsill. A few receipts and an outstanding payment due notice drift down as well. Ms. Ngcobo hands Angel the card. It is an invitation announcing a coming-of-age party, an *umemulo* ceremony for Angel's cousin, the daughter of Ms. Ngcobo's younger brother. Ms. Ngcobo expresses excitement about the party. Angel shows much less enthusiasm. Oblivious to her misgivings, Ms. Ngcobo invites us to attend. The party is being held the following Saturday. I agree, hoping that Angel will stay home for the full week. Chester and I say our goodbyes. On Monday morning, Angel is back inside Point Place.

The following Saturday, Chester and I again convene on the wooden bench of the Shangases' kitchen. Angel and her mother are in the bedroom, sifting through secondhand clothes. To pass the time, I flip through a family photo album, which features several pictures of Angel smiling, her cheeks plump and round. Chester nudges me, and I look up. I reach for my camera, but I am too late. Angel—dressed in an orange ruffled frock—has fled to the back room. A few minutes later, she reemerges wearing more citified attire, a miniskirt and matching crop top. A self-conscious grin lingers on her face.

Finally, with outfits in order, we leave the Shangase home to take a *kombi* to another part of the township. As we wind our way along the hills, I notice a change in scenery, indicating a gradual transition from an informal to a formal settlement. The dirt road becomes a paved one; dust no longer billows behind us. The front gates to homes are higher, the chicken wire replaced with metal bars. Ms. Ngcobo announces our destination, and we lurch to a stop in front of a modest ranch house. It belongs to her youngest sister, Tilly. She works at a bank and makes a decent living, which explains the nice dwelling. Aunt Tilly plans to attend the *umemulo* ceremony as well.

We enter the house. It is spacious, well lit, and uncluttered—the exact opposite of the Shangase home. I notice a complete living room set, as well as a television, DVD player, and surround-sound stereo speakers. Delighted by our presence, Aunt Tilly ushers us to the overstuffed chairs and couch, giving us little time to settle in before she launches into a rapid succession of questions, all directed at Angel: "Where do you live? Who do you stay with? Why don't you like your home? What troubles you there? Why do you pretend not to know me when I see you on the streets?" To this last question, Angel looks confused. Aunt Tilly ends her inquisition with an offer for Angel to stay with her in her large house, where she can have her own room. Angel does not answer; she merely smiles abashedly like her mother, who also is listening to the exchange.

Abruptly, Aunt Tilly changes the subject matter. She brings up the problem of her twenty-year-old son, who has not spoken in the last two years. She had him committed to a mental institution, but he was released after a few months for unspecified reasons. Now, instead of psychiatrists, Aunt Tilly relies on the help of herbalists and diviners. On hearing this, Chester perks up. His mother is an *isangoma* (diviner) and may know of a way to heal Aunt Tilly's son. Aunt Tilly contemplates Chester's suggestion. She also appraises his appearance, noting that his clothes are too nice for him to be staying on the streets.

Aunt Tilly leads us to one of the bedrooms to meet her son. She throws open the door and in a booming voice calls out, "Hello, my child, look who came to visit!" She urges him to greet us, but he only twitches, startled by the noise. Unnerved, I direct my attention to the rest of the room, where, at the far end, several buckets stand clustered together. I peer closer. They are filled with chunky brown water. Aunt Tilly explains that she will do anything to help her son, even if it means paying for expensive medicines. Suddenly inspired, she shakes him: "Speak! Speak, child! A special doctor has come all the way from the United States of America just to see you! You must talk!" As before, he does not answer.

Resigned to the silence, Aunt Tilly ushers us back to the living room. She pulls out a photo album, which contains pictures of her son as a child. She cannot understand the change in his behavior. Growing up, he was a normal, healthy boy with lots of friends. She looks over to Chester and Angel, who are engaged in a low conversation. "Is he her boyfriend?" she asks, but before I can respond, she inquires, "Perhaps my son would be happier in town, like them?" Angel lifts her head in alarm at this suggestion. To deter her aunt, she explains that the other kids would drive her son even crazier; they would cause him to do funny things, like sniff glue. Aunt Tilly nods her head knowingly. The doctors once told her that a drug overdose caused her son to lose his mind. She accepts their diagnosis yet attributes his mental illness to another intervening factor as well—the *amadlozi*.

Aunt Tilly believes that the *amadlozi* are fighting over her son, leaving him "mixed up." As a single mother, she neglected to perform certain rites that should have been conducted on the father's side of the family. The two lineages never united. Now her son does not know how to act properly. With this explanation, Aunt Tilly looks over to her sister, Ms. Ngcobo. I anticipate a similar justification for Angel's desire to leave home, but Aunt Tilly surprises me and does not refer to the ambiguous marital arrangement of Angel's parents. Instead she remarks on how good it is of me to treat Ms. Ngcobo like everyone else. Although she is the oldest, she is the poorest of all the siblings.

From Aunt Tilly's house, we walk a few blocks to the brother's house. We are late for the actual *umemulo* ceremony but arrive in time for the meal. On entering the house, Aunt Tilly announces to everyone that I am there to observe Zulu customs. She orders some younger girls to move aside and make room for me on the couch. All of them are dressed formally. The cousin is dressed best of all, in a cream-colored gown with ornate beadwork. Nobody greets Angel, who, in her miniskirt and crop top, looks miserably out of place. Angel ends up sharing a chair with Chester. Ms. Ngcobo asks for a plate of food from some of the women standing nearby. They inform her that plates will be passed out in due course. I immediately receive one. I try to give it to Ms. Ngcobo, but she tells me no, she will receive one next. Shortly thereafter I see Aunt Tilly eating. Even Chester has a plate, which he shares with Angel. Finally, Ms. Ngcobo receives a plate of food. All of us pretend not to notice the late offering.

A young woman places a hunk of roasted goat meat on the coffee table in front of us. Another young woman, one of the formally dressed girls, tears off a large piece for herself. The older women laugh at her audacity. She should have waited for them to take their share first. The tension around the coffee table lessens, enough so that Ms. Ngcobo feels no inhibition in taking a piece of meat for herself. After finishing the meal, she announces that it is time for us to leave. We walk across the street to the bus stop. Chester and I plan to return to Durban. Angel wants to join us, but she dares not step on the bus in front of so many discerning relatives. The bus arrives, and Ms. Ngcobo asks me to wait a moment. She fishes around in her purse and pulls out a chocolate mint. She places it in my hand and thanks me for bringing Angel back home. I board the bus. From the window, Chester waves goodbye and promises that he will speak to his mother about Aunt Tilly's son in a few weeks' time.

* * *

Chester's Home Situation

Chester's home is similar to Aunt Tilly's, although it is not as nicely furnished. The main house consists of a long rectangular structure. A small square house also sits on the property. This is where Chester sleeps when he visits his family, usually only for a night or two. I have been to Chester's home several times before and know what to expect: a grandmother who will put him to work. Chester accedes to all of Granny's demands. He fixes the busted front door, prepares lunch, and tells her amusing stories. For this particular visit, I bring Ofentse with me, because I plan to formally interview Chester's family. I still do not understand why he ran away from home at such a young age. As with many of the Point Place youth, the exact reasons are unclear.

We wait for Chester's mother in the living room. A series of framed photographs hang on the wall—portraits of deceased family members. Chester points out his grandfather, a policeman who was gunned down outside their home six years ago. He also shows me a picture of a smiling baby, the first child of his oldest sister. The baby died of a protracted illness. I know that Chester's father has passed away, too. I ask which one he might be. Chester explains that there are no photographs of his father, for he did not live with them but stayed in the home of his paternal grandmother a few blocks away. Chester's parents never married. Because of this, Chester prefers to use the name of his mother's family, Ndlovu. He speaks about his father's family with bitterness. Much of this relates to the fact that they do not support the children in the Ndlovu household even though Chester, his older sister, and his two younger brothers share the same father. As Chester notes, "Ever since my father passed away, they've not been taking care of us. You see, when we go to their house, we ask for shoes and clothes for school. They don't take care of it. Only my mother, my granny, and my sister are the ones who're taking care of us all."

The Ndlovu household survives on Granny's pension, child welfare grants, and the wages of the oldest sister, who works in town. The earnings of Chester's mother as an *isangoma*, although irregular, make up the difference. Occasionally Granny sells beer as well. These activities bring trouble, though. Young men, knowing Granny stays home alone, often kick down the front door. Drunk and determined, they threaten her: "Hey! Bring the money, you old lady!"

The presence of someone like Chester would deter such men, but he refuses to remain at home to "guard the plates." As he explains, "I don't want to sit at home just to look after my plate here. I, myself, want to give my mother a plate [of food]."

When Ofentse and I finally meet Ms. Ndlovu, she acknowledges that Chester first left home to help the family. Unlike the other neighborhood children who returned home after a day's work, however, Chester did not come back. Both Granny and Ms. Ndlovu want him to return home. Even after all these years, they have difficulty accepting his decision to live apart from them. As Ms. Ndlovu states, "Is there a parent who doesn't want their child at home? It's the child who doesn't want to stay at home."

To which Granny adds, "We'd be so happy if he returns here at home."

"He just comes and sleeps one day," Ms. Ndlovu explains.

Granny, in particular, is troubled by Chester's wanderings. She thinks he stays with "winkers," an allusion to prostitutes that makes Chester, Ofentse, and me laugh—to which Granny replies in a serious and hurt tone, "You're laughing. But we stay worried here in the house. We don't know if he's dead or in the hospital or in jail. We don't know what happens. We're asking in our hearts if he's dead." Granny's reference to death brings forth a new story from his mother.

Once, on the streets of Durban, three men beat up Chester. They bludgeoned him with a brick and stabbed him four times in the chest. The youth from Point Place phoned Ms. Ndlovu, saying that she must hurry to the hospital, because Chester might not live through the night. In hearing his mother retell the story, Chester asks, "Why don't you just say I was supposed to be here at home because somebody else passed away?" His injuries, I learn, coincided with the death of his sister's baby, the one in the photograph. To explain the reason for his misfortune, he adds, "You see, I was supposed to be here at home, but I didn't know. I didn't know about the baby's passing. So I didn't go home. That's why I was stabbed."

In subsequent conversations, Chester explains that the *amadlozi* deserted him. They were angered by his failure to return home during the baby's illness. He learned about the baby's death only after his mother visited him in the hospital. Recognizing the severity of his breach, he convinced the nurses to discharge him early. It was critical for him to return home to attend the baby's memorial service. Only then might he reconnect with the *amadlozi*. Only then might they look after him again on the streets.

Later I ask Ofentse why Ms. Ndlovu has trouble taking care of what is closest to her—her own children. She speaks with the *amadlozi*. Why can't she ward off misfortune? Why can't she convince Chester to stay at home? Ofentse expresses surprise at my line of questioning. She thought I knew: an *isangoma* can help others, but she cannot stop the forces that shape her own life. And so, before we leave the Ndlovu home, Chester's mother asks us to send a message to Angel. If Aunt Tilly decides to visit, she will need to bring two white candles, a R20 note, and an unwashed shirt belonging to her ill son.

*   *   *

In his introduction to *African Systems of Kinship and Marriage*, A. R. Radcliffe-Brown (1950) discusses kinship as a social relationship. Kinship, according to Radcliffe-Brown, is not constituted through biology. For even descent—the "physical" ties between parents and children—as he famously writes, "is recognized and reckoned" (1950:13). Kinship, in short, is a system of acknowledgment. Hence Radcliffe-Brown (1950:11) speaks of "rights and duties," the rules of behavior that serve to maintain the kinship system as a unified whole. His theorization of kinship as a social and not a biological construction fits well with the views of the Point Place youth, who, as seen in chapter two, frequently draw on idioms of kin to create reciprocal obligations of support and care. Of course, differences exist between their conceptualizations of kinship and Radcliffe-Brown's structural-functionalist theorizations. Radcliffe-Brown (1950:82–83) is primarily concerned with the continuity and stability of society, how the parts of a social structure function to maintain the whole. Thus he tends to present social institutions, like kinship, as intact harmonious systems. The kin relations of the Point Place youth, particularly in their homes, suggest a more fractured existence. Here they cannot choose ties of affiliation; nor can they reimagine or reinvent their kin designations. They can, however, renounce their filial obligations, which they do repeatedly by running away.

The home situations of Angel and Chester reflect this contentiousness among kin. Angel, for instance, fails to greet her aunt on the streets. Although her act is a seemingly small slight, it underscores a common expectation that youth should acknowledge their elders both in the home and outside of it. To counter this rebuff, Aunt Tilly asserts her moral and material domination by offering Angel a room in her house. The proposition is generous but also humiliating, because it draws attention to the impoverished circumstances of Angel's parents.[2] Aware of these status hierarchies, Angel does not reject her aunt's offer directly. Instead she gives a noncommittal smile and expresses her renunciation by returning to her father's home, and later on to the streets.

Chester, meanwhile, rejects his father's family altogether by using his mother's surname. His decision highlights the expectation that kin, even extended kin, should assist their dependents, yet this assistance is not one-way. As mentioned by Chester's mother, it is common for children in her neighborhood to look for work to help support their families. Anthropologists conducting research in Brazil, a country comparable to South Africa in terms of income distribution and inequality, often describe this situation as a class distinction between "nurturing" and "nurtured" childhood. For example, lower-class families living in shantytowns expect children to contribute their wage earnings to the household as well as perform menial chores. These are "nurturing" children, for they look after the everyday subsistence of their families. Middle- and upper-class children, meanwhile, lead a life relatively free from these obligations. Their parents provide for all their needs, often to excess, so they are designated as "nurtured" children (Goldstein 2003; Hecht 1998).

Chester's desire to support his family, and more specifically to give his mother a plate of food, reflects a similar class distinction. Poor youth in South African townships enact a nurturing childhood by seeking out work to help provide for their families. Still, Chester believes that his father's family is remiss in neglecting to recognize him and his siblings as dependent kin and thus entitled to material support—something he refers to by mentioning their failure to buy him and his siblings school shoes and uniforms, which would mark their childhoods as nurtured ones, too. Here, then, the nurturing/nurtured dichotomy is not absolute in its categorical distinction of class privilege. Rather, it reflects a shifting continuum of acknowledgment in which youth link material offerings to the acceptance—and in some cases rejection—of kin relations.

Certainly, the kinsfolk of the Point Place youth, as seen with Angel and Chester, recognize the material conditions that prompt their children to run away. They describe the poverty of their homes and the lack of available jobs. The basic income grants provided by the government lift their economic prospects only marginally. Related to these difficulties, they also remark on the absence of supportive kin, which usually means that a husband/father figure is deceased or estranged from the family.

In regard to his home situation, Chester is typical of the residents of Point Place. It is rare for their parents to be married or living together. Also as with Chester's family, it tends to be the case that when the Point Place youth are at home, they reside primarily with their mother and her kin. Despite normative ideals of patrilineal descent, their households are matrifocal in orientation. The presence of elderly family members such as grandparents is common, too. For with the high prevalence of HIV/AIDS, a substantial segment of the reproductive population—at the generational level of parents—has fallen ill or died.

I learn this most directly by visiting the homes of the Point Place youth, for the demographic surveys administered inside Point Place provided inconsistent answers about the marital and living status of their parents. For instance, many of the residents did not know whether their parents were married, due to various enactments of *ilobolo* and Christian ceremonies. Also, a large number of their parents were deceased or missing. In 2005, out of seventeen homes that I visited, not a single one included a married parent. Only in two homes—those of Angel and Jabulani—did the mother and father consider themselves to be in a committed long-term relationship.

Also, many of the Point Place youth who took part in the surveys were unsure whether their parents were still alive; they had left home when their parents were ill and had not seen or heard from them since. Additionally, many of these youth did not know at least one of their parents—usually their father—at all. Again, then, home visits offered the most reliable information. In 2005, in fourteen of the seventeen homes I visited, at least one parent was deceased or missing. By 2012, all seventeen homes had experienced the death of a parent—which included Angel's and Jabulani's fathers—and seven of them had experienced the death of two parents. The South African Census from 2011 corroborates these findings, as it reports an almost twofold increase in maternal and double orphanhood between 2001 and 2011 (Statistics South Africa 2012b:77).

Such numbers reflect the hardships of the Point Place youth's familial situations. Yet their kinsfolk are just as likely to refer to these difficulties as problems with the *amadlozi*. The *amadlozi*, as apical kin, structure the moral dominion of the home. In much the same way that senior kin members (like grandparents and parents) expect junior kin members (like children) to submit to an age-based hierarchy of rights and duties, the *amadlozi* expect the same from their descendants. If honored with special ceremonies and sacrificial rites, the *amadlozi* protect their descendants. If neglected, they in turn neglect, too.

The kinsfolk of the Point Place youth often remark on their failure to acknowledge the *amadlozi* properly in their homes. They want to rectify the situation, but this is a time-consuming and costly endeavor. It requires ritual specialists and sacrificial animals, like goats and cows. It also requires the participation of attendant kin, many of whom, like the Point Place youth, are missing or estranged from their homes. These rites of offering thus tend not to occur, and when they do, they usually occur only in part (cf. Ashforth 2005:209–219). Such is the case with the families of Jabulani and Liyanda, who, as I describe below, strive to reconcile their kin, living and deceased, but are unable to do so completely.

*   *   *

Jabulani's Home Situation

Ayize, who is twenty, spends the day walking the streets of Durban. She wears a flower-printed dress, clearly meant for an older matron. Her flip-flops, two sizes too big, slide off her feet with every other step. She has traveled to the city without money or food, looking for her older brother. She knows that he resides in the Point Area but is not sure exactly where. In the evening, Ayize finds shelter in a police station, where the officers provide her with a blanket and allow her to sleep on the waiting bench. In the morning they direct her to a downtrodden part of the Point. They have an idea where her brother might reside.

Jabulani is shocked to come across his younger sister standing outside the gates of Point Place. He regards her appearance with trepidation. Why is Ayize crying? Where is her baby? Ayize tells her brother everything that has happened to her over the last several months. Her story is not so different from the stories of the Point Place females.

Ayize left home a few months earlier, pregnant, to live with her boyfriend. He promised to provide for all her needs in town. Yet once the baby was born, he could not support them, so he took Ayize and the baby to the home of his mother, where he left them stranded in the countryside. To make matters worse, his mother made many demands of Ayize. They argued often, until one day the mother kicked Ayize out of the house. Ayize, with nowhere else to go, hitchhiked to Durban. She came alone, unable to bring her baby.

After hearing his sister's story, Jabulani promises that he will help her recover the baby. He decides that they need to secure the help of their own mother, Ms. Dlamini. They will visit her in the morning. Until then, Jabulani makes arrangements for Ayize to spend the night inside Point Place. He chooses the most respectable room possible (that of his best friend), not wanting to expose her to the drinking habits or bad behavior of the Point Place females. Early the next morning, he phones me. He asks whether I will take Ayize home, not to his mother's homestead in rural KwaZulu-Natal, but to an informal settlement known as Tin Town. I have been to Tin Town once before to meet his mother:

> *Jabulani directs my car along a narrow, sludge-mired path lined by homes constructed from mud and wattle and roofed with sheets of corrugated tin. An older woman regards us with an intense look of irritation. Her eyes dare me to make a single mis-turn, for one untracked spin of the tire will send mud flinging onto her drying clothes. I carefully navigate around the laundry lines. I have come to Tin Town to interview Jabulani's mother. Initially I am confused, for Jabulani told me that he grew up in the countryside. Tin Town, although hosting a few garbage-eating goats, does not match my idea of a rural homestead. I later learn that Ms. Dlamini works for the forest company; she lives in Tin Town intermittently, as it is close to her place of employment. From six in the morning until three in the afternoon, she cuts down weeds with a panga, working six days a week, earning R34 a day. It is backbreaking labor, yet Ms. Dlamini does not walk with a stoop. She stands tall. When I step out of the car with Ofentse, Ms. Dlamini clasps our hands. She thanks us for bringing Jabulani home to visit. I am humbled by her touch. Her palms bear the scars of a thousand minuscule incisions healed over with time.*

When Jabulani asks me to return to Tin Town, I readily agree to his request. I want to repay Ms. Dlamini for her kindness—kindness that cost her R34 in lost wages plus another R36 in gifts.[3] My second trip to Tin Town passes quickly. Ayize amuses us with her impressions of Point Place, where she found the girls terrifying. Jabulani adds his own embellishments to her impressions, telling stories that, while comedic, reveal sincere brotherly concern. He does not want Ayize to regard Point Place as more than a stopover. He need not worry: Ayize has no plans to return to Point Place, for she has other matters

Figure 12. Ofentse and I posed
for this photo during a visit to
Jabulani's mother. We were not
expecting cold weather, and
Jabulani's mother insisted on
buying us warm hats at the local
store.

on her mind. As we approach Tin Town, she becomes noticeably quieter.
How will she explain the missing baby to her mother?

I do not learn the end to Ayize's story until several weeks later. As predicted
by Jabulani, Ms. Dlamini takes careful action to reclaim the baby by securing
an affidavit for Ayize that recognizes her rights as the mother. With Ayize
in tow, Ms. Dlamini takes the affidavit to the boyfriend's home, where the
family submits to the request. They do not want to be arrested on kidnapping
charges. Still, the parting is not easy: the mother of the boyfriend cries when
Ayize takes the baby. To mitigate the ill will, Ayize and Ms. Dlamini linger
in the boyfriend's home. They agree to lunch, which delays their departure
until the late afternoon. Ms. Dlamini and Ayize reach Durban just as darkness falls.

Much to Jabulani's horror, Ms. Dlamini and Ayize spend the night inside
Point Place, planning to return to Tin Town the following afternoon. Until
then, they would like to see more of Durban. Jabulani, for his part, is desper-
ate for his mother and sister to leave Point Place. A rat has already chewed
off the rubber tip of the baby's bottle. So early in the morning, he pawns
his mother and sister off on Ofentse. He asks her—and, by tacit extension,

me—to show them the tourist sights. He is unable to join us, fearful that he will be fired for missing another day of work.

Over lunch, Ms. Dlamini narrates the life histories of her children. While she acknowledges the hardships of their upbringing, she also attributes their wanderings to forces beyond her control. The *amadlozi*, she explains, have made it difficult for her children to stay at home. "Growing up, my children didn't like their home. I saw it too late that they have the *amadlozi* inside of them." Ms. Dlamini does not attribute her children's waywardness to her own *amadlozi*. Rather, she believes the *amadlozi* from the Mbeles—their father's patrilineage—are causing the problems. As she explains, "They [my children] ran away. I didn't see it was the Mbele. Ayize's child is going to do it, too. When she's grown, she's going to be someone who doesn't hear. I must take my children to their father's homestead. They must burn *impepho* for my children so they can love their home and me."

With the reference to Ayize's baby, Ms. Dlamini remembers the difficulties of her own transition to motherhood. Like Ayize, she also experienced the theft of her offspring: "When I visited the Mbele homestead, they took Jabulani and his older sister from me. They said they were going to do a ceremony for them. They took them from me. I left their home alone, like Ayize." The story brings tears to her eyes, but she continues, "My mother came back with me to the Mbele homestead to fetch my children. Now they're mine." This statement, however, is not entirely true, for Ms. Dlamini's children keep running away.

Initially, Ms. Dlamini attributed these tribulations to her own *amadlozi*. To appease them, she decided to organize a ceremony for her deceased parents called a *buyisa*—a special rite of "return" that allows the departed to gain admittance into the spirit world. She financed the ceremony herself, collecting on the payout of her pension, which she used to buy a cow and several goats. With the remaining money, she decided to invest in Jabulani by sending him to driving school. The result was less than satisfactory, for he failed the final test. From this failure, Ms. Dlamini speculates that Jabulani's misfortunes must rest with his father's lineage, the Mbeles.

Although Mr. Mbele and Ms. Dlamini are not married, either by a Christian ceremony or by *ilobolo* (bridewealth exchange), they have five children together. Mr. Mbele watches the younger kids on the Dlamini homestead while Ms. Dlamini works for the forest plantations. Mr. Mbele's chronic illnesses, chest pains, and partial blindness limit his ability to find steady employment. In an attempt to remedy the situation, he has consulted numerous diviners for help. They tell him that he must return to his parents' homestead and build his own house. There he must slaughter a cow to placate

Figure 13. This homestead in rural KwaZulu-Natal belongs to Jabulani's mother, although for employment reasons she usually does not stay here. His two younger brothers and the daughter of his older sister typically stay here, as did his father before he passed away.

the *amadlozi*. As Ms. Dlamini explains, "If there can be a home for them, where they can live, the *amadlozi* will go in nicely." Only then might Mr. Mbele get better; only then might his children settle down.

Unfortunately, there are numerous difficulties attached to this undertaking. First, Mr. Mbele is too sick to travel that far, let alone build his own house. Second, for the ceremony to work, he must pay for it himself, yet he has no money of his own. His only hope is to secure a pension, a convoluted and time-consuming task. Lastly, to gain access to the homestead, he must negotiate with his brother. His parents have already passed away, and while Mr. Mbele should be entitled to the land, his brother's wife may block his efforts.

For Ms. Dlamini, these strained alliances provide the backdrop to her children's departures. She acknowledges that her strict rules—particularly her overuse of the switch—contributed to her children's unhappiness at home; nevertheless, her strictness does not fully account for why her children have so many problems settling down in life, especially Jabulani. Of all her children, he has stayed away the longest. At the age of twelve, he ran away from home. Ms. Dlamini did not hear from him for two years. To find him, she consulted a diviner, who told her that he was trapped in a dark place. Finally, in the second year, Ms. Dlamini received word of Jabulani's whereabouts. He was in prison.

"Why," Ms. Dlamini repeatedly asked Jabulani while she was visiting him in prison, "did you leave home?" He never gave her an answer. During this time, he also exhausted his mother's patience by telling the social workers that he was not supported at home. Infuriated by Jabulani's accusations, Ms. Dlamini asked her son whether he grew up "wearing the skin of a wild animal." To prove her financial stability, she agreed to a fingerprint test. The police matched her fingerprints to a database in Pretoria, which showed her employment record at the forest company. In the end, the magistrate sentenced Jabulani to one year in a reformatory school—an outcome that Ms. Dlamini found satisfactory: "I said you can lock him up for two years at this school. He can study there." And indeed, Jabulani learned quite a bit at the reformatory school; as Ms. Dlamini notes, that is where he learned how to speak English and be "clever," although not necessarily in a good way. At the end of the year, with a group of friends, he ran away to Durban.

Now twenty-four years old, Jabulani has spent his entire adolescent and adult life on the streets, in children's shelters, juvenile detention centers, prison, and Point Place. Nonetheless, while he ran away from home, he still remains close with his family. He visited his mother several times during my field research, bringing her the earnings from his paychecks. For her part, too, Ms. Dlamini continues to confer with diviners, recently spending R200 for consultations on how Jabulani might secure a permanent job as well as a nice girlfriend. She remains hopeful that despite the setbacks, he will find his way through the contending claims of Mr. Mbele's *amadlozi*.

*   *   *

Liyanda's Home Situation

Twenty-two-year-old Liyanda gives birth to a baby girl while staying at Point Place. Shortly thereafter she leaves Point Place, unable to support the baby without the help of her boyfriend, Siphiwe, who has been arrested for theft. Given the circumstances, she decides to take her baby to his family's home, which is located in a township outside the city. This arrangement lasts only a few weeks, though, for Liyanda cannot abide by the rules of Siphiwe's mother, Ms. Khumalo. She returns to Point Place with her newborn girl:

Whoosh! An immensely large woman pushes past me down the wind-
ing stairs of Point Place. She carries a blanketed bundle in her arms.
Moments later Liyanda follows, her steps small and slow. It takes me
a few seconds to piece together the ensuing scene. Siphiwe's mother
has come to Point Place to reclaim Liyanda's baby. A few days later,
social workers enter the building. They remove two other babies from
Point Place, which they take to a special home for abandoned chil-
dren. The Point Place girls can visit their babies anytime, but they
cannot remove them without the signature of a legal adult guardian.
State officials deem the girls unfit for motherhood. The fathers of the
babies, also living within Point Place, receive no consideration at all.
Yet, when they discover their babies are missing, they cry, too.

Liyanda makes regular appearances at Point Place, but she does not spend
the night. She does not want to give Ms. Khumalo another reason to request
adoption papers. Ofentse sympathizes with Liyanda's troubles. Mothers-in-
law, she tells me, are difficult. One day Liyanda comes up with a plan. She
asks Ofentse and me to visit the Khumalo home. Perhaps Ms. Khumalo will
be nicer if she meets us? We decide to bring Khaya—Ofentse's boyfriend—as
well. Khaya and Siphiwe used to work together, and we hope this connection
will ameliorate any ill will that Ms. Khumalo might feel toward us as Liyanda's
friends.

On our way to Siphiwe's home, Liyanda tells us that Ms. Khumalo is still
angry with her for making her spend the extra money to collect the baby
from Point Place, a journey that costs R6 each way. The fare seems like a
small payment, but even before we enter Siphiwe's home, I can tell that his
family is struggling. The Khumalo home consists of three shacks arranged
in a semicircle within a dirt yard. A series of clotheslines stretch from a lone
tree to a collapsing chicken-wire fence. Next to the tree, Ms. Khumalo is
washing laundry, vigorously engaged in her work. She looks up, surprised
by our presence. Quickly she collects herself and ushers us into her home.
Apart from a sofa chair, a couch, and a coffee table, the living room holds
very little in the way of furniture or decorative knickknacks. The walls are
bare. A large Valentine's Day card occupies an otherwise empty television
stand. On the floor, a chubby baby rests. She is well dressed, and her hair is
neatly plaited. Liyanda picks up her daughter for us all to admire. The baby
gurgles contentedly.

Ms. Khumalo asks for our surnames, attempting to identify our provenance. Soon she realizes that none of us—Ofentse, Khaya, or I—grew up in
KwaZulu-Natal, but she reassures us that she enjoys meeting people whose

backgrounds are different from her own. Ms. Khumalo's hospitality dispels any unease we might have felt at meeting Liyanda's adversary. She serves us mixed juice, apologizing for not having any snacks. She contemplates sending Liyanda to the store but then reconsiders; she decides that she would like Liyanda to hear what she has to say, particularly in front of us.

"I'm at a loss," Ms. Khumalo begins. "What can I do with Liyanda? She does not love her baby." At my look of surprise, Ms. Khumalo elaborates: "I know Liyanda is young, but she must show more responsibility toward her baby. This is why I went to town a few weeks ago, to request adoption papers from the social workers. I'm the one who takes care of the baby. I even buy formula for her. Last month I told Liyanda to stop breastfeeding. She goes up and down too much." Emboldened by our nods, Ms. Khumalo continues, "I allow this. I only ask for Liyanda to return home at night to spend time with the baby. Even if she can't afford to buy anything, Liyanda must show her baby a mother's love." Ms. Khumalo pauses. She turns away from us to address Liyanda directly. "I love the baby, Liyanda. It's better if you sign the papers. Then I know the baby is my responsibility, and I can plan for her future." None of us, including Liyanda, knows how to respond to Ms. Khumalo's heartfelt appeal.

Unexpectedly, a voice chimes in, "Liyanda, why don't you buy milk for the baby?"

"I'm not working!" Liyanda yells back.

"*Hawu.*" Ofentse expresses dismay at Liyanda's disrespectful tone.

Thump. A wizened figure emerges from behind a drawn curtain. She hobbles toward us. Khaya, Ofentse, and I all stand up to offer our seats. The old woman motions for us to sit down; she has another destination in mind. Whack! With her cane she hits Liyanda's chair, narrowly missing Liyanda's legs. Ofentse scolds Liyanda to stand up. She does so, reluctantly. To the rest of us, the old woman announces, "I'm the grandmother of Siphiwe." She asks for our surnames. Ofentse and I confuse her, because our surnames are indecipherable. Khaya rescues the name exchange; she recognizes his Xhosa background, having grown up in the same part of the Eastern Cape. From then on, the grandmother addresses Khaya exclusively. She asks him where he stays, and when he replies "Point Place," she gleefully responds, "So you know this gangster here," indicating Liyanda, "this crook!" The three of us—Khaya, Ofentse, and I—have difficulty suppressing our amusement. Khaya nods his head in affirmation. The grandmother presses on, blaming Liyanda for Siphiwe's arrest. In recollection of her grandson, her tone softens. She asks Liyanda, "Do you think you're the only one who loves Siphiwe? I also love Siphiwe. Do you hear me, Liyanda?" Liyanda does not respond.

Khaya sympathizes with the grandmother's suffering. He promises to attend Siphiwe's court hearing and will send word about bail. Liyanda interjects. She wants to attend the hearing as well. "No," Khaya shuts Liyanda down, "it's better to remain at home, otherwise you'll be tempted to stay in town." Ms. Khumalo thanks Khaya for his wisdom. The grandmother praises his surname. She also adds without hesitation, "I know those Gumedes, they're gangsters!"—another barb directed at Liyanda, whose last name is Gumede.

A scowl creeps over Liyanda's face. Her plan has gone awry. Khaya has switched allegiances, and Ofentse is on the fence. The tipping point comes with the changing of the baby's diaper, which brings on a new onslaught of accusations. Apparently Liyanda leaves the dirty diapers in a bucket, not bothering to wash them until they are all used up. Ofentse has a low regard for dirty diapers. She takes Ms. Khumalo's side, leaving Liyanda bereft of moral support. By the time we depart the Khumalo home, Liyanda has become silent, her lips tightly pressed in annoyance.

A few days later, Ofentse receives a phone call from Ms. Khumalo, who reports that Liyanda has left home with the baby. She is not at Point Place, either. Several more days pass before we learn her whereabouts. A social worker tells us that she helped Liyanda acquire the transport fare to return to the home of her maternal grandparents, the Zungus. Ofentse and I are impressed by Liyanda's initiative. We decide to phone her to find out how she is doing. Her grandfather, Mr. Zungu, answers the call. He thanks Ofentse profusely, assuming that we are the ones who encouraged Liyanda to return home. And I suppose in some small way, as Ofentse later points out, we did. Our visit to the Khumalo home made the situation so unbearable for Liyanda that she decided to go back to her own family. Mr. Zungu invites us to visit his homestead. We accept the offer, and embark on a trip that takes us up the northern coast and into the rural interior of KwaZulu-Natal.

Very little traffic passes by the Zungu homestead. My car chugs up the last stretch, cresting the top of a plateau. Several young children—alerted by the sputtering noise and billowing dust—come running outside. Liyanda walks behind them and stops, waiting for the dust to settle. She greets us with a smile, her daughter attached to her side. Already I can see that the Zungus' homestead is better off than the Khumalos', as the surrounding pastures support an abundance of livestock: cattle, goats, and sheep. Plowed fields cut across the landscape, and vegetables grow in a garden plot near the homestead. Liyanda takes us on a brief tour of the outer plots, then leads us to the inner circle: five rondavels clustered around a rectangular house. In between these dwellings, children run freely.

Figure 14. Pastures surrounding the homestead of Liyanda's grandparents.

Mr. Zungu and his wife look after these youngsters, who are their grand-children, eleven in total. Mr. Zungu expresses pride in what anthropologists might refer to as a "wealth in people." As he notes, the homestead keeps the family together. Pensions and child grants help with daily expenses, but their long-term subsistence derives from the land and livestock, and ultimately from helping each other. Mr. Zungu explains the generational continuity of his homestead. Originally it belonged to his grandfather, then to his father, who passed it on to his own three sons. As the oldest surviving son, at the age of sixty-three, Mr. Zungu is the household head (*umnumzana*). Still he defers to his wife of nearly forty-five years. Their stories, told in tandem, complement each other.

Mr. and Mrs. Zungu attribute Liyanda's wanderlust to the untimely death of her mother—their daughter. Liyanda ran away shortly thereafter. Yet, as Mr. and Mrs. Zungu note, their daughter's death does not fully account for Li-yanda's departure. In recent years a number of their children have died: three daughters and two sons, leaving the elderly couple with only one surviving daughter. Thus, like Liyanda, most of their grandchildren have experienced the loss of a parent. Still, in some respects Liyanda's situation is unique, at least in terms of kin affiliation, for she retains the surname of her father's lineage: Gumede.

Mr. Zungu elaborates, "We're the Zungu family. Liyanda is a Gumede. She's my daughter's child. Here at home, I'm the grandfather. The Gumedes took out two cows when Liyanda was born. They paid for her. But her parents never married." The Gumede family, in other words, paid the fines for the pregnancy (*ihlawulo*) but never completed the bridewealth exchange (*ilobolo*). Liyanda therefore grew up in the home of her mother's family, the Zungus. Most likely she will continue to live with them, for her father has also passed away, making the completion of *ilobolo* improbable. Yet, while Liyanda keeps the surname Gumede, this difference does not diminish her standing in the Zungu homestead. Mr. and Mrs. Zungu treat Liyanda as an equal among their grandchildren.

If anything, Liyanda occupies a privileged position in the Zungu homestead. Mrs. Zungu explains, "My daughter used to buy Christmas clothes for us. She also dressed her own child, Liyanda. We lost the mother of Liyanda. We lost her. There's no other child that's going to be like her, not even the boys. She knew her home." When Liyanda's mother was alive, she worked in Durban. She kept Liyanda with her until Liyanda reached school age. The mother then sent her to the Zungu homestead. Liyanda never liked school, so her grandparents allowed her to return to Durban to stay with her mother. As Mr. Zungu puts it, "Liyanda got used to Durban just like that." Eventually Liyanda's mother became too ill to look after her daughter, and she sent Liyanda back to the home of her parents. But Liyanda, now used to township life, had changed. Her unchecked adolescent sexuality challenged the conservative values of the Zungu household. As Mr. Zungu elaborates, "When Liyanda came back here, she only cared about boys. This thing got into her. She became naughty. She also started stealing. We really argued then." Mrs. Zungu adds that her husband hit Liyanda. Shortly thereafter, Liyanda stole R400 from her grandfather. She took a *kombi* back to Durban, where she stayed on the streets, in children's shelters, and in Point Place for nearly two years. Unlike her mother, Liyanda forgot her home—at least until she had her own child.

Mr. and Mrs. Zungu express great concern about the baby's future. They want to perform special rites, like *imbeleko*,[4] that would introduce the baby to their *amadlozi* and protect her from illness and harm. This is complicated, though, because so many families are involved. Liyanda's baby will retain the surname Khumalo. The Khumalo family, however, needs to compensate Mr. Zungu with a cow. Mr. Zungu says that he will split the cow with Liyanda's father's family, the Gumedes. Still, as he explains, "They [the Gumedes] don't

have more power than me. I have the power because Liyanda stays with me."
Thus Mr. Zungu will be the one to perform the ceremony for Liyanda's baby.
Only then will the baby receive the full recognition of the Zungus' *amadlozi*.
For her part, Liyanda is not overly concerned with these negotiations. She
already has voiced her claim to the baby—not by a surname but by her first
name. Liyanda calls her baby Nomusa, a name that she chose inside of Point
Place,[5] a name that she chose to complement the masculine name of Ofentse's
three-year-old son, Musa.

*   *   *

Inside Point Place, kinship opens up possibilities for everyday survival. It
creates ties of reciprocity; it resolves conflicts; it connects youth in times of
distress. As kin, the youth of Point Place indicate a willingness to endure the
uncertainties and risks of their shared poverty. They do not extend this same
willingness to their homes. In the home, kinship often divides rather than
unites. It represses and constrains. The Point Place youth cannot reinvent
the terms of their relatedness. They are subject to the dictates of their elders,
to the disparaging remarks of loftier relatives, to the conservative values of
the homestead economy. So to leave the problems of the home, these youth
set off for better opportunities, for new dwellings and more accommodating
abodes like Point Place.

Yet, while the Point Place youth renounce their filial obligations, they
recognize the intervening authority of their kin attachments, because even
outside the home, the *amadlozi* hold sway. And a breach with them is no
trivial matter. It nearly kills Chester. It severely hampers Jabulani, who fails
to secure a steady job or a girlfriend. From the perspective of their kinsfolk,
such wanderings reflect more than the waywardness of youthful disobedi-
ence. They reflect the strained affiliations of the past. The arrival of newborn
babies, as seen with Liyanda and Ayize, also makes the attenuations of the
home apparent. Babies need to belong to a lineage, or malevolent forces, like
ill will and sickness, might prevail.

Notably, the Point Place youth do not concern themselves with these matters directly. They leave it to the specialized knowledge of their kinsfolk.
They are the ones who set up the rites of reconciliation and reunification,
the ceremonial offerings and sacrifices to the *amadlozi* that maintain generational continuity in the home. Thus, to characterize kinship as repressive
in the home is not entirely accurate, for it protects and perpetuates life,
too. Hence, at varying times, Angel, Chester, Jabulani, and Liyanda return
home, sometimes with apologies and their earnings from the city, which their
kinsfolk accept. These material contributions, nonetheless, are sporadic and

meager, signaling intentions of goodwill rather than a substantial or ongoing investment in the maintenance of the home.

In this regard, there are some parallels with the migrant "absconders" discussed in chapter four, those who forsake their home responsibilities for individual pleasures in the labor compounds, townships, and cities (Mayer 1961; Moodie 1994). Here, though, as anthropologist Hylton White (2001:468, 2004:156) notes, a distinction can be made between the absconder and the thug (*tsotsi*).[6] Whereas the absconder looks after his interests to the detriment of his home-based kin, the *tsotsi* diverts and destroys life by preying on the gainful employment of others. Jabulani's incarceration and Chester's stabbing point to the violent lifestyle associated with the *tsotsi* figure. The insults directed at Liyanda and the disapproving looks at Thulile's funeral reveal that females are not excluded from this category, either. Moreover, their unregulated sexuality—often stigmatized as prostitution—challenges gendered constructions of docility and respectability in the home. Angel feels this approbation, too, when she attends her cousin's *umemulo* ceremony wearing a revealing crop top and miniskirt.

Yet, while the *tsotsi* figure, in the popular imagination, invokes an image of moral depravity and destruction, this book provides an alternate view, one more in keeping with the day-to-day routines of *nakana*. The cherish-ing of babies within Point Place suggests a profound desire to propagate life, not destroy it. The street and home thus are not at odds with one another; nor are they distinct spheres of living. Rather, they work to reinforce one another. The Point Place youth leave home to seek out new opportunities and return home to protect its lifeline—the babies. For with the recognition of the *amadlozi*, babies unite the intervening generations, youth and their elders—even if only temporarily.

Conclusion

There are many different endings to the stories of the Point Place youth. Some have moved on to nightly paying shelters, usually the males, while others, usually the females, have found lovers who have apartments in the city center. Some have secured employment, informal and contract-based, and some have become mothers and fathers, raising their children in the homes of their kinsfolk. These are happy and hopeful endings, but there are sad ones, too. Many of the Point Place youth have died. Many have been sent to prison for crimes they have and have not committed. Many have succumbed to their addiction to drugs far more debilitating than glue. Many have returned to the streets because they have nowhere else to go. The police repeatedly have entered Point Place, oftentimes with warrants for criminal activities, evicting as many as they could legally.

I learn about much of this in the United States. The older males phone me, the ones who work and can afford the airtime: "Call back!" they shout into the phone. "The police are coming!"

How can they be calling me in the middle of an eviction? All the same, I phone Ofentse. Sometimes she is standing there with the callers, amused by the stories of her friends.

Invariably she declares, "*Baqamba'manga*," which means "They're telling lies." They think these lies will bring me back to Point Place. They do not believe that I am far away.

Ofentse's explanation makes me smile. How could I forget? *Uqamba'manga*, which means "You tell lies," is a declaration of jest and seriousness, a declaration so common with the Point Place youth that it accompanies almost every utterance, even the mundane ones: I'm going to the store. *Uqamba'manga.* I saw Jerry wearing a new tracksuit. *Uqamba'manga.* Xolile ate your meat pie. *Uqamba'manga.* I promise I'm coming back. *Uqamba'manga.*

This last statement I made with absolute conviction eighteen months into my field stay. I was returning to the United States for the December holidays. The Point Place youth did not believe that I would be coming back. *Uqamba'manga,* they told me, but I was triumphant. They would see! So my goodbyes were not sad; they were not much of anything.

Beauty and Angel accompanied me to the bus stop. It was crowded that day, the city center already filled to capacity with holiday shoppers and beachgoers. I crossed the street and looked back. Angel was nearby, but Beauty lagged behind. She had stopped to greet an older woman sitting on the pavement, her legs outstretched, a cup of change by her feet. I was impatient with the delay. When Beauty caught up to us, she explained that the older woman was a friend of her mother's. They used to sit together, collecting money on the streets of Durban. The woman remembered Beauty as a child.

I paused on hearing Beauty's revelation. I nearly missed the bus. It was one of the rare times that Beauty spoke about her past to me. I knew her mother had died when she was young. Apart from this, I knew very little about her childhood. She never offered much information, and I never felt comfortable asking. I do not know why she shared this encounter with me, the disclosure about her mother's past as a street beggar. She could have made something else up or said nothing at all. Perhaps she thought I would not come back? I boarded the bus and waved goodbye. Angel and Beauty waved back.

After the holidays, I returned to Durban as promised. Beauty, I learned, had passed away before New Year's Day. It surprised me more than any other death at Point Place, although I am not sure why. Beauty had been sick for a long time. She had gone to the tuberculosis hospital. She came back not much changed, but I thought she would be okay. She had been strong enough to walk to the bus stop that day. Beauty's aunt came to Durban to fetch the body. I am not consoled. I call Ofentse, who is in Johannesburg visiting her own family, to tell her what happened. When she hears what I have to say, she responds, *"Uqamba'manga"*: "You tell lies." She drops the phone.

Ofentse returns to Durban shortly thereafter. We speak about Beauty only a little. The other youth at Point Place do not bring up her name, for they believe that referring to the dead causes stress and bad luck. Several weeks pass like this. In the end, Ofentse's son, Musa, breaches the silence. Only three years old, he knew Beauty for his entire life. He asks for her. The first time I hear it, I am taken aback. Ofentse explains that Beauty is no longer with us, but Musa insists. He points to Angel. He wants her to pick him up, and

Angel is delighted. She is always trying to win Musa's affections. She bribes him with candy and balloons. She wants to be his favorite girlfriend. On this day I think that Musa may be confused.

Musa's mistake is not uncommon. I have often heard outsiders—usually charity donors—mix up Angel's and Beauty's names. They were the same age and had the same slight build; they were inseparable as friends, having spent years together on the streets, in Thuthukani, and at Point Place. They even stayed together at the tuberculosis hospital. Angel convinced Beauty to join her when nobody else could. So when Musa calls Angel "Beauty," I attribute it to his young age and impressionable associations. Ofentse corrects him, but in the days that follow, Musa keeps referring to Angel as Beauty. It is odd, because he knows everyone else by the correct name. Several more weeks pass before Ofentse realizes what is happening. She hears Angel whisper into Musa's ear. Ofentse assumes that Angel is promising her son the usual treats, such as ice cream, chips, and trips to the park, but instead Angel is asking him to call her Beauty. And Musa obliges, happily commemorating their deceased friend.

* * *

Angel's articulation of relatedness—of "standing for" Beauty (*ukumela*)—conveys a powerful sentiment of social belonging that organizes the day-to-day living of the Point Place youth. When Beauty was alive, Angel addressed her as her sister. She linked herself to Beauty as closely as she could, and now that Beauty has passed away, Angel minimizes this distance by claiming her name. For Angel there is no contradiction in this realignment of relatedness, as long as it brings the self and the other together. There is utility in the obligations of these associations—of standing for one another (*ukumelana*) as kin, friends, and lovers. Yet there is an affective dimension to this connectivity, too, one not based on purely material concerns. Angel joins herself to Beauty after her death because she wants to remember her friend. This brings her happiness, which she extends to a three-year-old boy who misses Beauty, too. Angel's actions impart the shared reciprocities of *nakana*—of taking notice and caring about another person.

This helps explain why—despite the ongoing violence of evictions, arrests, drug addictions, physical abuses, illnesses, and deaths—youth continue to cohabitate in Point Place. Certainly many of them lack better options to secure safe and affordable shelter, a predicament that they share with the urban poor throughout the Third World (Davis 2006:30). In regard to formal dwellings, very little exists in South African cities to accommodate the destitute.[1] Public housing is not available in Durban. Also, without reliable income, tenement housing or "hand-me-downs" in which owners sublet to renters are too expensive.[2] So are hostels and flophouses. Nightly paying shelters cost between R18 and R25 for a bed and upwards of R50 for a room.[3] They also are prohibitive in their regulations, as they turn out patrons during the day and do not offer those who are paying the base rate lockers for their personal belongings. The managers also tend to espouse Christian doctrines of salvation, which many youth on the streets find too moralizing in their rhetoric.

The Point Place youth thus largely follow the informal options available to them. From an institutional perspective, they may be characterized as squatters, and when out on the streets as pavement dwellers (Davis 2006:30). Historically, in South Africa, the sociopolitical framing of squatters and pavement dwellers has been one of legislated oppression, aimed at removing Africans, especially the unemployed, from their tenuous hold on urban living. Even prior to apartheid rule, the 1910 Public Health Act and 1934 Slums Act revealed directives (couched in terms of sanitation and disease) that promoted race- and class-based segregation at the expense of the black urban poor. The 1950 Group Areas Act and 1951 Prevention of Squatting Act, both implemented during apartheid rule, continued to disenfranchise Africans from urban areas, offering the state broad powers to evict and relocate "undesirables" to peripheral settlements. Housing policy, in short, was more about segregating and controlling the black underclass than about providing adequate shelter. Nonetheless, while highly repressive, these acts never were uniform or coherent in their application (Maylam 1995:34). I venture to say that the same is true even in post-apartheid South Africa, where the spatial regulation of people through housing policy is an incomplete and contradictory project of state control.

The most recent legislation to reveal these contradictions was the 2007 KwaZulu-Natal Elimination and Prevention of Re-Emergence of Slums Act. Its name effectively conveyed its intent; specifically, the Slums Act allowed municipalities to evict occupants from vacant land and derelict buildings. It also mandated that private owners maintain their properties or face fines and imprisonment. Essentially, it targeted anyone who could not afford formal housing, as well as those who could not keep their property in good condition. The implications of the Slums Act were profound, as KwaZulu-Natal accommodates a large number of households that live in informal dwellings. A standard definition of informal dwellings, provided by the 2011 Census, describes them as makeshift structures constructed from found materials—like corrugated iron, plastic, and cardboard—that are not approved by local authorities and not intended as permanent abodes (Statistics South Africa

2012b:80). In shorthand, they may be referred to as shacks or, in isiZulu, as *imijondolo.*[4]

From the position of the South African state, shacks are spontaneous, unplanned dwellings. This spontaneity often means that infrastructural services—like piped water, electricity, toilets, and refuse removal—are nonexistent. Even so, these shelters offer the possibility of an improved life, as their proximity to urban centers provides opportunities for employment as well as better access to schools and hospitals. Not surprisingly, in KwaZulu-Natal, the Durban metropolitan area accommodates the largest number and proportion of households living in shacks, which the 2007 Community Survey puts at 105,000, a figure that does not account for shacks in the backyards of properties, in which case the number would be substantially higher (Housing Development Agency 2012:14).

Given the magnitude of informal dwellings in KwaZulu-Natal and the scope of mass evictions, razzings, and arrests, the 2007 Slums Act did not go unopposed. Abahlali baseMjondolo, a shack dwellers' movement in Durban, challenged the legislation on the basis that it contravened the South African Constitution, which stipulates that everyone has the right to access adequate housing. The state also must take reasonable measures to help individuals realize this right.[5] In their appeal to the Durban High Court, Abahlali base-Mjondolo lost the case, with the judge proclaiming, "The Act makes things more orderly and it must be given a chance to show off its potential."[6] Fortunately, the potential of the Slums Act was short-lived, for Abahlali base-Mjondolo then took its case to the Constitutional Court, which repealed the legislation in 2009.[7]

On paper, the retraction of the Slums Act signals the government's commitment to housing rights in South Africa. It is an affirmation of the right to shelter as well as the right to life. In practice, though, not much has changed for the Point Place youth—prior to, during, or since the revocation of the Slums Act. They continue to face punitive arrests, physical assaults, and unlawful evictions. If the police do not put them in prison, they drive them far outside the city, leaving them to walk back by foot. "They throw us away," one young man remarked to me in 2013 when I asked why he no longer resides inside Point Place. Afraid to stay in the building, he sleeps on the streets and, when he has money, in overnight shelters. This young man's situation reveals the lived disparities of housing rights in South Africa, where forced removals continue not just as physical violations but as emotional dislocations, too. To be thrown away (*lahla*) signals the very real possibility of not being able to return from the violence of these rejections.

Housing security thus remains a struggle for the urban poor in South Africa. Still, the case of Point Place provides cautious optimism for the future of informal shelters in city centers. These settlements exist because large numbers of youth—seeking employment, companionship, and autonomy—refuse to relinquish their right to urban living. They do so, moreover, from a social perception that does not turn inward but extends out to include others in similarly vulnerable circumstances. Subsequently, the number of youth who take refuge in informal shelters is not dwindling. It continues to grow.

And here is the crux of Point Place. It accommodates large numbers of destitute youth in the midst of urban renewal projects aimed at "revitalizing" the city center. Its existence reveals that informal shelters are not antithetical to the commercial interests of private developers or the security concerns of the state. Nor are informal shelters antithetical to the creative making of public spaces. If anything, they are integral to these processes. For, as seen with Point Place, it is possible for youth to come together to create culturally expressive forms of social life not only for the privileged few, but for anyone who is looking for shelter and, along with it, a sense of belonging under a shared roof.

Glossary

This is a guide to some of the meanings of commonly used terms in this book. I have dropped the prefix *uku-* for most verbs to help the English reader distinguish the stem of these words in the text. I have left the prefixes on the nouns. The definitions provided in this glossary are largely taken from the *English-Zulu, Zulu-English Dictionary* (Doke et al. 1999). Some of the terms here also reflect street slang and languages other than isiZulu.

abaphansi	"those who are down below," another name for the ancestors
abaqwayizi	prostitutes, "winkers"
amabutho	Zulu age-set regiments
amadlozi (sing. *idlozi*)	ancestors, shades
amalaka	the inner throat or tonsils
amaqhikiza	girls of marriageable age, supervisors of younger girls' courting practices
amasi	curdled milk
amatshipa	"the cheap ones," migrant workers who do not support their homes with their wage earnings
buyisa	a special rite of return that allows the deceased to gain admittance into the spirit world
emasokweni	"the place of the lovers," STI clinic
fa	to die, to come to an end
ihlawulo	"damages," fines paid to an unmarried woman's family for impregnating or deflowering her
ililaka	the soft palate of the mouth
ilobolo	bridewealth

imali yokuqoma	a lover's fee
imijondolo	shacks
impepho	a dried plant of everlasting flowers that is burned to cleanse the air and to appease the ancestors
imvilapho	an external lesion or sore
insizwa	a young man, a hornless ox or bull, often associated with vigor
intombi	a full-grown girl, a girlfriend
inyanga	healer
isangoma	diviner
isifebe (pl. *izifebe*)	bitch, prostitute
isigebengu	gangster
isithembu	polygyny
isithunzi	living spirit, shadow
isoka (pl. *amasoka*)	a successful male lover, a boyfriend
izifenqo	witticisms
jola	to be in love with someone
kila	to entrap a girl in speech
kipita	to cohabitate, "to keep it," a sexual living arrangement that is viewed negatively by the general population
kombi	a minivan taxi
lahla	to throw away, to abandon, forsake, desert
mealie-meal	cornmeal
nakana	to care about, to take notice of one another
nakekela	to take care of, to look after someone (usually when they are ill)
panga	machete
phanda	to beg, steal, hustle
qoma	to accept love, to choose a lover
shebeen	an unlicensed drinking establishment
shela	to propose love
sjambok	a whip
soma	to have sex between the thighs
takkies	shoes
thanda	to love, to like
tikoloshe	a hypersexual being that is a "familiar" of a witch, often sent by a witch to carry out witchcraft
tsotsi	thug
ugogo	"grandmother" in isiZulu; when used as a name, it is "uGogo"
ukuma	to stand
ukumela	to stand for
ukumelana	to stand for one another
ukumuma	to stand in the way

ulaka	anger, wrath, passion
umakoti	bride
umcako	a chalky white mineral that is consumed, thought to aid digestion and to prevent pregnancy
umemulo	coming-of-age ceremony for a young woman
umnumzana	the male head of a household
umuthi (pl. *imithi*)	tree, shrub, herbal substances, sometimes used for occult purposes

Notes

Introduction

1. Local newspaper headlines, which appeared a few days later, sum up these initiatives as well: "Joint Plan of Attack Pledged against Murky Underworld" (Newman 2004b); "Dodgy Areas to Be Tackled One by One" (Newman 2004a); "eThekwini Declares War on Crime" (Metro 2004). The *Daily News* in its coverage of the summit reported, "As the municipality steps up its no-holds-barred campaign to ruthlessly enforce the city's by-laws, more than 400 buildings in the [central business district] alone have been identified as 'sick'" (Madlala 2004).

2. The Gini index measures the level of inequality, in terms of income or wealth, within a country. A Gini coefficient of zero indicates perfect equality. In 2009 the World Bank reported the Gini coefficient for South Africa as 63.9. The income share of the highest 10 percent was 51.7 percent, while the income share of the lowest 10 percent was 1.2 percent. GINI Index (World Bank estimate), http://data.worldbank.org/indicator/SI.POV.GINI, accessed March 19, 2013.

3. The apartheid government—associated with white minority rule—came into power in 1948 with the election of the National Party. Known for its discriminatory policies, the National Party implemented a regime of racial segregation that affected all aspects of political, social, and economic life in South Africa.

4. This figure reflects an expansion of the unemployment rate to include people not actively searching for a job.

5. The expanded unemployment rate for black South Africans is 46.3 percent, compared to 10.2 percent for white South Africans. The expanded unemployment rate for women is higher, too. For black women it is 52.9 percent, compared to 8.1 percent for white men (Statistics South Africa 2012b:51–52).

6. As a caveat regarding ahistorical, atomized, and romanticized notions of youth agency, anthropologist Deborah Durham (2008:154) cautions against using the concept too generally. Rather, as she writes in relation to youth, "We must ask what kind

of agency they might have, how they come by it and exercise it, and how their agency relates them to others and to their society."

7. Mandrax, the brand name by which methaqualone is known in South Africa and Europe, is a potent barbiturate. (The U.S. brand name is Quaalude.) To make their high cost-effective, street youth will crush the Mandrax tablet and sprinkle it on top of dagga, which they light and smoke through the stem of a broken glass bottle.

8. This request coincided with the 2000 International AIDS Conference in Durban, which prompted a citywide "cleanup" campaign, including the sweeping up of children into street shelters. The 2000 conference also was defined by the political stance of South African president Thabo Mbeki, who denied that there was a causal link between HIV and AIDS. President Mbeki's denial had profound implications for street youth, who, as I discuss in subsequent chapters, rarely seek HIV testing.

9. I drop the prefix *uku-* to make the verb stem *nakana* distinguishable to the English reader. Except for the monosyllabic verb stem *ukuma* and its related concepts, *ukumelana* and *ukumuma*, I drop the subject prefix *uku-* with verbs I discuss in subsequent chapters as well.

Chapter One. Shelter Hopping

1. Boers are white South Africans of mainly Dutch descent who primarily speak Afrikaans.

2. "Step to Keeping Children off the Streets," http://www.lhcfoundation.org/news, accessed March 9, 2004; archived at https://web.archive.org/web/20041230220332/ http://www.icare.co.za/news.php?id=39&which=articles, accessed March 7, 2015.

Chapter Two. Standing (K)in

1. In the mid-nineteenth century, Sir Henry Maine diverged from biological understandings of kinship as based on sexual procreation to posit kin relations as a social contract (Parkin 2004:30), which could include "artificial" ties like adoption (Maine 1861:27).

2. Sidney Mintz and Eric Wolf's (1950:341) discussion of *compadrazgo* in Latin America presents a classic example of ritual kinship. The *compadrazgo* system is a set of personal relationships between individuals who participate in the ritual of Catholic baptisms. It orders a network of horizontal relations (between social classes) and vertical relations (across social classes) that impart varying degrees of emotional, spiritual, and material support to those who enter into these relationships (Mintz and Wolf 1950:355).

3. In many respects, I value the modifier "fictive" because it highlights the productive possibilities and innovations of kin relationships. Ultimately, though, I refrain from using the term in my writing because it produces an inherent paradox. The modifier "fictive" draws attention to the manufactured work of *all* kin relationships yet simultaneously posits the fictive version as less real or true, not because these ties are less enduring but because they represent a contrast with "genuine" kinship: a genealogical model based on cognatic (blood) and affinal (marriage) relations. As

David Schneider (1984:172) notes, even fictive kin assumes the primacy of biogenetic substance. It is a simulated genealogical tie, positioned within the conventional parameters of a dominant kinship ideology that still has roots in popular folk theories of blood and marriage.

4. The exchange rate of the South African rand to the U.S. dollar averaged about 8:1 during most of my field stay.

5. Most of the Point Place residents identify their ethnic background as Zulu (approximately 75 percent), with the majority of them coming from the surrounding townships of Durban and the rural areas of KwaZulu-Natal. Those who are not Zulu tend to come from the provinces of the Eastern Cape, Free State, and Gauteng. The interethnic solidarity of the Point Place youth stands in marked contrast to their demonstrated xenophobia toward foreign African nationals.

6. My discussion of sexual relationships focuses only on heterosexual couples; homosexuality is highly stigmatized inside Point Place, making it difficult to discuss the topic openly in casual conversations or interviews.

7. I discuss *phanda* in greater depth, from a gendered perspective, in chapters three and four.

8. Social reproduction theory has been influential in the fields of anthropology and youth studies. One representative study is Paul Willis's (1977) ethnography *Learning to Labour: How Working Class Kids Get Working Class Jobs*, which explains how societal inequalities are reproduced in schools as British youth enact an oppositional culture that paradoxically keeps them in working-class positions, thus reinforcing the status quo. More recently, Cindi Katz's (1991, 2004) scholarship on Sudanese youth provides valuable insights about the resilience of social reproduction and its potential for exploitation, especially in the context of global capitalism. As Katz (2001:718) writes, "Social reproduction is vexed because [. . .] it is focused on reproducing the very social relations and material forms that *are* so problematic. Social reproduction is precisely not 'revolutionary,' and yet so much rests on its accomplishment, including—perhaps paradoxically—oppositional politics." The Point Place youth face this predicament as they reproduce the social norms of their upbringings in the face of broad-scale inequalities. These norms, though, often are misinterpreted by the state as oppositional or criminal, thus further marginalizing the youth, who in turn seek status and support from each other.

9. This is a veiled reference to being HIV positive. Inside Point Place, formula milk is considered a status symbol, so the other youth are unaware of this mother's HIV status.

10. This is not to suggest that all sib relationships in South Africa withstand the stress of AIDS. Rather, my intention is to show how the Point Place youth, contrary to popular expectations, are able to imagine relationships that are based on a shared sense of commonality and equality. For them, this often takes on the idiom of siblinghood. Sexual relationships, unlike sib relationships, are seen as vectors of HIV transmission and hence, due to stigmas of sexual promiscuity and irresponsibility (Meiberg et al. 2008), tend to break down in the face of AIDS.

Chapter Three. Love, Betrayal, and Sexual Intimacy

1. According to Statistics South Africa (2008:24), in 2006, tuberculosis was the leading cause of death for those between the ages of fifteen and forty-nine, reportedly contributing to 20.1 percent of deaths within this age group. While the Point Place youth were extremely reluctant to discuss HIV/AIDS in personal terms, they often revealed their tuberculosis status, as TB was prevalent inside Point Place.

2. HIV prevalence is the proportion of individuals in a population who have HIV at a specific point in time. It applies to all cases, new and old, and usually is given as a percentage.

3. HIV incidence is the proportion of people who become infected with HIV during a specific period of time. It applies only to the number of new cases.

4. Statistics South Africa (2011:2) reports that KwaZulu-Natal is the second most populous province in South Africa, home to 10.8 million people, or 21.4 percent of the South African population.

5. Statistics South Africa (2011:4) reports that in 2005, the estimated number of people fifteen years and older who were receiving antiretroviral treatment was 101,416. In 2010, it was 1,058,399.

6. *Emasokweni* is the locative form of *isoka*, which in isiZulu refers to a successful male lover. In his discussion of the *isoka* figure, Mark Hunter (2005, 2010) notes its changing significations over time. Increasingly today, in the face of AIDS, the persona of *isoka*—and more specifically the *isoka lamanyala* (dirty lover)—takes on negative connotations of male infidelity and irresponsible promiscuity (Hunter 2010:53, 165–166).

7. For recent anthropological discussions of love and material consumption in southern Africa, see the works of Mark Hunter (2002, 2009, 2010) and Jennifer Cole (2004, 2009).

8. Certainly feelings of love may develop from relationships that begin with commodity transactions, for example, those popularly known as "sugar daddy" relationships. The Point Place females also may have boyfriends from back home. On the whole, however, they express greater feelings of love for their Point Place boyfriends, which they connect to domestic support and companionship.

9. Another linguistic extension of the verb *naka* is *nakekela*, which in isiZulu translates as taking care of or looking after someone. The Point Place youth generally use this expression when they are referring to illnesses. For example, in one interview, Ofentse asks a respondent how she took care of her sister who was having convulsions: "*Kade umanakekela kanjani?*" (How did you take care of her?) Similarly, Angel uses the verb *nakekela* to explain the treatment she received at the tuberculosis clinic: "*Ngijabule kakhulu ngoba ngafika ngizacile. Ngingakwazi ukuhamba kahle. Ngafika eFOSA bangisiza. Banginikeza amapilisi. Bangifeeda ngokudla. Banginakekele futhi ngifunde ukuthi kumele u-respect umuntu.*" (I'm very happy because when I went there I was thin. I didn't know how to walk properly. When I arrived at FOSA, they helped me. They gave me tablets. They gave me food. They cared for me, and they taught me to respect people.) In another interview, I ask a young woman why the

Point Place females do not go to the clinic when they develop an STI. She responds, "*Ayankwa futhi abayinakekeli*" (Ashamed, and they don't look after themselves). Here *nakekela* is constructed in the negative sense of not looking after oneself, which leads to further illness.

10. Mark Hunter (2010:16) presents an analytical distinction between material and romantic love by drawing on a notion of "provider" love, which he describes as "expressions of love enacted through cooperation and mutual assistance." As he is careful to point out, though, provider love and romantic love always work in tandem. Hunter's analytical use of provider love closely corresponds to my discussion of *nakana*.

11. Recent studies show that while nonmarital cohabitation is increasing in Kwa-Zulu-Natal, the general population tends to view these arrangements negatively (Hosegood et al. 2009; Posel and Rudwick 2014). This can be seen in the derogatory term *kipita*, which means to cohabitate but literally translates as "to keep it" (Posel and Rudwick 2014:283). In interviews with the Point Place youth, they tend to describe their living arrangements as "staying with" (*hlala na-*) someone or "staying together" (*hlalisana*). Their use of the verb *hlala* (to stay) may reflect the fact that many of their rooms include not only lovers but also friends and, occasionally, siblings from their homes.

12. In isiZulu: "*Kumele uhlale naye. Umenzele yonke into ayifunayo. Umuwashele kodwa naye akawashele. Umenzele yonke into. Uma ekunaka nawe umunake.*"

13. Another way of thinking about this reciprocal recognition can be seen in Ann Swidler and Susan Cotts Watkins's (2007:150) article about transactional sex in Malawi. As they write, "Just as women need patrons to provide them with material benefits, men need clients who provide them with an outward display of power, prestige, and social dominance and an inward sense of behaving morally."

14. Other studies in KwaZulu-Natal also note the tendency of couples to not use condoms when feelings of love and trust are expressed (Hunter 2010; Preston-Whyte et al. 2000), especially when they are involved in a marital or cohabitating union (Maharaj and Cleland 2005).

15. Again, my discussion of sexual relationships focuses on heterosexual love, because of the stigmatization and therefore the secrecy surrounding homosexuality within Point Place. The subject of homosexuality comes up most often in discussions of prison life and gang affiliations, specifically the 28s. When sent to prison, the Point Place youth primarily identify with the 26s, a rival gang of the 28s. The difference between the two gangs, they claim, is that "the 26s kill for money. The 28s kill for boys." For a comprehensive social history of the 26s, see van Onselen's (1982a, 1982b, 1984) body of work, *Studies in the Social and Economic History of the Witwatersrand, 1886–1914* and *The Small Matter of a Horse*. For a contemporary study of the 28s, see Jonny Steinberg's (2004) book *The Number*.

16. In my interviews, I never directly asked a respondent whether she was a prostitute. Our conversations on commercial sex emerged from other discussions aimed primarily at understanding how the girls supported themselves financially.

17. In the *English-Zulu, Zulu-English Dictionary, phanda* is defined as to "scratch up, dig by scratching." Its secondary meaning is to "sound for information," as in to "pump" (Doke et al. 1999:645). See also Wojcicki 2002a:356.

18. I have not been able to trace the meaning of *amabunja.* "O" is shorthand for *Ou,* which in Afrikaans derives from the word "old" and refers to a guy or fellow; and "i.k." is shorthand for *isoka,* which in isiZulu refers to a man with many girlfriends.

19. For similar findings on the material differences between sex linked to consumption and sex linked to subsistence, see the work of Mark Hunter (2002).

20. I conducted this interview with Simosihle in English, because she speaks it fluently.

21. Apart from Zodwa, only four other youth asked me to accompany them to a clinic for an HIV test. All of them were female. Three of the girls spent a significant amount of time in Point Place. The fourth girl, the youngest and estimated to be twelve years of age, preferred to stay on the streets and in children's shelters. Out of the five girls, three tested positive, one tested negative, and one tested false positive. The false positive tested negative on follow-up tests but then, in 2013, tested HIV positive.

22. Given the stigma of AIDS, I never directly asked whether a parent had died from it. Some youth offered the information on their own. Others merely said that their parent had passed away after a long illness. During my research, out of a survey of 163 youth who spent time at Point Place, 14 (approximately 9 percent) indicated that they did not know the living status of one or both parents; 42 (approximately 26 percent) indicated that one parent had died; and 31 (approximately 19 percent) indicated that both parents had died. This is a crude survey of parental deaths, as different conceptions of kinship may have shaped these responses. Additionally, youth may have concealed the living status of a parent for personal reasons, including distrust of me as a researcher with a clipboard. Still, the numbers— oftentimes confirmed through in-depth interviews and corroborating information from friends, lovers, siblings, and other kin—reveal the immense rate of death at the generational level of parents.

23. UNICEF defines an AIDS orphan as a child under the age of eighteen who has lost a mother or father to an AIDS-related illness. Because of the potential impact on funding, orphan statistics often do not distinguish whether a child has lost one parent or both parents to AIDS.

24. In a 2008 study, the HSRC (2009:46) reported that condom use has increased over time. In KwaZulu-Natal, in 2002, the proportion of people aged fifteen years and older who had used a condom during their last sexual encounter was 26.7 percent; in 2005, it was 36.3 percent; and in 2008, it was 66.2 percent.

25. Adam Ashforth (1999:52) describes a similar scenario in the township of Soweto: "I have many times heard women deriding the idiocy of boys who think they can buy themselves a girlfriend for the price of a burger and coke." For Ashforth, such incidents reveal underlying assumptions that men treat women like property and sexual access can be purchased for a price. Women, of course, do not always agree to these terms, especially if the compensation is paltry.

26. People Opposing Women Abuse, www.powa.co.za/Display.asp?ID=2, accessed September 20, 2007; archived at https://web.archive.org/web/20070324231339/http://www.powa.co.za/Display.asp?ID=2, accessed March 12, 2015. This statistic is an extrapolation based on an assumed ratio of unreported to reported sexual assaults.

27. South African Police Service (SAPS), www.saps.gov.za/statistics/crimestats/2006/_pdf/category/rape.pdf, accessed September 20, 2007. The United Nations Economic Commission for Africa (2009: 68) discusses these statistics as well. Moreover, these numbers represent cases of rape reported to the SAPS; if the numbers are extrapolated to unreported cases from other studies, the actual incidence could fall between 110,000 and 490,000 rapes over the course of one year (Vetten 2007:429).

28. The Point Place males never speak about rape in personal terms but do acknowledge that these assaults occur on the streets, in children's shelters, and in prison.

29. Only one case of rape was reported inside Point Place during my two years of fieldwork (2003–2005). Upon learning of the assault, the Point Place males beat the accused into near-unconsciousness. They then deposited him in front of a police station, forcing him to confess his crime against the girl to the police.

30. This conversation emerged in reference to media reports of baby rape in South Africa.

31. The isiZulu verb *lahla* has a secondary meaning, which is to "abandon, forsake, desert" (Doke et al. 1999:444).

Chapter Four. Love, Respect, and Masculinity

1. Following the work of Robert Morrell (1998:607), my designation of a dominant masculinity is not meant to imply that there is a single or uniform way of becoming a man. I do not view masculinity as an essential gender identity but as a social construction subject to incremental and radical contestation and therefore subject to change. For an overview of hegemonic masculinities in South Africa that includes detailed summaries of scholars' analytical and empirical contributions, see the article by Morrell et al. (2012), "Hegemonic Masculinity/Masculinities in South Africa: Culture, Power, and Gender Politics."

2. I am indebted to the scholarship of Mark Hunter (2010), who has delineated the historical trajectories of the *isoka* and *umnumzana* figures, connecting them to changing "geographies of intimacy" and the broader political economy of KwaZulu-Natal from the nineteenth century to the present day.

3. The *English-Zulu, Zulu-English Dictionary* defines *isoka* as a "young man who has passed through the circumcision school; one old enough to commence courting." The secondary meaning is a "girl's fiancé" (Doke et al. 1999:763).

4. These entitlements connect to Ashforth's (1999) discussion of masculinity in Soweto. As he explains, men often treat women like property. For example, boyfriends pay for access to sexual services (through gifts), are expected to protect their girlfriends from intruding threats, and gain status by engaging in multiple sexual conquests. While the Point Place males never explicitly refer to their girlfriends as property, they do express a sense of entitlement to the bedrooms, and thus to their girlfriends' productive and reproductive capacities.

5. Rachel Jewkes and Robert Morrell (2010), writing about gender inequality in South Africa, note that ideal forms of femininity for African women often entail expectations of acquiescence, which can help them secure social and material rewards. Cultural values like respect, obedience, and passivity also undergird normative expectations of femininity.

6. Similar associations appear with the female equivalent, *intombi*, a full-grown girl, yet her sexuality is more regulated than an *insizwa*'s. The emergence of virginity-testing ceremonies in KwaZulu-Natal points to some of these social controls (Leclerc-Madlala 2001; Scorgie 2002).

7. In his obituary for Eileen Krige, John Argyle (1995:92) notes that Krige's (1936) first book, *The Social System of the Zulus*, is not an ethnography in the traditional sense of in-depth fieldwork, in that much of her research, as she acknowledges in the preface, is "a synthesis of earlier published materials," and supplementary information is included from correspondence courses with Zulu students. Thus Argyle (1995:93) refers to Krige's work as "distance" fieldwork.

8. In addition to his regulation of marriage, Shaka's centralization of the *amabutho* provided ample opportunity for the exploitation of age-sets. From a materialist perspective, the consolidation of male bodies—housed in military barracks—lent itself to the ready appropriation of surplus labor. Conscripted into labor-tribute parties, young men worked for the paramount and his chiefs (Guy 1979:11–12; Wright 1978:24). The *amabutho* essentially perpetuated a system of precapitalist patriarchal dominion whereby warriors, in order to achieve *umnumzana* status, became agents and subjects of state predation. In sum, those in positions of authority, namely patriarchal elders, controlled the productive (labor) and reproductive (marital) powers of young men.

9. This cultivation of a combative warrior masculinity found affirmation in later instances of political violence, as seen with the Zulu faction fights and hostel confrontations of the late 1980s and early 1990s (Mamdani 1996).

10. Vilakazi (1962:52) notes that in conversations about love, Christian girls refer to their lovers through the euphemism "we are like that" rather than "we are sweethearts." He thus draws attention to the sense of secrecy and sin associated with premarital sexual attachments among "modernized" youth.

11. During one of my home stays in rural KwaZulu-Natal, an elderly *induna* (headman), his wife, and their children recounted this love proposal to me. Other variations exist in townships and on college campuses.

12. *Soma*, also referred to as *hlobongo*, received a great deal of attention from mid-twentieth-century anthropologists. The social utility of the practice ensured that pubescent girls would not become pregnant before marriage. Yet *soma* was not only about the regulation of female fertility; it also helped young men defer the obligations of marital commitment. It enabled them to *shela* many girls without having to face the repercussions of paying for seduction damages. The practice of *soma* channeled the potential dangers of youth sexuality into a nontransgressive outlet (Gluckman 1950:187; Krige 1936:158; Vilakazi 1962:55–56).

13. During one of my home stays in a township in KwaZulu-Natal, a group of high school students, boys and girls, recounted this love proposal to me.

14. isiZulu nomenclature addresses these formal lineage interests as well. A suitor who wishes to marry does not *shela* a bride. Rather, he asks permission from his parents, a process known as *ukucela*. If they are in agreement, they send a request to the bride's family through a go-between messenger (Reader 1966:179).

15. A group of college students, young men and women, recounted this love proposal to me while I was studying isiZulu at the University of KwaZulu-Natal in Pietermaritzburg.

16. From the perspective of those living in the rural areas, these young men rejected their filial obligations by spending their money in town and in the mining compounds, where they drank, gambled, and consorted with town women. Across the expanse of South Africa, these workers acquired the derogatory name of *amatshipa*, a phonological derivative from English meaning "the cheap ones" (Mayer 1961:6; Moodie 1994:142).

17. To receive lighter sentences or to be placed in Excelsior (a juvenile detention center) rather than prison, the youth of Point Place often obscure their real ages and claim that they are "minors" even though they may be older than eighteen. This strategy tends to lose effectiveness by the time they reach the age of twenty.

Chapter Five. Residing with the Spectral

1. Two accounts claim that Yogi found the red candle while jogging along the Durban beachfront.

2. uGogo is a common Zulu name for a grandmother. In South African popular culture, grandmothers are often portrayed as beloved and respected figures. The success of the Vodacom cell phone advertising campaign—which deploys the now-iconic phrase "*Yebo Gogo*" [Yes, Grandmother]—conveys this high regard.

3. When speaking to a person directly in isiZulu, the noun prefix, in this case the "u," is dropped.

4. One account claims that Yogi actually transformed into a black cat.

5. The religious backgrounds of the Point Place youth, all Christian, vary by denomination, with many of them claiming affiliations to Anglican, Methodist, Presbyterian, and Catholic churches. A large number also follow Zionist and Apostolic practices, a merging of African traditional religions and Christian faith healing. Their selection of religious practices was of particular concern to Hilda, a Catholic missionary, who often remarked that the Point Place youth joined churches offering food and other types of assistance but quickly left when donations ran dry. The Point Place youth, meanwhile, prefer not to join Pentecostal churches because they frequently asked for monetary contributions during services.

6. *Umuthi* (pl. *imithi*) means "tree" or "shrub" in isiZulu. When used in medicine, it can include noxious as well as curative substances, depending on the intent of the person's application (Ngubane 1977:22).

7. I translate *idlozi* (pl. *amadlozi*) as "ancestor" and "shade," using the terms interchangeably. Berglund (1976:29) would fault this decision, as he exclusively translates *idlozi* as "shade": "One reason for not using the word ancestor is that the English idiom suggests ascendants who are dead (according to Western concepts) and, as

a result, there is a distance between them and the living . . . This is not descriptive of Zulu concepts which [. . .] assume a very close and intimate relationship and association within the lineage between the departed and the survivors." I appreciate Berglund's analytical insights yet also am mindful of my respondents' general use of *idlozi*, which they translate as "ancestor."

8. The *amadlozi* also are commonly referred to as the *abaphansi*—those who are down below (Ngubane 1977:50–51; Sibisi 1975:48).

9. In his book *Witchcraft, Violence, and Democracy in South Africa*, Adam Ashforth (2005:223–224) describes the *isithunzi* as "a sort of life force" as well as "the inner, hidden, invisible domain of personhood" comparable to breath (*umphefumulo*). He distinguishes the *isithunzi* from *umoya*, which he claims corresponds more closely to Christian understandings of the soul. Ashforth nonetheless cautions against any rigid differentiation of these concepts, for they often are used interchangeably in ritual and linguistic practices.

10. Peter Geschiere (1997:2), conducting anthropological research in Cameroon, also remarks on this apparent disconnect between expectations of modernity and practices of witchcraft. The oft-repeated statement "Where there is electric light, witchcraft will disappear" belies the actual experiences of his research assistant, who frequently encounters occult forces while residing in town.

11. Anthropologist Isak Niehaus (2001, 2002), conducting long-term field research in the province of Limpopo, provides excellent ethnographic accounts of popular understandings of witches.

12. In recent years, anthropologists have duly noted the dramatic surge—or perceived surge—of occult economies in southern Africa (Ashforth 2000; Auslander 1993; Burke 2000; Comaroff and Comaroff 1999a; Gulbrandsen 2003; Jensen and Burr 2004). For a lively discussion on this topic, see also the back-and-forth exchange between anthropologists Jean and John Comaroff (1999b) and Sally Falk Moore (1999).

13. As Ashforth (2005:14) notes, "Stories of witches, as with most stories, are recounted with deliberate efforts to stimulate laughter. Good stories are rewarded with guffaws. The fact of laughter, however, does not detract from the importance of the information."

14. Adam Ashforth's (2005:3) scholarship highlights the profound connections between spiritual insecurity and all other facets of life in South Africa. As he writes, "It is related to, but not reducible to, other forms of insecurity such as poverty, violence, political oppression, and disease."

Chapter Six. Homecomings

1. The ethnographic scholarship on street youth in developing countries is replete with examples of youth living on the streets to support the home—either through their street earnings or through their absence, which helps mitigate household expenditures like food, clothing, and school fees (Aptekar 1988; Flynn 2005; Hecht 1998; Kilbride 2000; Márquez 1998).

2. Ofentse experiences this humiliation in her family, too. She is much younger than her siblings, and when she was a child, one sister who married well repeatedly made overtures to bring Ofentse into her home. The sister later also offered to adopt Ofentse's son, a proposition that Ofentse found horrifying in its implications that she could not provide adequately for him. As Ofentse explains, if accepted, the proposition would create ties of indebtedness to her sister, whom she finds overbearing, arrogant, and annoying.

3. To keep us warm, Ms. Dlamini bought wool caps for me and Ofentse. She also prepared tea and cookies for us, and as we were leaving, she attempted to reimburse me for the gasoline costs.

4. Typically, the father's family conducts the ritual by slaughtering a goat and making a bracelet (*isphandla*) from its skin for the baby; given Liyanda's estrangement from the Khumalo family, however, Mr. Zungu decides that he will perform the ceremony for the baby. At a later date, the Khumalo family may perform the ritual as well.

5. Mark Hunter (2010:145–147) also discusses the "politics of naming" babies, linking these spiritual discussions to material considerations, in which young unmarried women often prefer that their baby assume the surname of their lover so they can receive financial support from his family—a process that connects to broader strategies of "making a living" in contemporary South Africa.

6. The *tsotsi* figure is often referred to as an *isigebengu* (gangster) in isiZulu.

Conclusion

1. According to the Housing Development Agency (2012:23) in South Africa, "formal dwellings include house or brick structure on a separate stand, flat in a block of flats, town/cluster/semi-detached house, house/flat/room in backyard and a room/flatlet on a shared property."

2. In 2013, friends staying in tenement housing in the center of Durban reported monthly rents of R2300 and R2500, not including electricity or water. That rate was for a bachelor flat.

3. These prices reflect the 2013 going rate for an overnight shelter.

4. On a national scale, the 2011 Census reports that approximately 13.6 percent of households in South Africa can be considered informal dwellings (Statistics South Africa 2012b:57).

5. The South African Constitution 1996, Chapter 2: Bill of Rights, http://www.justice.gov.za/legislation/constitution/bill-of-rights.html, accessed March 16, 2015.

6. KZN High Court Upholds Slums Act, January 30, 2009, http://mg.co.za/article/2009-01-30-kzn-high-court-upholds-slums-act, accessed June 11, 2013.

7. Landmark Judgment in Favour of Poor, October 18, 2009, http://mg.co.za/article/2009-10-18-landmark-judgment-in-favour-of-poor, accessed June 11, 2013.

Works Cited

Aptekar, Lewis
1988   Street Children of Cali. Durham, NC: Duke University Press.

Argyle, John
1995   Eileen Jensen Krige (1905–1995). Natalia 25:92–95.

Ashforth, Adam
1999   Weighing Manhood in Soweto. CODESRIA Bulletin 3 & 4:51–58.
2000   Madumo: A Man Bewitched. Chicago: University of Chicago Press.
2005   Witchcraft, Violence, and Democracy in South Africa. Chicago: University
    of Chicago Press.

Auslander, Mark
1993   "Open the Wombs!" The Symbolic Politics of Modern Ngoni Witchfinding. In
    Modernity and Its Malcontents: Ritual and Power in Postcolonial Africa. Jean Co-
    maroff and John Comaroff, eds. Pp. 167–192. Chicago: University of Chicago Press.

Beazley, Harriot
2003   Voices from the Margins: Street Children's Subcultures in Indonesia. Children's
    Geographies 1(2):181–200.

Berglund, Axel-Ivar
1976   Zulu Thought-Patterns and Symbolism. Bloomington: Indiana University Press.

Burke, Charlanne
2000   They Cut Segmentsi into Parts: Ritual, Murder, Youth, and the Politics of
    Knowledge in Botswana. Anthropological Quarterly 73(3):113–120.

Carsten, Janet
2004   After Kinship. Cambridge: Cambridge University Press.

Christiansen, Catrine, Mats Utas, and Henrik E. Vigh, eds.
2006   Navigating Youth, Generating Adulthood: Social Becoming in an African
    Context. Stockholm: Nordiska Afrikainstitutet.

Cole, Jennifer

2004   Fresh Contact in Tamatave, Madagascar: Sex, Money, and Intergenerational Transformation. American Ethnologist 31(4):573–588.

2009   Love, Money, and Economies of Intimacy in Tamatave, Madagascar. *In* Love in Africa. Jennifer Cole and Lynn M. Thomas, eds. Pp. 109–134. Chicago: University of Chicago Press.

Comaroff, Jean, and John Comaroff

1999a   Occult Economies and the Violence of Abstraction. American Ethnologist 26(4):279–303.

1999b   Response to Moore: Second Thoughts. American Ethnologist 26(2):307–309.

Connell, R. W.

1995   Masculinities. Berkeley: University of California Press.

Connell, R. W., and James W. Messerschmidt

2005   Hegemonic Masculinity: Rethinking the Concept. Gender and Society 19(6):829–859.

Davis, Mike

2006   Planet of Slums. London: Verso.

De Boeck, Filip

2004   On Being *Shege* in Kinshasa: Children, the Occult and the Street. *In* Reinventing Order in the Congo: How People Respond to State Failure in Kinshasa. Theodore Trefon, ed. Pp. 155–173. London: Zed Books.

De Boeck, Filip, and Alcinda Honwana, eds.

2005   Makers and Breakers: Children and Youth in Postcolonial Africa. Oxford: James Currey.

Delius, Peter, and Clive Glaser

2002   Sexual Socialisation in South Africa: A Historical Perspective. African Studies 61(1):27–54.

Diouf, Mamadou

2003   Engaging Postcolonial Space: African Youth and Public Space. African Studies Review 46(1):1–12.

Diversi, Marcelo

2006   Street Kids in Nikes: In Search of Humanization through the Culture of Consumption. Cultural Studies/Critical Methodologies 6(3):370–390.

Doke, C. M., D. M. Malcolm, J. M. A. Sikakana, and B. W. Vilakazi

1999   English–Zulu, Zulu–English Dictionary. Johannesburg: Witwatersrand University Press.

Dorrington, R. E., L. F. Johnson, D. Bradshaw, and T. Daniel

2006   The Demographic Impact of HIV/AIDS in South Africa: National and Provincial Indicators for 2006. Cape Town: Center for Actuarial Research, South African Medical Research Council and Actuarial Society of South Africa.

Durham, Deborah
2004   Disappearing Youth: Youth as a Social Shifter in Botswana. American Ethnologist 31(4):589–605.
2008   Apathy and Agency: The Romance of Agency and Youth in Botswana. *In* Figuring the Future: Globalization and the Temporalities of Children and Youth. Jennifer Cole and Deborah Durham, eds. Pp. 151–178. Santa Fe: School for Advanced Research Press.

Flynn, Karen Coen
2005   Food, Culture, and Survival in an African City. New York: Palgrave Macmillan.

Geschiere, Peter
1997   The Modernity of Witchcraft: Politics and the Occult in Postcolonial Africa. Peter Geschiere and Janet Roitman, trans. Charlottesville: University Press of Virginia.

Gluckman, Max
1950   Kinship and Marriage among the Lozi of Northern Rhodesia and the Zulu of Natal. *In* African Systems of Kinship and Marriage. A. R. Radcliffe-Brown and Daryll Forde, eds. Pp. 166–206. London: International Africa Institute.

Goldstein, Donna
2003   Laughter out of Place: Race, Class, Violence, and Sexuality in a Rio Shantytown. Berkeley: University of California Press.

Goody, Esther
1982   Parenthood and Social Reproduction: Fostering and Occupational Roles in West Africa. Cambridge: Cambridge University Press.

Gulbrandsen, Ornulf
2003   The Discourse of "Ritual Murder": Popular Reaction to Political Leaders in Botswana. *In* Beyond Rationalism: Rethinking Magic, Witchcraft and Sorcery. Bruce Kapferer, ed. Pp. 215–231. New York: Berghahn Books.

Guy, Jeff
1979   The Destruction of the Zulu Kingdom: The Civil War in Zululand, 1879–1884. London: Longman.

Hansen, Karen Tranberg
2008   Localities and Sites of Youth Agency in Lusaka. *In* Youth and the City in the Global South. Karen Tranberg Hansen, ed. Pp. 98–124. Bloomington: Indiana University Press.

Hart, Keith
1988   Kinship, Contract, and Trust. *In* Trust: Making and Breaking Cooperative Relations. Diego Gambetta, ed. Pp. 176–193. New York: Basil Blackwell.

Hecht, Tobias
1998   At Home in the Street: Street Children of Northeast Brazil. Cambridge: Cambridge University Press.

Hosegood, Victoria, Nula McGrath, and Tom Moultrie
2009   Dispensing with Marriage: Marital Partnership Trends in Rural KwaZulu-
       Natal, South Africa, 2000–2006. Demographic Research 20(13):279–312.

Housing Development Agency
2012   KwaZulu-Natal: Informal Settlements Status. Johannesburg: Housing Devel-
       opment Agency.

HSRC
2009   South African National HIV Prevalence, Incidence, Behaviour and Com-
       munication Survey 2008: A Turning Tide among Teenagers? Cape Town: HSRC
       Press.

Hunter, Mark
2002   The Materiality of Everyday Sex: Thinking beyond "Prostitution." African
       Studies 61(1):99–120.
2005   Cultural Politics and Masculinities: Multiple Partners in Historical Perspective
       in KwaZulu-Natal. Culture, Health, and Sexuality 7(4):389–403.
2009   Providing Love: Sex and Exchange in Twentieth-Century South Africa. In
       Love in Africa. Jennifer Cole and Lynn M. Thomas, eds. Pp. 135–156. Chicago:
       University of Chicago Press.
2010   Love in the Time of AIDS: Inequality, Gender, and Rights in South Africa.
       Bloomington: Indiana University Press.

Isolezwe
2003   Kutakulwe izingane ebezidayisa ngomzimba [Crime tackled: Children who
       were selling their bodies]. October 31.

Jackson, Michael
1996   Introduction: Phenomenology, Radical Empiricism, and Anthropological
       Critique. In Things as They Are: New Directions in Phenomenological Anthro-
       pology. Michael Jackson, ed. Pp. 1–50. Bloomington: Indiana University Press.

Jensen, Steffen, and Lars Burr
2004   Everyday Policing and the Occult: Notions of Witchcraft, Crime, and the
       People. African Studies 63(2):193–211.

Jewkes, Rachel, and Robert Morrell
2010   Gender and Sexuality: Emerging Perspectives from the Heterosexual Epi-
       demic in South Africa and Implication for HIV Risk and Prevention. Journal of
       the International AIDS Society 13(6):1–11.

Katz, Cindi
1991   Sow What You Know: The Struggle for Social Reproduction in Rural Sudan.
       Annals of the Association of American Geographers 8(13):488–514.
2001   Vagabond Capitalism and the Necessity of Social Reproduction. Antipode
       33(4):709–728.
2004   Growing Up Global: Economic Restructuring and Children's Everyday Lives.
       Minneapolis: University of Minnesota Press.

Kaufman, Carol E., and Stavros E. Stavrou
2004   "Bus Fare Please": The Economics of Sex and Gifts among Young People in Urban South Africa. Culture, Health, and Sexuality 6(5):377–391.

Kilbride, Philip, Collette Suda, and Enos Njeru
2000   Street Children in Kenya: Voices of Children in Search of a Childhood. Westport, CT: Bergin & Garvey.

Kleinman, Arthur, and Joan Kleinman, eds.
1996   Suffering and Its Professional Transformation: Toward an Ethnography of Interpersonal Experience. Bloomington: Indiana University Press.

Krige, Eileen Jensen
1936   The Social System of the Zulus. Pietermaritzburg: Shuter & Shooter.

Lawrence, Denise L., and Setha M. Low
1990   The Built Environment and Spatial Form. Annual Review of Anthropology 19:453–505.

Leclerc-Madlala, Suzanne
2001   Virginity Testing: Managing Sexuality in a Maturing HIV/AIDS Epidemic. Medical Anthropology Quarterly 15(4):533–552.

Maddy, Richard E.
2001   Fictive Kinship in American Biomedicine. *In* New Directions in Anthropological Kinship. Linda Stone, ed. Pp. 285–302. Lanhan, MD: Rowman & Littlefield.

Madlala, Bheko
2004   Crime Dens Demolition: City Blitz on "Sick" Buildings. Daily News, October 1: 4.

Magazine, Roger
2003   Action, Personhood, and the Gift Economy among So-Called Street Children in Mexico City. Social Anthropology 11(3):307–318.

Maharaj, Pranitha, and John Cleland
2005   Risk Perception and Condom Use among Married or Cohabiting Couples in KwaZulu-Natal, South Africa. International Family Planning Perspectives 31(1):24–29.

Maine, Sir Henry
1861   Ancient Law. London: John Murray.

Mains, Daniel
2007   Neoliberal Times: Progress, Boredom, and Shame among Young Men in Urban Ethiopia. American Ethnologist 43(4):659–673.

Maira, Sunaina, and Elisabeth Soep, eds.
2005   Youthscapes: The Popular, the National, the Global. Philadelphia: University of Pennsylvania Press.

Mamdani, Mahmood
1996   Citizen and Subject: Contemporary Africa and the Legacy of Late Colonialism. Princeton: Princeton University Press.

Márquez, Patricia
1998 The Street Is My Home: Youth and Violence in Caracas. Stanford: Stanford University Press.

Mauss, Marcel
1990 The Gift: The Form and Reason for Exchange in Archaic Societies. W. D. Halls, trans. New York: W. W. Norton.

Mayer, Philip
1961 Townsmen or Tribesmen: Conservatism and the Process of Urbanization in a South African City. London: Oxford University Press.

Maylam, Paul
1995 Explaining the Apartheid City: 20 Years of South African Urban Historiography. Journal of Southern African Studies 21(1):19–38.
1996 Introduction: The Struggle for Space in Twentieth-Century Durban. *In* The People's City: African Life in Twentieth-Century Durban. Paul Maylam and Iain Edwards, eds. Pp. 1–30. Pietermaritzburg: University of Natal Press.

Meiberg, Annemarie, Arjan E. R. Bos, Hans E. Onya, and Herman P. Schaalma
2008 Fear of Stigmatization as Barrier to Voluntary HIV Counselling and Testing in South Africa. East African Journal of Public Health 5(2):49–54.

Metro
2004 eThekwini Declares War on Crime. October 1: 1.

Mintz, Sidney, and Eric Wolf
1950 An Analysis of Ritual Co-Parenthood (*Compadrazgo*). Southwestern Journal of Anthropology 6(4):341–368.

Moodie, Dunbar
1994 Going for Gold: Men, Mines, and Migration. Berkeley: University of California Press.

Moore, Sally Falk
1999 Debate: Reflections on the Comaroff Lecture. American Ethnologist 26(2):304–306.

Morrell, Robert
1998 Of Boys and Men: Masculinity and Gender in Southern African Studies. Journal of Southern African Studies 24(4):605–630.

Morrell, Robert, Rachel Jewkes, and Graham Lindegger
2012 Hegemonic Masculinity/Masculinities in South Africa: Culture, Power, and Gender Politics. Men and Masculinities 15(1):11–30.

Narayan, Kirin
1993 How Native Is a "Native" Anthropologist? American Anthropologist 95(3):671–686.

Nattrass, Nicoli
2007   Disability and Welfare in South Africa's Era of Unemployment and AIDS. *In* State of the Nation: South Africa 2007. Sakhela Buhlungu, John Daniel, Roger Southall, and Jessica Lutchman, eds. Pp. 179–200. Cape Town: HSRC Press.

Newman, Latoya
2004a   Dodgy Areas to Be Tackled One by One. Mercury, October 1: 4.
2004b   Joint Plan of Attack Pledged against Murky Underworld. Mercury, October 4: 4.

Ngubane, Harriet
1977   Body and Mind in Zulu Medicine: An Ethnography of Health and Disease in Nyuswa-Zulu Thought and Practice. London: Academic Press.

Niehaus, Isak
2001   Witchcraft, Power and Politics: Exploring the Occult in the South African Lowveld. London: Pluto Press.
2002   Perversion of Power: Witchcraft and the Sexuality of Evil in the South African Lowveld. Journal of Religion in Africa 32(3):269–299.

Nyawo, Nomsa
2005   When Days Are Dark, Friends Are Few. METRObeat 78:22–24.

Parkin, Robert
2004   Descent and Marriage. *In* Kinship and Family: An Anthropological Reader. Robert Parkin and Linda Stone, eds. Pp. 29–42. Malden, MA: Blackwell Publishing.

Peletz, Michael G.
1995   Kinship Studies in Late Twentieth-Century Anthropology. Annual Review of Anthropology 24:343–372.

Posel, Dorrit, and Stephanie Rudwick
2014   Ukukipita (Cohabiting): Socio-Cultural Constraints in Urban Zulu Society. Journal of Asian and African Studies 49(3):282–297.

Preston-Whyte, Eleanor, Christine Varga, Herman Oosthuizen, Rachel Roberts, and Frederick Blose
2000   Survival Sex and HIV/AIDS in an African City. *In* Framing the Sexual Subject: The Politics of Gender, Sexuality, and Power. Richard Parker, Regina Maria Barbosa, and Peter Aggleton, eds. Pp. 165–190. Berkeley: University of California Press.

Radcliffe-Brown, A. R.
1950   Introduction. *In* African Systems of Kinship and Marriage. A. R. Radcliffe-Brown and Daryll Forde, eds. Pp. 1–85. London: International African Institute.

Reader, D. H.
1966   Zulu Tribe in Transition: The Makhanya of Southern Natal. Manchester: Manchester University Press.

Samara, Tony Roshan
2005   Youth Crime and Urban Renewal in the Western Cape. Journal of Southern African Studies 31(1):209–227.

Schneider, David
1984   A Critique of the Study of Kinship. Ann Arbor: University of Michigan Press.

Scorgie, Fiona
2002   Virginity Testing and the Politics of Sexual Responsibility: Implications for AIDS Intervention. African Studies 61(1):55–75.

Sibisi, Harriet
1975   The Place of Spirit Possession in Zulu Cosmology. *In* Religion and Social Change in Southern Africa: Anthropological Essays in Honour of Monica Wilson. Michael G. Whisson and Martin West, eds. Pp. 48–57. Cape Town: David Philip.

Stack, Carol
1974   All Our Kin: Strategies for Survival in a Black Community. New York: Harper and Row.

Statistics South Africa
2008   Mortality and Causes of Death in South Africa, 2006: Findings from Death Notification. Pretoria: Statistics South Africa.
2011   Statistical Release: Mid-Year Population Estimates. Pretoria: Statistics South Africa.
2012a   Quarterly Labour Force Survey: Quarter 3 (July to September), 2012. Pretoria: Statistics South Africa.
2012b   Statistical Release (Revised): Census 2011. Pretoria: Statistics South Africa.

Steinberg, Jonny
2004   The Number: One Man's Search for Identity in the Cape Underworld and Prison Gangs. Johannesburg: Jonathan Bell Press.

Strathern, Marilyn
1988   The Gender of the Gift: Problems with Women and Problems with Society in Melanesia. Berkeley: University of California Press.

Swidler, Ann, and Susan Cotts Watkins
2007   Ties of Dependence: AIDS and Transactional Sex in Rural Malawi. Studies in Family Planning 38(3):147–162.

Taylor, Lawrence
2001   Tunnel Kids. Tucson: University of Arizona Press.

UNAIDS
2006   2006 Report on the Global AIDS Epidemic. Geneva: UNAIDS.
2008   2008 Report on the Global AIDS Epidemic. Geneva: UNAIDS.

United Nations Economic Commission for Africa
2009   African Women's Report 2009: Measuring Gender Inequality in Africa: Experiences and Lessons from the African Gender and Development Index. Addis Ababa: United Nations Economic Commission for Africa.

van Onselen, Charles

1982a   Studies in the Social and Economic History of the Witwatersrand, 1886–1914, vol. 1: New Babylon. New York: Longman.

1982b   Studies in the Social and Economic History of the Witwatersrand, 1886–1914, vol. 2: New Nineveh. New York: Longman.

1984   The Small Matter of a Horse: The Life of "Nongoloza" Mathebula, 1867–1948. Johannesburg: Ravan Press.

Verheijen, Janneke

2013   Balancing Men, Morals and Money: Women's Agency between HIV and Security in a Malawi Village. Leiden: African Studies Centre.

Vetten, Lisa

2007   Violence against Women in South Africa. *In* State of the Nation: South Africa 2007. Sakhela Buhlungu, John Daniel, Roger Southall, and Jessica Lutchman, eds. Pp. 425–447. Cape Town: HSRC Press.

Vigh, Henrik E.

2006   Social Death and Violent Life Chances. *In* Navigating Youth, Generating Adulthood: Social Becoming in an African Context. Catrine Christiansen, Mats Utas, and Henrik E. Vigh, eds. Pp. 31–60. Stockholm: Nordiska Afrikainstitutet.

Vilakazi, Absolom

1962   Zulu Transformations: A Study of the Dynamics of Social Change. Pietermaritzburg: University of Natal Press.

Waetjen, Thembisa

2004   Workers and Warriors: Masculinity and the Struggle for Nation in South Africa. Champaign: University of Illinois Press.

Warner, Michael

2002   Publics and Counterpublics. Public Culture 14(1):49–90.

Weiss, Brad

2009   Street Dreams and Hip Hop Barbershops: Global Fantasy in Urban Tanzania. Bloomington: Indiana University Press.

Weston, Kath

1991   Families We Choose: Lesbians, Gays, Kinship. New York: Columbia University Press.

White, Hylton

2001   Tempora et Mores: Family Values and the Possessions of a Post-Apartheid Countryside. Journal of Religion in Africa 31(4):457–479.

2004   Ritual Haunts: The Timing of Estrangement in a Post-Apartheid Countryside. *In* Producing African Futures: Ritual and Reproduction in a Neoliberal Age. Brad Weiss, ed. Pp. 141–166. Leiden: Brill.

Wilk, Richard R., and Robert McC. Netting

1984   Households: Changing Forms and Functions. *In* Households: Comparative and Historical Studies of the Domestic Group. Robert McC. Netting, Richard R. Wilk, and Eric J. Arnould, eds. Pp. 1–29. Berkeley: University of California Press.

Willis, Paul

1977   Learning to Labour: How Working Class Kids Get Working Class Jobs. Farnborough: Saxon House.

Witness

2003   Point Place Has Floors Closed. October 31: 3.

Wojcicki, Janet Maia

2002a   Commercial Sex Work or *Ukuphanda*? Sex-for-Money Exchange in Soweto and Hammanskraal Area, South Africa. Culture, Medicine, and Psychiatry 26:339–370.

2002b   "She Drank His Money": Survival Sex and the Problem of Violence in Taverns in Gauteng Province, South Africa. Medical Anthropology Quarterly 16(3):267–293.

Wright, John B.

1978   Pre-Shakan Age-Group Formation among the Northern Nguni. Natalia 8:22–30.

Index

Page numbers in *italics* denote terms found in the glossary.

EMILY MARGARETTEN is an assistant professor of anthropology at Ripon College.

Interpretations of Culture in the New Millennium

The University of Illinois Press
is a founding member of the
Association of American University Presses.

Composed in 10.5/13 Adobe Minion Pro
by Lisa Connery
at the University of Illinois Press
Manufactured by Sheridan Books, Inc.

University of Illinois Press
1325 South Oak Street
Champaign, IL 61820-6903
www.press.uillinois.edu